INSPIRE JUSTICE

365-day devotional
on poverty and justice

D0111556

Canadian Bible Society
The Word. For Life.

www.biblesociety.ca

World Vision

For Children. For Change. For Life.

www.worldvision.ca

For more information about how you can help meet the world need for the Word of God write

Canadian Bible Society
The Word. For Life.

10 Carnforth Road, Toronto
Ontario, Canada M4A 2S4
Tel: (416) 757-4171
Toll free: 1-800-465-2425
www.biblesociety.ca
www.biblescanada.com

World Vision is a Christian relief, development, and advocacy organization dedicated to working with children, families, and communities to overcome poverty and injustice. As followers of Jesus, we are motivated by God's love to serve all people regardless of religion, race, ethnicity, or gender. For more information on how you can make a difference in the life of someone living in poverty, please contact:

World Vision

For Children. For Change. For Life.

1 World Drive
Mississauga, ON L5T 2Y4
Tel: 905-565-6100
Toll-free: 1-866-595-5550
www.worldvision.ca

Bible passages: **Contemporary English Version** © American Bible Society: Psalms and Proverbs © 1991, 1992; New Testament © 1991, 1992, 1995; Old Testament © 1995.
The Least of These (Devotionals):
© 2010 American Bible Society / © 2012 Canadian Bible Society

ISBN 978-0-88834-984-2
70100108 InspireJustice 365-day devotional   CBS-2013-1M
701001078-WV InspireJustice 365-day devotional – World Vision Ed
                                                               CBS-2013-1M

Printed in Canada

Poverty, war, famine, disease; there are a lot of things in this world that are unsettling. While the solutions aren't always so clear to us, God's Word can be a frequent reminder that everything is under God's control and that in the end, he will bring justice to all who have been oppressed.

GETTING THE MOST FROM GOD'S WORD \\

As you embark on taking a journey, we encourage you to engage with God's Word following these four steps so that your life may be touched and changed in the most meaningful way.

Pray with focus and openness to see what God has for you. God, connect with me here, as I seek You in your Word.

Read the selected section of Scripture slowly. Take note of intriguing words and phrases. Read them a second time.

Reflect on what strikes you as you read. What does this passage of Scripture teach you about God's values?

Respond to the passage. Speak to God directly about what's on your mind and heart. Look for ways to live out what you've uncovered.

Day 1 | *Courage*

PRAY: God connect with me here, as I seek you in your Word.

READ: Matthew 28.1–10 — Have you ever experienced both fear and joy at the same time? It's an odd but exhilarating mixture of emotions! For some it happens when they jump out of a plane with nothing but a parachute keeping them from plummeting to earth. For others, it happens when they get up to sing in church.

Jesus told the two women in today's reading to find the disciples and tell them to meet him in Galilee. Although frightened, they didn't allow their anxiety to keep them from doing what the Lord asked. There are many circumstances that may hinder us emotionally from doing God's will. Some Christians are married to unbelievers who have negative feelings toward the church. Others are timid about sharing their faith with unsaved friends and coworkers because they don't want to be ridiculed. But God is able to overcome all of these circumstances – all you have to do is ask.

REFLECT: When you're sharing the Good News of salvation with others, He will provide you with the ability and the opportunity to proclaim His message. This is an excellent certainty and conviction to establish in your life as a new year is about to unfold!

RESPOND: Ask God to give you the courage and wisdom to tell others about Him and to share His love with those in need.

Lord, I pray that you will not only give me the chance to witness to friends and neighbours but also that you will provide me with both the courage to speak and the wisdom to say the right things.

TO KNOW MORE:
Psalm 103 and Hebrews 2 \\

Day 2 | *Empathy*

PRAY: God connect with me here, as I seek you in your Word.

READ: 1 Corinthians 9.19-23 — One of the most valuable traits a person can have is the skill and desire to understand and have sympathy for another person's point of view. Whether the environment is a boardroom, courtroom or living room, the ability to seek common ground makes each party involved feel vital and appreciated. It doesn't mean that anyone compromises his or her convictions; it just makes the opportunity for a peaceful solution more likely. Christians need to find common ground when they have disagreements with others in order to more easily solve their problems. If you're having difficulty resolving a situation, don't resort to name calling or accusations. Instead, turn to God's Word and pray that the Holy Spirit will open your heart to His guidance and direction. In this way you can also be an effective witness rather than a detriment to the spreading of the Gospel.

REFLECT: Paul was willing to concede his Christian liberties whenever necessary in order to bring people to Christ. This is the type of empathy we should have when sharing our faith with others – not being judgmental, on the one hand, or condescending, on the other, but in all things exhibiting loving and gracious attitudes.

RESPOND: Ask God to give you a heart for others so you can effectively deal with conflicts and, in the same way, share His plan of salvation in a kind and sensitive way.

Lord, help me to find peaceful solutions to any problems I am having with others and give me the insight and patience I need to see another person's point of view so I can be an effective witness for you.

TO KNOW MORE:
Ezekiel 34 and Galatians 6 \\

Day 3 | *Success*

PRAY: God connect with me here, as I seek you in your Word.

READ: Proverbs 11.19 — Do you envy people you work with or see people on the news who seem to acquire worldly success effortlessly? These "fortunate" individuals seem to have the so-called Midas Touch when it comes to turning any opportunity into a financial bonanza. Too often, though, their success is built by cheating or misleading others and the intent of their hearts is evil; they deserve your prayers, not your jealousy. The Bible says that their lives will end in destruction. It's important to keep our hearts and minds focused on Jesus Christ. Only then will we find true success. The riches and glory of those who live only to please themselves is fleeting and meaningless when compared to the eternal rewards awaiting those who commit their lives in faithful service to the Lord.

REFLECT: In Deuteronomy 30.15-18 Moses tells the Israelites, as they are about to cross the Jordan River into the Promised Land, that they could choose "life and success or death and disaster" (CEV). While it may appear that God ignores the behaviour of those who succeed through underhanded dishonesty, this isn't the case. It's important that, as Christians, we treat everyone with integrity and openness.

RESPOND: Ask God to help you become truly successful – the kind of achievements that bring eternal glory and not temporary satisfaction.

Lord, help me to replace my desires for respect and material success with a keen hunger for righteousness and a love for those around me.

TO KNOW MORE:
1 Chronicles 29 and 1 John 3 \\

Day 4 | Hardships

PRAY: God connect with me here, as I seek you in your Word.

READ: 2 Corinthians 1.3-7 — Many people believe that whenever God comforts us, our hardships instantly disappear. But if that were true, people would turn to God only to be relieved of pain, not to love Him. We must understand that comfort can also mean receiving the strength, encouragement and hope to deal with difficult times.

It's also important to note that verse 5 assures us that as we suffer with Christ, we will also receive His marvellous comfort. What a wonderful promise! So wonderful, in fact, this passage reveals that the blessings we receive are so great we will have an abundance of "comfort" to share with others. In this way God gives us the great joy of both receiving His love and then offering it to those who need it the most.

REFLECT: The more we suffer, the more comfort God can give us. Allow God to reassure you. Remember that every trial you endure will help you endure future hardships better—and to more effectively minister to others who are going through difficult times.

RESPOND: Ask God to relieve the stress you are feeling about personal circumstances, to help you accept whatever He desires for your life so that you will have opportunities to share His mercy with others.

Lord, I pray that you comfort me as I face difficulties so that I can, in turn, be a faithful witness to those going through similar circumstances.

TO KNOW MORE:
Micah 7 and Philippians 2 \\

Day 5 | *Easy*

PRAY: God connect with me here, as I seek you in your Word.

READ: Proverbs 14.12 — Get rich quick! This time-worn promise has been offered for generations to those who want a shortcut to the easy life. Yes, the "wide and pleasant road" seems to offer many options and require few sacrifices. Easy choices, however, should make us take a second look at possible alternatives, as today's brief passage warns.

Ask yourself these questions before rushing to take the easy way into an opportunity or out of a situation: Is the solution attractive because it allows me to be lazy? Am I doing this because it will let me continue with my current life-style and perhaps save my reputation? Do I prefer to follow the easy path because it requires no moral restraints? If you can answer in the affirmative to any of these questions, it's time to turn to God and His Word before proceeding one step further.

REFLECT: The right choices typically require hard work and self-sacrifice. Don't be trapped by apparent shortcuts. Don't think that there is a magic solution that will help you gain riches or get out of problems you have created. A Godly life, one that is marked by loving Him and loving others with the same fervour as you do yourself, is what will lead to true peace and ease.

RESPOND: Ask God to help you to base your decisions in life on the truths of His Word and on the guidance of His Holy Spirit.

Lord, forgive me when I allow my desires for instant gratification or freedom from a situation keep me from doing what is right.

TO KNOW MORE:
Obadiah 1 and James 1 \\

Day 6 | *Youth*

PRAY: God connect with me here, as I seek you in your Word.

READ: Luke 2.40-50 — She sure is a smart kid – she'll be running a corporation one day! I'm guessing he'll find a cure for the common cold by the time he's a teenager! These are just a couple variations on the many types of proud statements parents (and grandparent) often make about their children. Whether our observations are based on reality or not, most of us believe our kids can do almost anything.

But what leads to true success in life? What can a child learn from a young age that will set them on the road to greatness in God's eyes? For answers, let's look at what happened in today's reading. The fact that Jesus demonstrated wisdom beyond His years is not surprising since he stayed in close contact with his Heavenly Father. James 1.5 says, "If any of you need wisdom, you should ask God, and it will be given to you. God is generous and won't correct you for asking" (CEV). This is the type of advice you can offer a young person which will be truly beneficial and help them become "spiritual prodigies" as they grow into adulthood.

REFLECT: Regardless of the circumstances a young person in your life is facing – whether bright with promise or daunting and uncertain – encourage them to ask God for good judgment and insight. He is always happy and willing to give wisdom to those, both young and old, who ask and believe.

RESPOND: Lovingly share with a young person in your life that he or she will grow more and more in wisdom each day if they walk faithfully with God and regularly turn to His Word.

Lord, I pray for wisdom and faithfulness for (Name) and ask that you will protect and keep (him/her) in your loving care throughout their life.

TO KNOW MORE:
Isaiah 11 and 2 Timothy 2 \\

Day 7 | *Encouragers*

PRAY: God connect with me here, as I seek you in your Word.

READ: 1 Thessalonians 5.5-11 — Have you ever run a lengthy race? A 12.5K, a 25K or even a 50K trek? For those who have, you know that somewhere along the way your body starts crying out for you to stop as your legs ache, your throat burns and your lungs gasp for air. This is when cheering friends and fans are most valuable. Their encouragement helps you push through the pain to the finish.

In the same way, Christians should encourage each other. A word of encouragement offered at the right moment can be the difference between finishing well and collapsing along the way. Observe your family members, friends at church or those in a Bible study. Be sensitive to their needs and the moments when they'd love to have someone pray with them and offer supportive words in the name of Jesus.

REFLECT: Paul reminded the church in Thessalonica that "Christ died for us, so that we could live with him, whether we are alive or dead when he comes. That's why you must encourage and help each other" (1 Thessalonians 5.10-11a CEV). Your words and actions can be a breath of fresh air for those who need someone to "cheer" them on as they run life's often difficult road.

RESPOND: Ask God to help you become an encourager – someone who supports the goals and aspirations, the needs and security, the faith and convictions – to other believers, in His holy and precious name.

Lord, I pray that you will encourage me to be a constant source of encouragement to those around me and those I encounter throughout my life.

TO KNOW MORE:
Psalm 139 and Ephesians 4 \\

Day 8 | *People*

PRAY: God connect with me here, as I seek you in your Word.

READ: Genesis 1.26,27 — God said, "Now we will make humans, and they will be like us. We will let them rule the fish, the birds, and all other living creatures."

Many have argued over what it really means to be "made in God's image," but at the very least, it indicates something profoundly significant about humans. To mistreat people is to forget this crucial fact: they are made in the image of God. This affects not only who we are, but how we behave.

These words in Genesis help us understand that each of us – every man, woman and child – bears God's stamp. As we understand and live this out, our lives reflect the One who created us. Instead of oppressing others, we empower them; instead of standing idle, we get involved. We stand up for justice, speak out for the powerless, and love the unloved.

Why? Because we take after our Father in Heaven.

REFLECT: What if you were to wear a badge all the time that said "made in God's image"?

RESPOND: Build up a picture of what God is like. Every time you read the Bible, write down what it tells you about God, perhaps in a journal.

Lord, I look at the stars at night, and I wonder why you care about us. I look at the earth, and I wonder why you've given us such immense responsibly. You are ruler and yet you trust us to rule. You are amazing.

TO KNOW MORE:
Genesis 1.26,27; Genesis 1;
Colossians 1.15-27; Matthew 22.15-22 \\

Day 9 | *Power*

PRAY: God connect with me here, as I seek you in your Word.

READ: Psalm 72.1-7 — As someone once said to Spiderman, "With great power comes great responsibility." We are reminded of this in the Psalmist's beautiful prayer for the king. In a world where so many leaders show favouritism towards the wealthy and powerful, the king is to be honest and fair – particularly to the poor and the homeless. He is to punish their oppressors. His leadership is to be like falling rain that makes the grass grow.

Leadership in government and business today is often equated with the creation of wealth, prosperity, and growing the economy. This Psalm calls for the creation of justice. In Israel, each new king was expected to write out a copy of God's law to remind him to rule the kingdom according to what God requires (Deuteronomy 17.18-20). God's job is to provide the grass. The king's job is to help it grow.

When and where are you in conversation with those of power, wealth and authority? To what do you hold them accountable? What efforts do their institutions make to alleviate poverty?

REFLECT: What if you were to write out the entire Bible (or even one of its books)? How would that help you remember what God wants you to do? Imagine one of your leaders rolling up his or her sleeves and helping build a house for a person with no home.

RESPOND: Try to sum up God's law from this Psalm. Write it out so that it fits on one side of a sheet of paper. Keep it near you and read it several times a day.

Please help our leaders to be honest and fair like you, our God, especially towards the poor and the weak. Guide the leaders of the world to work for peace and justice so that all people can live in safety and with dignity.

TO KNOW MORE:
Psalm 72.1-7; Psalm 72; Deuteronomy 17.8-20; John 19.33-40 \\

Day 10 | *Literacy*

PRAY: God connect with me here, as I seek you in your Word.

READ: Luke 10.25-28 — "What is written in the Scriptures? How do you understand them?" asks Jesus (10.26). Or in other versions, "How do you read it?" Of course, to read the Scriptures right – to read anything right – first you have to be able to read.

Poverty and illiteracy go hand in hand. The poor, the homeless, and refugees have difficulty accessing education. Not being able to read, write or count means more than missing out on the latest best-seller. It means not being able to get a decent job. It means that you are vulnerable to being cheated. It means that you cannot easily claim things to which you have a right.

Don't just think "overseas" either. Illiteracy is rampant in industrialized nations, particularly in prisons where there is a huge link between criminal behaviour and lack of literacy skills.

God wrote down his commandments for Moses. Jesus read and quoted the Scriptures. No one needs to be able to read to meet Jesus, but think about what they are missing! Don't you think Jesus would like people to be able to read about him?

REFLECT: Remember your own experience of learning to read. Imagine every child in the world being able to read and write in his or her own language.

RESPOND: You're reading this, so perhaps you could help someone else learn to read: at school or a local library, at home, or at church. How many different ways can you find to give away books? Consider underwriting the cost of a student's textbooks, pencils, and other school supplies.

Lord, turn me into a lifelong student of your Word.

TO KNOW MORE:
Luke 10.25-28; Deuteronomy 11; Joshua 1.1-9; 8.30-35 \\

Day 11 | *Body*

PRAY: God connect with me here, as I seek you in your Word.

READ: 1 Corinthians 12.19-26 — The Corinthian church was divided by envy, factions, and sinful behaviour. But one of its main problems was the belief that certain members of the church were not very important, that these members could be ignored or discarded.

Paul pictures the church as a body made up of many parts, yet functioning as a unit. It is based on varieties of skills and gifts and on mutual interdependence. Even the weaker parts of the body are important and deserve respect.

The Bible describes people honestly. Paul himself was not an impressive speaker (2 Corinthians 10.10,11). He seems to have had a disability or a recurring illness, but that didn't stop him (2 Corinthians 12.7-10; Galatians 4.13,14). In the Old Testament, Moses had a speech problem (Exodus 4.10). It's not about ability or disability, but about the gift bestowed on you by God. Sometimes people with disabilities are barred from participation, set aside, or hidden away, but God says everyone can play a part in the body of Christ.

REFLECT: Imagine your own life five years from now. How do you envision using the gifts God has given you? What gifts do you see in other people? What opportunities do they need to experience to make the most of their gifts?

RESPOND: Develop an appreciation for people who are very different from you. Do you know people with disabilities in your church or in your community? Talk to them. Find out about their lives. How can you help them? And, just as importantly, how can they help you?

Lord, help me to notice the gifts you've given to people around me – my friends, my family, co-workers, and people at church. Help me find ways to encourage them to use their gifts to serve you and others.

TO KNOW MORE: 1 Corinthians 12.9-16; 1 Corinthians 12; Romans 12.3-8; 1 Peter 4.7-11 \\

Day 12 | *Food*

PRAY: God connect with me here, as I seek you in your Word.

READ: Leviticus 19.9,10 — It's one of those parental clichés: "Eat your dinner! People are starving in India/Africa/China/some other place." But like most clichés, it contains a spoonful of truth. In the United States of America nearly 30 million tons of food is thrown away every year. And in one of Canada's largest cities, every month, residents toss out nearly 17.5 million kilograms of food. Just think of it. The food we place in our shopping carts or what we order in restaurants will never see the inside of our stomachs. It will be scraped into trash cans or will just sit in a dark corner of the fridge until, years beyond its sell-by date, it starts to evolve into an entirely new life form.

Leviticus shows us a different way to deal with unwanted food. It was not to be wasted, but put to good use. Jesus collected leftovers too – presumably so they could be given away.

Our parents were right. People are starving around the world. So eat your greens.

REFLECT: What is God asking you to leave behind for the poor? A portion of your pay-cheque? Your food? Your time?

RESPOND: Give thanks at every meal and finish your greens. Take an inventory of the contents of your fridge and plan how you're going to use them. Invite someone to dinner who may have trouble making ends meet. Find out what it costs to feed a family for a week in another part of the world. Send that amount to a charity that provides food for that country.

Rain on the hills, grass for cattle, plants for our food, grain for our health, oil for our skin, and sweet fruit to cheer us up. All this comes from you, Lord God, for all of us to share.

TO KNOW MORE:
Leviticus 19.9,10; Ruth 1-2 \\

Day 13 | *Tree*

PRAY: God connect with me here, as I seek you in your Word.

READ: Deuteronomy 20.19-20 — Here, tucked away in a chapter of military rules for the Israelites, is an intriguing piece of ecological planning. "When you are attacking a town, don't chop down its fruit trees," says God.

In other words, don't destroy something you're going to need. Trees take a long time to grow, but a short time to cut down. Short-term thinking has long-term consequences.

Trees feature heavily in the Bible. They provide food (Deuteronomy 24.20,21), serve as memorials (Genesis 21.33), supply building materials (1 Chronicles 14.1), offer shade (Zechariah 3.10; John 1.48), and even stand as landmarks (Genesis 12.6). There are rules about planting and cultivation (Leviticus 19.23-25).

Exploitation of forests has had devastating results. Deforestation has caused severe shortage of firewood, forced animals out of their natural habitats and led to adverse soil erosion.

The roots of trees go deep. Wield the axe wisely, one day you might need that tree.

REFLECT: Picture a map showing the forests and woodlands of your province. Imagine the green areas spreading. Look at trees around you now. Imagine them in 200 years.

RESPOND: Plant a tree.

I will put down my roots in your house, Lord God. Make me flourish like a palm tree; strong like a cedar of Lebanon. Keep my spirit fresh and healthy, fruitful in old age.

TO KNOW MORE:
Deuteronomy 20.19,20; Genesis 2.15-17;
Genesis 3; Revelation 22 \\

Day 14 | *Children*

PRAY: God connect with me here, as I seek you in your Word.

READ: Matthew 19.13-15 — It was common for parents in Jesus' day to bring their children to teachers and elders to be blessed. But the disciples view this as a distraction: "We're on a mission here. People to see, places to go. Can't be distracted by kids."

Jesus, however, rebukes them. He says these children are models for the citizens of the Kingdom and he welcomes them. Welcoming them is like welcoming Jesus himself (Matthew 18.1-5).

He also gives stern warnings about anyone who causes them to fall into sin (18.16). The abuse, neglect, oppression and exploitation of children can do exactly that: tripping them up an ensnaring them in sin, self-destructive behaviour, shame, despair and rage.

It's a rescue mission: go find them, save them from the hands of those who would exploit them, give them what they need to flourish and, most of all, bring them into the presence of Jesus.

REFLECT: Every time you see an adult, try to imagine him or her as a child. Every time you see a child, imagine that child as the best adult he or she can be.

RESPOND: When you see children you know, give them some attention. Look into their eyes and say their name. Make them feel like they matter.

Pray for the children you see – for their future, for them to grow up healthy, happy, and hopeful.

Thank you, Lord, for the blessing of children: their noisy singing, their loud laughter, their enthusiasm and energy, their loyalty, and love. They are gifts from you, of strength and joy.

TO KNOW MORE:
Matthew 19.13-15; Matthew 18.1-14; Deuteronomy 6 \\

Day 15 | *Land*

PRAY: God connect with me here, as I seek you in your Word.

READ: Proverbs 23.10-11 — Throughout the world, land is highly valued. Good locations, fertile land, mining rights – whatever the attraction, people will do what they can to get hold of it. Some governments and powerful business interests think nothing of driving people from their land, bulldozing houses, and redrawing boundaries. Even traditional lands are taken from those who have looked after it for generations.

Victims of land loss are usually the poor who cannot afford the legal fees to fight their case.

Who will defend their rights? We see that such helpless people have a defender in God. This passage from the Proverbs wars against moving the stones that mark the boundaries of another's land. In the world of ancient Israel, God is often understood to be a person's next of kin, the one who can act as their redeemer. Part of the redeemer's role was to buy back family land that had been lost. God takes that part and will fight on behalf of his family.

Who will fight for these people? Who will be their defender? God will. And, perhaps, we will too.

REFLECT: Imagine a world where no one fights over land. Everyone is content with their own territory. Everyone shares resources fairly. Everyone respects one another's needs.

RESPOND: Get to know which people are dispossessed. Where in the world are they? How do they live and survive?

Our Lord, I know that you defend the homeless and desire that the poor be given justice. May I become someone you can rely on to help make your desires a reality.

TO KNOW MORE:
Proverbs 23.10-11; Jeremiah 22 \\

Day 16 | *Toilet*

PRAY: God connect with me here, as I seek you in your Word.

READ: Deuteronomy 23.12-14 — You can't say the Bible's not about real life. Out in the desert, God gives clear, exact commands about cleanliness. "Set a place outside the camp to be used as a toilet area. And make sure that you have a small shovel in your equipment." Not a bad rule for life.

Why did this matter? Partly it has to do with holiness and purity: in the culture of the time, the person approaching God had to be clean. But also it's common sense: properly disposing of waste is an important way of keeping clear of disease.

This passage also shows that God cares about all aspects of human life; God knows us and knows how we function – in every sense of that word. God is not shy or embarrassed; the One who created us knows all about sanitation. Sadly, many people in the world cannot obey this simple instruction. Living in slums with open sewers, they have, literally, nowhere else to go. And so disease, infection, and death are real threats to community life.

God knows that people need simple things like proper toilets, or at least shovels.

REFLECT: What would your world be like if all the sewers stopped working? Imagine every home in the world had a clean toilet, just like yours.

RESPOND: Have a look down a drain. Then imagine sleeping next to it. Place a coin box in your bathroom and every time you use the toilet, pay a "toilet toll." At the end of the month send it off to a charity that builds toilets for people who need them.

You know my deepest thoughts, Lord. Nothing is hidden from you!

TO KNOW MORE:
Deuteronomy 23.12-14; Leviticus 15.1-15; Colossians 2.8-23 \\

Day 17 | *Persecution*

PRAY: God connect with me here, as I seek you in your Word.

READ: Luke 21.10-19 — The path of following Jesus often leads to persecution. For those who've grown up in a culture of freedom and choice, it is easy to forget that there still exist places where certain decisions can result in oppression, exclusion, persecution, and even death.

Jesus makes plain the consequences of such choices. He warns his followers that they will be persecuted by both religious and secular authorities. For some, their own families will turn against them. They will be hated because of their loyalty to Him. And this is indeed what happened to Peter, Paul, John, and James, not to mention many others down the years whose names were never recorded.

In North America, we may be scorned or ridiculed, but we are rarely arrested for our faith. In many countries, however, thousands of Christians share this exact fate. Jesus knew that his followers would be persecuted because of their faith; but just because it's anticipated it doesn't mean it's acceptable.

REFLECT: Imagine yourself sending a card to a Christian in prison. Picture the expression on their face as they hold it in their hands. Imagine them being released and reunited with their family. It can happen!

RESPOND: Read about those who suffer persecution. Don't let their stories – and lives – disappear without a trace. Put up pictures of persecuted Christian brothers and sisters on your wall. Request an email prayer alert from an organization that works to help persecuted Christians.

Have mercy, Lord, on those who are mistreated. Keep them strong and rescue them from death.

TO KNOW MORE:
Luke 21.10-19; 2 Timothy 3; Romans 8.31-39 \\

Day 18 | *Victims*

PRAY: God connect with me here, as I seek you in your Word.

READ: Matthew 2.16-18 — Voices crying, women weeping. An army sweeps through Bethlehem, carrying out orders. But surely every victim had a mother, and just as surely, every mother cried.

This scene has been replicated throughout history. In the 1970s and 1980s, thousands of citizens "disappeared" in the dictatorships of Argentina and Chile. In Chile, mothers protested by dancing alone, without partners, to symbolize their missing sons. In Argentina, mothers marched around the Plaza de Mayo in Buenos Aires, carrying photographs of those who were missing.

From the massacre of villages to genocide and ethnic cleansing, each victim leaves behind someone who grieves. They have children who mourn and mothers who weep. And they have a Father in heaven who demands justice. Deep grief will be eased. Justice will be done. In the meantime, we need to speak up for the victims. Shall we dance?

REFLECT: Imagine you've just heard of the Bethlehem massacre in the news. What do you do? Imagine families being reunited with lost relatives. Imagine people dancing together joyfully once more.

RESPOND: Let the plight of others move you to tears. Celebrate the fact that you are free and can take action without being overcome by despair. Write, make phone calls, send emails, give money, pray. Matthew quotes from Jeremiah 31.15. Read Jeremiah 31.16-20.

Does it give you hope?

Lord, when I'm brought low with despair, help me to praise you again. Revive me so that I may be an instrument of peace and justice.

TO KNOW MORE:
Matthew 2.16-18; Psalm 2; Joel 3.17-21; Revelation 16.1-7 \\

Day 19 | *Tools*

PRAY: God connect with me here, as I seek you in your Word.

READ: 1 Samuel 13.19-21 — Ancient Israel's neighbours, the Philistines, were cultured people, good at metalwork, an advantage that allowed them to oppress the Israelites for long. Iron was valued for its strength and hardness and was used to make objects such as axes, chisels, hoes, ploughs, and weapons. The Philistines kept the iron-working technology to themselves, making Israel dependent upon them for repairing their agricultural tools. The Israelites had no choice but to pay exorbitant prices for these services.

Withholding technology is a means of controlling other nations. Technologically advanced nations may well say, "It's all ours and we'll allow you some of it, but only if you can pay. This way we can keep you poor, and charge you high prices at the same time." People can be starved of technology, just as they can be starved of food. They can be denied the opportunity to develop the tools they need to advance. What can be done to make the tools of technology accessible to those for whom such access barred? Some cities and communities provide wireless access as a way to make this service equitable. What would it take to expand such access to technology throughout the world?

REFLECT: What would the world be like if everybody had the same equipment at their fingertips as you have—at work and at home?

RESPOND: People in developing nations don't have money for essential items. Work with friends to raise the funds needed to cover the cost of one of these piece of equipment—a loom, a sewing machine, a water purifier, a computer—and donate it to an organization that will provide these items to those who need of them.

God, you desire the best for all people and you protect the poor. Use me to advance their well-being, further their plans, and help them achieve self-sufficiency. Guide me in your ways. Make me like you, Lord.

TO KNOW MORE:
1 Samuel 13.19-21; Judges 4; Isaiah 2.1-5 \\

Day 20 | *Bible*

PRAY: God connect with me here, as I seek you in your Word.

READ: Matthew 4.2-4 — Jesus, fasting for 40 days in the desert, is tempted by the devil to turn stones into bread. He counters the temptation with a quotation from Scripture (Deuteronomy 8.3). You see, there are other kinds of hunger. Humans need more than the physical; they need love and respect. They need to hear from God.

Throughout the world there are people who are hungry for the Word of God, either because they have no Scriptures in their language, Bibles are too expensive to own, or because the Bible is banned in their country. People in such places treasure each scrap of the pages of the Bible they can get their hands on. They memorize verses and treat each page like gold leaf.

Meanwhile, most of our homes are well-stocked with Bibles. But do we value the ones we own? One of the services we can offer people is to feed them the Word of God, providing them with spiritual nourishment they need. People need both bread and Bibles.

REFLECT: What would happen if all Bibles of the world were suddenly dusted off and regularly read?

RESPOND: Choose a Psalm and start memorizing one verse a day. Learn how you can help provide them with God's Word at www.biblesociety.ca

Lord, I enjoy pleasing you. Thank you for revealing yourself through your Word. Your law is in my heart. I am happy and willing to listen and obey.

TO KNOW MORE:
Matthew 4.2-4; Deuteronomy 8; Psalm 119.1-16 \\

Day 21 | *Water*

PRAY: God connect with me here, as I seek you in your Word.

READ: Isaiah 41.17-20 — Planet Earth could be renamed Planet Water. Although 75% of the Earth's surface is water, only 1% is drinkable. Nations battle to keep this resource to themselves, building huge reservoirs and constructing dams to divert it for their own needs. Even at home, drought restrictions remind us to think carefully about our use of this precious substance.

In this passage from Isaiah, God promises water: the barren desert will burst forth with growth. The prophet's words show the importance of water and the difference it can make in people's lives.

Lack of water – or being forced to drink unhealthy water – is the biggest single cause of disease and death in the world today. Giving people clean water allows them to flourish. Crops can be grown, communities can be developed, families can bathe and children who otherwise would spend all day finding water, have a chance to get an education.

Water can bring life to barren lives just as it can cause the desert to bloom.

REFLECT: All over the world, dry land becomes lush and green; everyone is clean and healthy; every child is in school. How did that happen?

RESPOND: Find out how you can conserve water in your household. Drink. Wash. Flush. Every time you use water, give thanks.

You, Lord, can turn deserts into lakes and scorched land into flowing streams. Help us work with you to channel water towards people who desperately need it.

TO KNOW MORE:
Isaiah 41.17-20; Exodus 17.1-7; John 4.1-42 \\

Day 22 | *Mission*

PRAY: God connect with me here, as I seek you in your Word.

READ: Luke 4.15-21 — Imagine the scene: Jesus back in his home town, where he grew up as a boy and learned the builder's trade. Someone says to him, "So, what are you doing with yourself these days?"

Here, in the synagogue, he answers the question. He unrolls the scroll and reads from Isaiah 61.1,2. This, says Jesus, is the Jubilee, the year of the Lord's favour, the year of forgiveness, the expression of God's love for the poor. It is Jesus' plan, his job description, his statement of intent. He has come to bring good news for all who suffer – the poor, the imprisoned, and the blind. He sets the pattern and calls people to the banquet with God.

But Jesus brings more to the party. Good news for the poor can also include someone to lift them out of poverty. Good news for the homeless is the love of God – and a roof over their heads. As followers of Jesus, this is our mission. We tell people about the saving love of Jesus, and we show them what he is like.

REFLECT: Envision your special mission as a follower of Jesus. How can you live in a Christ-like manner so that he will be exalted and your light will shine in dark places?

RESPOND: Write out your mission statement or manifesto, and then put into action for 21 days. By that time it should become second nature to you.

God our Father, thank you for Jesus who has given us a window into your ways. Thank you for your love. You give a helping hand to everyone who falls.

TO KNOW MORE:
Luke 4.16-21; Isaiah 61; Acts 9 \\

Day 23 | *Addiction*

PRAY: God connect with me here, as I seek you in your Word.

READ: Proverbs 23.29-35 — Another unexpected discovery in the Bible: an ancient account of a hangover as a vivid depiction of the effects of drinking – the fighting, the hallucinations, the loss of memory, and the strange craving to do it all again.

Dependence on alcohol and addiction to nicotine and heroin are destroying many lives. People who drink in response to stress or unhappiness may be showing early signs of alcoholism. People drink or take drugs to dull the pain, but the descent can be traumatic. Addiction leads to violence, poverty, sickness, isolation and break-up in families. Smoking may seem harmless but nicotine is an addictive drug and is the hardest to give up with devastating long-term effects.

What can we do? We can also protest the cynical exploitation of the world's poor by cigarette and alcohol companies. We should do all we can to change things for people who seek comfort in addictive substances, poverty, oppression, loneliness, feelings of insignificance, stress, and abuse.

REFLECT: Imagine if all the hurting people became members of God's Kingdom and were loved by his family, they'd feel valued and their lives would have purpose and joy. Isn't that a reason to invite them into the family?

RESPOND: Think about behaviours and activities that take up a large amount of your time and energy. Could any of these be considered compulsive or obsessive? Do they cause you to turn away from God?

Lord, when I am lonely and troubled, have pity on me. When my awful worries keep growing, rescue me from sadness. Remove from my life those things that separate me from you and keep me from experiencing healthy relationships with others.

TO KNOW MORE:
Proverbs 23.29-35; Romans 6; Ephesians 4.17-32 \\

Day 24 | *Differences*

PRAY: God connect with me here, as I seek you in your Word.

READ: Galatians 3.23-39 — Paul lived in a rigidly structured society. A person's birth defined everything: their status, family life, and job. There was some room for movement where a slave would become free, but most people's lives were set from their birth. Then along comes Christ, whom Christians "put on" like new clothes, and believers find they're part of a brand new, extended family. The early Church did not abolish a person's identity—Jews were still Jews, slaves still beholden to their masters, women still obliged to fill their limited roles within the community—but new roles and opportunities opened up for everyone who was part of God's family. In a special way, all were now equal.

Paul declares that the gulf between Jews and Gentiles has been bridged by Christ and there is neither male nor female. Even gender is no barrier. The radical nature of Christianity has no room for racism, classism, or sexism. There is only the family. Each member has a different function, their own identity; but all are clothed by God's love.

REFLECT: Galatians 3.27 might be suggesting that early Christians symbolically took off their old clothes before being baptized and put on a new set afterwards. What "clothes" are you going to change into as a Christian? Imagine a church that is truly representative of all the people who live in the community. Imagine the diverse worship styles and kinds of outreach the members could experience.

RESPOND: Find ways of reaching out to those not represented in your church. Where is the bridge-building going to start? How can you help it along? Pray for those in your church who are fearful of change and distrustful of people different from themselves. Pray for those who've been excluded or made to feel unwelcome.

Lord, you don't want anyone left out of your family. Keep us united so that the world will turn and worship you.

TO KNOW MORE:
Galatians 3.23-29; Ephesians 2.11-3.21 \\

Day 25 | Restoration

PRAY: God connect with me here, as I seek you in your Word.

READ: Isaiah 58.6-12 — What does it mean to worship God? Singing songs in church? Sharing food with the hungry? It's not "either/or," but "both/and." Here God calls people to worship him by bringing liberty to the oppressed, feeding the starving, clothing the naked.

God wants lives of restorative worship. Restoration means more than slapping a bandage on a wound. The society pictured by Isaiah has not been "patched up." Instead, there is an emphasis on wholeness, on permanent change, on bringing people back into complete health – mind, body, and spirit.

Changing the life of the homeless means more than offering temporary solutions, more than a bed for the night. It means looking at employment, security, health – deeper issues that when addressed, bring lasting changes. So, not just a patch of land, but a well-watered garden. Not just a roof over someone's head, but a home. Not just water but restorative healing peace.

REFLECT: Imagine and plan an event that allows the whole person to encounter God: a fitness session that ends in food and worship; a "free advice day" with prayer, and a free clothing exchange. Mix and match to make your own interesting experience that meets people's physical, mental, and spiritual needs.

Think of one thing you have done on occasion to help others. Imagine doing it regularly until the end of your life!

RESPOND: You can't do everything, so mark a date in your diary to reflect on whether you're using your energies wisely.

Lord, bring encouragement to those in need. Show all who claim to be your disciples what is pleasing in your eyes. Make us truly grateful and show us how we can help the poor and give them a reason to shout your praises.

TO KNOW MORE:
Isaiah 58.6-12; Isaiah 58; Matthew 5.1-16; Luke 19.1-9 \\

Day 26 | *Pennies*

PRAY: God connect with me here, as I seek you in your Word.

READ: Mark 12.41-44 — Jesus is sitting in the temple courtyard, watching wealthy landowners and rich pilgrims visiting Jerusalem for the Passover, casting their money into the large, trumpet-shaped offering bowls. Then along comes a widow, her poverty obvious from her dress. She throws in two tiny copper coins – the smallest coins in circulation.

Not impressive. But she has given all she had. She has less money than the others, but is far richer in spirit and understanding. The story follows a stinging attack on religious leaders who were oppressing the poor (Mark 12.38-40). Yet the people they are cheating are godlier than the rest of them put together.

It's not the money, but the motive; not the amount, but the attitude; not, perhaps, a question of how much we give away, but rather how much we keep for ourselves. This woman could have kept one f the coins for herself.

She didn't have to make a gift at all. But she chose to give all she could to God. How does Jesus' rebuke of the rich challenge us to examine those policies which bring us comfort at the expense of others?

REFLECT: What do you think God could do if you offered the contents of your bank account or your home to be used to further God's work in the world?

RESPOND: Be generous in your giving. Think of how much God has given you and be willing to give it back to him in thankfulness. God loves a cheerful giver.

I will praise you, Lord God, with a song and a thankful heart and will seek to do what is pleasing to you.

TO KNOW MORE:
Mark 12.38-44 ; Acts 4.32-5.16; 2 Corinthians 8 \\

Day 27 | *Immigrants*

PRAY: God connect with me here, as I seek you in your Word.

READ: Jeremiah 22.1-5 — The court during Jeremiah's time was a place of oppression and inequality. King Jehoiakim forced the people to pay higher taxes (2 Kings 23.35). The burden fell heavily on the most marginalized – widows, orphans, and the foreigners in the land.

But God had given rules on the fair treatment of refugees and immigrants. They were to be treated with kindness (Leviticus 19.33–34); fairness (Leviticus 24.22); care and support (Leviticus 25.35-37); and equality (Numbers 9.14).

Now, conveniently, the king and his court were forgetting God's commands, forgetting how their ancestors had similarly once been an exploited immigrant labour force in Egypt. What do we forget about refugees? That they are individuals, loved by God; that our actions as a nation have helped create imbalances of power that result in a world where some people end up becoming refugees? Do we, too, forget God's Words?

REFLECT: You've been granted an audience with the highest authority in the land. You have 15 minutes to speak your mind. What are you going to say?

RESPOND: Pray for groups in your community who welcome and support widows, orphans, immigrants, refugees, and victims of violence.

Find out where in your community special services are offered to immigrants (such as, learning English, becoming acclimated to the community, etc.) and befriend someone new to your neighbourhood.

Lord, you see and hear everything; you instruct the nations and give knowledge to help us all. Correct us, teach us, bless us.

TO KNOW MORE:
Jeremiah 22.1-5; Exodus 5; Deuteronomy 24.10-22 \\

Day 28 | Refuge

PRAY: God connect with me here, as I seek you in your Word.

READ: Numbers 35.9-28 — Numbers 35 talks about the provision of safe towns. The idea was simple: six towns were accessible from any point in the country (three on each side of the Jordan River)and offered asylum for all—free citizens, immigrants, or even visitors (35.15).

Anyone who had killed someone with a lethal instrument was assumed to have deliberately committed murder, and anger was no excuse (v.20). But if it was an accident, the person could go to the safe town and be protected from revenge by the victims' family, thus preventing the situation from escalating. This legislation provided two things necessary for every justice system: protection from revenge and the promise of a fair hearing. In our world, many people are assumed to be guilty because of the family they come from, their tribe, race, nationality, or appearance. Justice involves hearing both sides of the story. We need to make sure that those who are accused of crimes get a fair hearing. We need to make sure they live safely, free from "street justice' or vigilantism.

REFLECT: You have been appointed a judge. What principles would you insist upon? Have you ever judged or even punished someone unfairly? Imagine what you could do to make amends.

RESPOND: Pray for those who work in the justice system. Find out about advocacy work, speaking up for other people. Support a shelter that provides safe harbour for runaways and victims of domestic violence.

Lord, you are the refuge of everyone who has been wrongfully accused of a crime. Help me to be an advocate for people who lack the skills and means to defend themselves against false accusations. Give wisdom and compassion to all people who serve in the courts and criminal justice system.

TO KNOW MORE:
Numbers 35; Numbers 35; Joshua 20 \\

Day 29 | *Passion*

PRAY: God connect me here, as I seek you in your Word.

READ: Amos 3.13–4.3 — The prophets didn't pull any punches. If you see God as a reasonable, easy-going sort of person, then read the words he gave his prophets! They burn the tongue and blister the mouth. Old Testament prophets could be direct and blunt.

The part of Samaria that Amos describes was prosperous and famous for its agriculture. Here the cows are not in the fields, but in the homes!

The people live like cattle, without any spiritual dimension. It's almost an animal existence. But destruction is on its way. The Assyrians are coming, and they have a taste for beef. So God gives them a blast. It's the prophetic equivalent of a cattle-prod.

So is it OK to be outraged? Is it right to be rude? Only the passionate use impassioned language. God gets angry because he cares. Sometimes tough language is the only language that will be heard. God needs to shock people out of their complacency and, occasionally, we all need a poke to get us moving in the right direction.

REFLECT: Have you ever become really angry about injustice? What did you do? Would it be appropriate to use tough language?

RESPOND: Read your way around the world in 80 days: pick up a magazine article or click on a web site – a different country each day. Reflect on what you've learned about the needs of the poor and needy in three months' time.

You, Lord God, are not pleased with acts of injustice. Give me the courage to speak with boldness your word of truth.

TO KNOW MORE:
Amos 3.13–4.3; 2 Kings 13.10-25 \\

Day 30 | *Cash*

PRAY: God connect with me here, as I seek you in your Word.

READ: Matthew 6.24 — Who's your master? God or Money? People or possessions?

We live divided lives. We know where our heart should be – it should be in serving God. But so often we spend more time and devotion on our other master: money. We are wage slaves, worshippers at the shrine of wealth, dreaming of lottery-sized windfalls, buying stuff we don't need with money we don't have.

The Bible is realistic. We need money to live. People need to earn a living. But there's a difference between working for a living and living to work. There's a difference between earning money and worshipping it. Billions of people survive on less than $2 per day – it's vital, therefore, that we work out how much is "enough". Our heart should be with God, not in the shop window, the savings account, or the investment portfolio.

Jesus reminds us that we can take nothing with us. But we can store up treasure in heaven (Matthew 6.19-21). Our heart should be with our heavenly treasure, not our earthly wealth.

We need to master money before it masters us.

REFLECT: How much is enough? What's the least you could live with?

RESPOND: Keep a journal of your spending for one month. Where does the money go? Find out how far $10 will go in different places of the world. Check out Psalm 119.36; Matthew 6.24-33; Luke 16.10-12.

You give yourself to me freely so that I can experience the richness of your love forever. Help me to serve you with humbleness and gratitude.

TO KNOW MORE:
Matthew 6.34; Matthew 6.19-34; 1 Timothy 6 \\

Day 31 | *Prison*

PRAY: God connect with me here, as I seek you in your Word.

READ: Hebrews 13.1-3 — The early Church spent a lot of time visiting fellow Christians who were in jail because of their faith. They brought them necessities like food, drink, and clothing. It was not easy. Apart from the cost, there was the risk that people associating with imprisoned Christians would be arrested. Despite the dangers, the writer of Hebrews urges us to take the risk. It's an essential part of Christian living.

Care for prisoners goes beyond "looking after our own." In recent times, Christians have dared to care for prisoners. Reformers changed the conditions in prisons, arguing for humane treatment. Christians are engaged in radical, transformative work with offenders whom society has forgotten. Christianity is a religion based on repentance and hope. Where are those two qualities more needed than in prison? All prisoners need prayer, compassion, and a chance to encounter Christ.

REFLECT: Imagine visiting two prisoners: one who was arrested for leading a protest in which no one was hurt, the other for robbing a convenience store to support a drug habit. How would you minister to the needs of both of these very different prisoners? What would your prayers be for each of them?

RESPOND: Send a card at Christmas or Easter to someone in prison. Let them know you are thinking of them.

Find out how you can participate in a prison visiting ministry.

Donate towards the distribution of *The Key to Freedom Bible* — a prison ministry Bible that is distributed in prisons across Canada. http://www.biblesociety.ca/prison_bible

Even if others cannot hear me, or will not listen, I know you will, Lord. Hear the cries of those in prison. Hear my cry for them, too.

TO KNOW MORE:
Hebrews 13.1-3; Matthew 25.31-46; Acts 16.16-40 \\

Day 32 | *Prayer*

PRAY: God connect with me here, as I seek you in your Word.

READ: Mark 11.15-19 — The traders were not wrong in themselves. They offered a useful service by providing people – many of whom had come a long way – from having to bring their own animals for sacrifice. But they charged high prices. And they charged exorbitant rates to change the pilgrims' cash into the official temple currency.

No wonder Jesus was angry. The temple was supposed to offer people a way to encounter God, not charge them a massive booking fee. It was a rip-off religion. And the rip-off wasn't just religious either. The temple was the centre of Israel's economic life. It had become the central bank of Israel. The position of high priest made its occupant wealthy. There was even cattle-trading taking place in the outer temple courtyards. Where people of all nations were supposed to be free to pray, prayers were drowned out by the clamour of trade. When money shouts, other voices get lost. But as Jesus points out, prayer is more important than profit.

REFLECT: How can you make sure your local church is a place of prayer for all people?

RESPOND: See what you can find out about the temple in Jerusalem. Who built it? What was it for? What went wrong? (See 2 Samuel 7.1-17, 1 Kings 5-6; 9.1-9; Psalm 84; Jeremiah 7)

Lord, there are people who need to know you. There are people who need to learn how wonderful you are. Give them a spirit of openness and trust. Let them experience your presence. Help us to open the doors for them and welcome them in.

TO KNOW MORE:
Mark 11.15-19; Isaiah 56.1-8; Jeremiah 7.1-29 \\

Day 33 | *Peace*

PRAY: God connect with me here, as I seek you in your Word.

READ: Psalm 120.6-7 — Ever felt on your own? Ever felt as though no one was listening to you? Ever felt despised and ignored? Welcome to the world of the peacemaker. Often it seems as if violence is the only solution the world trusts. We are quick to resort to violence, always looking for the opportunity to lash out, launch missiles, or blow up innocent bystanders. Of course, sometimes evil must be resisted and the vulnerable protected by force. But that has to be a last resort, not an immediate response.

We should look for peaceful solutions. This is not weakness; arguing for peace is hard work. Take the writer of this psalm: he's tired, he's disillusioned; he's lived too long among these people. He just can't take it anymore. "Love your enemies," says Jesus (Matthew 5.43-45). "Do your best to live at peace with everyone," says Paul (Romans 12.18).

So we keep on going. Where there is conflict – in our world, in our communities, in our homes – the Christian way is to talk, to bring people together, to understand and, if possible, address grievances. We must speak out for peace among people who often speak only of war. It's a tough struggle. Peace, ironically, is worth fighting for, but not only with guns.

REFLECT: Where in your community is peace needed most? Where in the larger world? How can you help bring it about? Ask God.

RESPOND: Use the Internet or read a book to find out how peacemakers work. What qualities are needed to be a successful peacemaker?

Lord, I want to be your child and to live at peace with people, encouraging others to do the same. Help me to be full of kindness and truth.

TO KNOW MORE:
Psalm 120.6-7; Psalm 20; 2 Chronicles 20.1-29 \\

Day 34 | *School*

PRAY: God connect with me here, as I seek you in your Word.

READ: The Bible depicts wisdom as something to be valued, cherished, and sought after. People are to search for it and collect it. Learning is something that should be life-long.

But this is not some abstract knowledge. Wisdom is practical. The word translated as "wisdom" basically means "skill". It describes the skill of the craftsman in the tabernacle (Exodus 31.6) or the judicial abilities of kings (1 Kings 3.28). It is knowledge and learning and craft– the stuff that helps people live to their full potential– "life skills" as we may say today.

Wisdom gives you the ability to make wise choices, to discern what is right. It helps you understand the meaning, spot the patterns in the swirl of events around you. All these things show why human beings need to learn. It's not just learning for learning's sake; it's helping people to live, giving them choices (and helping them to choose). To deny people an education is to starve them of wisdom. They cannot grow the skills they need: they cannot learn a trade or craft; they do not have the wisdom they need to find the way out. They really do have to learn the hard way.

REFLECT: If you could design the perfect curriculum for the next generation, what subjects and skills would you make sure were included?

What would your life be like if you could not read or write?

RESPOND: Learn a new skill that enables you to help others, such as cooking and planning meals, making clothes, or making home repairs.

Lord, make me a student of the past and a teacher of the future. Help me to learn from others and pass on their wisdom to the next generation.

TO KNOW MORE:
Proverbs 1.1-7; Proverbs 1, 2 \\

Day 35 | *Home*

PRAY: God connect with me here, as I seek you in your Word.

READ: Luke 2.5-12 — Ah, Christmas! Think of the Christmas cards with the cozy stable, well-behaved animals, adoring shepherds and worshiping wise men.

Except the word usually translated as "inn" (verse 7) is the Greek word *kataluma*– which can also mean guest room or upper chamber. So forget the firs-century hotel, forget the grumpy innkeeper. It was in a very difficult, very harsh reality that God's son made his entrance on the world's stage: a peasant house where animals were kept and fed inside the home alongside the family. Joseph and his teenage bride stayed in a home so cramped that there was no room upstairs with the rest of their host's family; the only place to lay the baby was downstairs in the animals' feed box.

A small town in Palestine, a peasant's home, a helpless baby in the animal's feeding trough. The newborn Son of God is asleep.

REFLECT: Think of the images you've seen of sick babies and desperate mothers in run-down villages or refugee settlements. Now picture them in your house with all the comforts that you enjoy. Why shouldn't they have what you have?

RESPOND: Find out if there's a church or community-sponsored event near you that raises funds for the homeless. Sign-up and put the date in your calendar.

Prepare a meal or provide entertainment at a homeless shelter. Ride along in a van that delivers meals, clothing and blankets to homeless people who don't wish to go to a shelter. Offer them your prayers and friendship.

Lord, do you see the plight of those who are without a home? See how their lives are ebbing away. Please find them a place where they can settle. Thank you for your unfailing love and the wonderful things you do.

TO KNOW MORE:
Luke 2.5-12; Leviticus 25; Psalm 84 \\

Day 36 | *Sword*

PRAY: God connect with me here, as I seek you in your Word.

READ: Isaiah 2.2-4 — Weapons live on after the war is ended. Depleted uranium, land-mines, and unexploded shells. The peace treaty might have been signed, for many, the war never ends. This glorious passage (echoed in Micah 4.3) paints a picture of a society beyond warfare, the "last days" when nations listen to God instead of trying to blow each other up. It's not that there are no issues. It's just that firing missiles is no longer the way to deal with them. Here, the "peace dividend" in the last days brings agricultural growth, instead of military spending.

Wherever there are countries, there is military spending. Armaments are big business today. Many countries across the globe – wealthy and not so wealthy – spend large portions of their budgets on their military. But what if a small percentage of the military budget had been spent on infrastructure or development instead? What would the world look like without weapons?

REFLECT: Imagine a world with no weapons, but plenty of warm, well-fed people.

RESPOND: Let your government know what kind of world you want.

Lord, help those with power to exercise it wisely and with compassion. Help every nation and every person to consider the devastating consequences of war and to seek peaceful means for resolving conflicts. Help us to make the world a safer place for future generations.

TO KNOW MORE:
Isaiah 2.2-4; Isaiah 11; Joel 3 \\

Day 37 | *Weights*

PRAY: God connect with me here, as I seek you in your Word.

READ: Leviticus 19.35-37 — Heavenly behaviour, apparently, can be really down-to-earth. The book of Leviticus sees holiness expressed not only in terms of ritual and sacrifice, but in terms of simply doing the right thing. This chapter begins with a call to holiness and ends with telling people to make sure their scales are accurate!

Stealing can be subtle. Just tip the scales in our favour; shave a penny or two off a worker's pay; add some extras to the bill; make the packaging a bit fatter; or make the filling a bit thinner. The Bible condemns dishonest measures (Hosea 12.8; Proverbs 20.23; Amos 8.5; Micah 6.10,11). It's cheating; it's wrong. And it's the poor who suffer most from dishonest practices, the poor who cannot afford to fight such injustices in court. Fair trade means trading fairly with people and that business ethics should be, well, ethical. It means everyone working according to the same set of measurements.

It was the priests who were supposed to check that the scales were accurate (Exodus 30.13,24). What does that say about the role you and your church should play in seeing that fairness is done?

REFLECT: Are there ways, large or small, in which you cheat people? Even if you don't own the business, how you conduct yourself as an employee can make a difference. If your friends could see you at work, would they be satisfied that you treat every customer, client, and co-worker fairly?

RESPOND: Use the Internet to learn more about "fair trade" merchandise. Set yourself a challenge to buy fairly traded goods for every area of your life.

Lord, turn me into someone who is accurate and generous, honest in business, lending freely to others.

TO KNOW MORE:
Leviticus 19.35-37; Deuteronomy 25.13–16; Amos 8 \\

Day 38 | *Widow*

PRAY: God connect with me here, as I seek you in your Word.

READ: James 1.26,27 — True religion works from the inside out. What you believe is expressed by what you do.

Widows and orphans were some of the neediest people in ancient society. No benefit payments or welfare in those days. A woman without a husband could not go into business (not very easily), and children without parents had no one to look after them. Caring for such people was one of the hallmarks of the early Church. Even their enemies took notice.

Find the powerless and give them power, find the hungry and feed them. This is what good, true religion looks like.

Where is the widow or orphan around you? What are you doing to encourage agencies and institutions to provide transforming experiences to help them overcome their impoverishment? How does your church community assure that its worship practices embrace a vision for fully supporting the needy, and challenging agencies and institutions to offer greater care? What can Christians do to make sure that their actions speak as eloquently as their words on behalf of the marginalized?

REFLECT: Where there are orphans, picture whole families. Where there are widows and widowers, picture caring husbands and wives.

RESPOND: Increase the size of your "family." Include others who need to belong to a group of caring individuals. Read Matthew 25.36,43; Galatians 5.6

Our God, from your sacred home, you take care of orphans and protect widows. You find families for those who are lonely. Help me to see them and become a welcoming part of that family.

TO KNOW MORE:
James 1.26-27; Psalm 82; 1 Timothy 5.1-16 \\

Day 39 | *Obedience*

PRAY: God connect with me here, as I seek you in your Word.

READ: Acts 5.29-42 — It's interesting to notice how often the Christians of the early Church were in prison. Apostle Paul was falsely accused and jailed many times. Faced with unjust, ungodly laws, Christians sometimes need to follow the path of civil disobedience. Jesus was outraged by the corrupt practices of the money-changers in the Temple who were exploiting the poor. The early Christians sometimes staged protests refusing to worship the Roman Emperor. Here, Peter and the apostles lay down the ground rules: we must obey God rather than people. When the two come into conflict, God wins.

The Church has played a prominent role in civil disobedience in the past. Christians helped with the Underground Railroad that saved the lives of thousands of escaping slaves in North America. In World War II, Christians organized shelter for Jews escaping the Nazis. Christians have been prominent campaigners against apartheid, discrimination and war, and have worked to achieve prison reform, good health care, and public education for all.

There are higher laws. The demands of God are to be given priority over the demands of people and human institutions. The apostles were tried, abused, beaten. Why? Because they obeyed a higher calling from God.

REFLECT: What would cause you to protest against an unjust human law? What steps would you need to take first?

RESPOND: Go on, stick your neck out. Support a group whose action or campaign you can wholeheartedly agree with.

Lord, sometimes people need to have courage to be obedient to you above all else. This is true for those with power, and those without. I, too, need courage. You are an awesome God. Protect the rights of all, especially those who are oppressed.

TO KNOW MORE:
Acts 5.22-29; 1 Samuel 15; John 15.1-17 \\

Day 40 | *Redeemer*

PRAY: God connect with me here, as I seek you in your Word.

READ: Job 19.13-27 — Job lost everything except faith. Alienated from his friends and family, he scratched out a barebones existence on a garbage heap outside the city. And he cried to God for some kind of explanation.

What he wanted was not revenge, but justice. He wanted to leave behind a true, permanent record. He cried out for someone not to forget him, to set the record straight. He was a victim and he wanted to have things put right.

The Hebrew word translated here as "Savior" is *goel* ("redeemer"). A *goel* had the duty to seek justice for a murdered kinsman (Numbers 35.12-28). He had the responsibility to buy back the inheritance of a dead relative, which could mean redeeming someone from slavery or even marrying the widow to provide her with an heir. God is depicted as a *goel* of oppressed individuals (Proverbs 23.10,11) or even an oppressed nation (Exodus 6.6; Isaiah 43.1).

There are millions of people who sit in suffering like Job, longing for someone to tell the truth. In the slums of the world, in the garbage dumps outside the cities, in the prisons and the torture chambers, in the refugee camps, they need a redeemer. They need hope. They need someone to speak for them.

REFLECT: You could speak up for the millions who suffer. You could be their spokesperson. How could you do it?

RESPOND: Do whatever it is you do best: write, speak, volunteer, give–so that people know their Savior lives, so that they see God.

Lord, defend and protect oppressed men and women and nations! Keep your promise and save their lives.

TO KNOW MORE:
Job 19.13-27; Leviticus 27; 1 Peter 1.1-12 \\

Day 41 | *Talk*

PRAY: God connect with me here, as I seek you in your Word.

READ: Jeremiah 9.1-6 — Shortly before the collapse of Judah, no one could be trusted.

Prophet Jeremiah had enemies everywhere. Every conversation was a trap, every meeting a potential threat. From top to bottom, society was corrupt. People had taught themselves to tell lies, heaping sin upon sin and deceit upon deceit, refusing to acknowledge God.

Fast-forward 2,500 years, nothing much has changed for millions of Christians in the world today. They cannot talk about their faith or invite people to meet Jesus. In danger from their friends and families, the subjects of suspicion and lies, they trust in God because no one else is trustworthy.

Many people in the world are denied free speech. Their media is not free; they have no independent press. We can help their voices to be heard. We can raise the issues they cannot raise themselves. We are wealthy with freedom. Let us donate some to them.

REFLECT: Imagine being watched all the time. What sort of person would you become?

Picture a time when there is no pretense – what you see is what you get – and all the secret police are out of a job!

RESPOND: Which places in the world are threatened by free speech? Why? Find out. Learn what it means to be diplomatic. Find out how to write polite but effective letters to influential people.

Lord, help me to build trust in my family, church, and community by first putting my trust in you, the One who knows all my needs and seeks my welfare. Guide my actions and my words. Help me to be honest and fair in all my dealings.

TO KNOW MORE:
Jeremiah 9.1-6; Jeremiah 9; James 3.1-12\\

Day 42 | *Plague*

PRAY: God connect with me here, as I seek you in your Word.

READ: Mark 1.40-45 — Leprosy was the most feared disease of the ancient world. Considered ritually unclean, lepers were prevented from entering Jerusalem for fear of tainting the "Holy City." By law they had to cover their faces and cry out "Unclean! Unclean!" (Leviticus 13.45,46). Some considered lepers to be morally dubious, the victims of divine judgment. Jesus wants none of this. He is not afraid to touch the sickly man, unafraid to express his compassion. Seeing this, the crowds flock to him.

Today leprosy has been joined by diseases such as AIDS and pandemic viruses. As lepers experienced in biblical times, AIDS sufferers are viewed as having brought their misery on themselves. But even if that is sometimes true, there are millions of men, women and children who have simply been infected by others. Either way, Jesus still reaches out to them. We, too, need to share with them, not shun them, to restore their self-respect. We should reach out to them, not pretend they don't exist.

REFLECT: If only the world were free of all sickness and people did not waste away at a tragically early age. Imagine all those bodies, strong and healthy, able to participate fully in family life.

RESPOND: Pray for a swift end to the twenty-first-century devastation of HIV/AIDS.

Pray for the scientists struggling to develop better treatments and find a cure for HIV/AIDS, and for those who are ill or have lost loved ones to the disease.

Lord, there are people today who know what it is to be isolated because of illness. They lie on their beds, unable to move. Savior, please move to their aid and inspire those who are healthy to take action on their behalf.

TO KNOW MORE:
Mark 1.40-45; Leviticus 13.38-59; Numbers 5.1-10 \\

Day 43 | *Abuse*

PRAY: God connect with me here, as I seek you in your Word.

READ: Genesis 38.1-30 — Tamar is a Canaanite who marries into Judah's family. When her husband dies, she marries the brother, as custom dictates, to "carry on the line." But he cheats her, putting his own pleasure above God's promise to the patriarchs that they should father a mighty nation.

When Onan dies, Judah promises his next son to Tamar, but he doesn't mean it. So Tamar is trapped. She is an isolated, childless widow far from her own clan. Technically betrothed to Shelah, she cannot marry anyone else. She has been used and is now useless. So, disguised as a prostitute, she traps Judah, using his seal and staff as proof of identity.

This is the tale of a woman trapped into subservience and slavery. Lied to and betrayed by the men around her, Tamar is forced into prostitution. She is the forerunner of the victims of lies and broken promises. The morality of this tale is murky, but Tamar's courage and ingenuity are praised in the story. Tamar knows her duty and does it. So powerful is her example, that this lonely, desperate woman is even mentioned in the genealogy of Christ (Matthew 1.2-6a).

REFLECT: You have a daughter. What is your vision for her life?

RESPOND: Pray for the young people in your life. Add your voice to those fighting to stop the abuse of women and children through sex trafficking.

Lord, people who abuse others are behaving as if you are wearing a blindfold. They rely on fear to prevent their victims from crying out for justice. Give your people boldness to expose the wickedness of abusers and compassion to defend and support the helpless.

TO KNOW MORE:
Genesis 38.1-30; Psalm 34 \\

Day 44 | *Trapped*

PRAY: God connect with me here, as I seek you in your Word.

READ: Psalm 142.1-7 — Choice. It's a religion in the West. We're the customers and we demand lots of choices. So you can't just buy a coffee; you've got to choose from a roster of about 40. Look on the shelves of the supermarket: 20 kinds of cat food, 40 kinds of shampoo, 60 kinds of toilet paper.

Choice is a luxury that the poor cannot afford. They take what they can get. You don't get many lifestyle choices when you're concentrating on staying alive.

In this passage, the psalmist calls out to God to rescue him from the trap. He is trapped, imprisoned, hunted. "I am completely helpless," he cries (verse 5). Well, not quite. There is one choice left, one choice for everyone: the choice to follow God. "You are my choice," writes the psalmist. "You are my place of safety."

So think of this the next time you stand in front of the stacks of cat food at your supermarket. Poverty and faith go hand in hand; for many people in the world, God is the only choice they have.

REFLECT: Look around you. What choices are available to you today? Imagine you own a painting call "Freedom." What would you see in the picture?

RESPOND: There may be people living near you who feel trapped for one reason or another. Look at the expressions on their faces. Let them see your smile. Is there anyone who needs you to walk beside them?

Help, Lord! There are people who are frightened, trapped, imprisoned, hunted. Rescue them so they can praise your name.

TO KNOW MORE:
Psalm 142.1-7; Deuteronomy 30.11-20;
Joshua 24.14-28; Ephesians 1.1-14 \\

Day 45 | *Health*

PRAY: God connect with me here, as I seek you in your Word.

READ: Matthew 10.5-15 — Clearly, Jesus is giving his disciples a preaching mission. They are to tell everyone the good news. It also sounds like a medical mission. Heal the sick, cure leprosy, cast out demons – a mission to restore wholeness and health, to repair people who are physically, mentally, emotionally and spiritually broken.

The apostles are not to take money with them, nor store money. The business of heaven is not-for-profit. They are issuing invitations, not invoices.

Medical care is big business and cost of treatment is a barrier to healing for the poor. Pharmaceutical companies spend millions on research, development and promotion. But there are millions of poor people who lack access to basic medicine. Many companies are making efforts to give the poor their necessary medicines. How can we encourage them to do more?

REFLECT: Well-stocked medicine cabinets; warm, dry beds; privacy; speedy attention; specialist expertise. Pray that all people would be able to receive such care.

RESPOND: Estimate the worth of medicines in your house and donate an equivalent amount of money to a program providing medical aid to the poor.

Work with a church group to find the most urgent health issues in your community from a public health nurse and address these needs.

Lord God, when I am healthy, remind me that my health is a gift from you; help me to be grateful. When I am ill, help me to seek your face. Attend to the needs of all who need your healing presence, especially those with chronic and severe illnesses and those struggling with limited resources. Restore them to wholeness.

TO KNOW MORE:
Matthew 10.5-15; Exodus 15.22-27; Luke 10.29-37; Isaiah 6 \\

Day 46 | *Chains*

PRAY: God connect with me here, as I seek you in your Word.

READ: Deuteronomy 26.4-10 — The speech tells a story. Each individual worshipper recounts his/her shared history: a homeless Aramean gives birth to a mighty nation which becomes enslaved and God rescues them. The moment defines the relationship between God and Israel.

Slavery existed in several different forms in biblical times. At its worst, slavery was a life of unremitting exploitation and punishment. At its best, it was like being part of an extended family. Slaves never forgot that they were once owned as mere objects.

In our time, "officially" slavery has been abolished and unofficially, people are still enslaved in many parts of the world. Chains come in many forms. People are shackled by low wages as well as by leg irons. People are enslaved today because of human trafficking. According to the RCMP, 800-1200 people are trafficked in Canada each year, where a girl can be sold for $15,000 and can earn $40,000 per year for her owner. An estimated 1.3 million children are currently enslaved in the sex trade around the world.

God is a mighty Liberator. Wherever slavery exists in the world, God still wants us to set people free. We too have been freed from our slavery to sin.

REFLECT: Look at your clothes. Under what work conditions do you imagine they were made?

RESPOND: Learn about products from companies that mistreat their workers. Write a letter or email of protest to that company and commit to buying only products that are fairly traded.

Lord, throughout history You rescued people out of the deepest darkness and broke their chains as they prayed to you. Do it again today, Lord.

TO KNOW MORE:
Deuteronomy 26.4-10; Deuteronomy 26: Philemon 1 \\

Day 47 | *Women*

PRAY: God connect with me here, as I seek you in your Word.

READ: John 4.3-26 — Midday. The sun is at its hottest. A Samaritan woman comes to the well to fetch water and finds a stranger there. A Jew speaks to her and asks for a drink. A single Jewish man talking to an unchaperoned woman! And a Samaritan at that!

Doesn't he know the rules? There are lots of rules that guide behavior, designed to keep people in their place, to keep women at the well. They are denied education and employment, status and respect; some are little more than slaves.

It was the same in Jesus' day, but he had no time for rules. Throughout his ministry, he showed a special regard for women who were among his followers (Luke 8.1-3). They supported him – even when his closest male followers had deserted him (Mark 14.50). He rewarded their faith (Matthew 9.20-22). Jesus gave women a value and attention that was radically different in the socially rigid hierarchies of first-century Israel. Why? Because the water of life was for everybody. Of that, Jesus was certain.

REFLECT: What do the girls and women do in your household? What choices do they have? Compare that with how women are treated in other parts of the world.

RESPOND: Don't be afraid of such a vast subject. Dive right in and use the Internet to find out about women's rights. Be a revolutionary! Treat everyone with the same kindness that Jesus did.

Lord, you created every person in your image and you've given each of us special gifts. Help us to value ourselves and one another. Help us to assure that no one is denied a chance to contribute to the great work of loving and serving you.

TO KNOW MORE:
John 4.3-26; John 4.39-42; Luke 1.39-56; 1 Samuel 2.1-11 \\

Day 48 | *Convenience*

PRAY: Make me mindful, O Lord, of my many blessings.

READ: Genesis 3.17-19 — What is the hardest work you've ever had to do to get something to eat? Maybe you've spent an entire day in the kitchen preparing a special meal for someone's birthday. Maybe you've caught a fish for dinner. Or maybe you've had a bag of potato chips get stuck in a vending machine and had to keep rocking the heavy apparatus back and forth until the bag finally fell.

In this era of fast food, convenience stores and microwaveable meals, the only time many of us associate sweat on our brow with dinner time is when we're eating a spicy burrito. And most of us have never gone hungry so we don't think too much of the fact we're able to eat whenever and whatever we please. The flip side, of course, is that those who have gone without eating for a long period of time and who don't know where their next meal is coming from have a much greater appreciation for food.

Set aside a single day and consider each bite you take. Think about what went into producing it, the luxury of its sweet or savory tastes and how many minutes it took to earn the money it cost. Soon you'll begin to appreciate the blessing of nourishment and understand why many in the world never frivolously take their next bite, let alone their next meal, for granted.

REFLECT: We're probably all familiar with the image of a homeless person holding a sign that reads WILL WORK FOR FOOD. How about you? Are you willing to work for food? Not for yourself, but for those who do not have enough. Are you willing to give your time and energy, the sweat of your brow, to collect and deliver food for the needy?

RESPOND: Consider becoming involved with a Christian charity that provides meals to those in need.

Lord, help me to see the needs of the hungry and show me ways I can help minister to them in your name.

TO KNOW MORE:
Genesis 3; Ecclesiastes 2, 3 \\

Day 49 | *Sowing*

PRAY: Cleanse the thoughts of my heart, O Lord, so I can serve you with pure intent and plant seeds of mercy in your name.

READ: 2 Corinthians 9.9-10 — Have you ever planted seeds? You stick them in dark, rich dirt and wait for the sprouts to push through. You watch the progress until the plant is too large to fit in the little cup; then you transplant it into a bigger pot. You know that certain things need to happen in order to get a harvest: seeds, planted properly; enough nutrients, water, sun and protection from pests; and patience as you wait for the plant to mature.

Keep these principles in mind as you read Paul's words today. In the context of advice to the Corinthian Christians about giving, Paul expands the concept beyond giving money. The principle Paul quotes (from Psalm 112.9) says that godly people give generously to those in need and their good deeds will never be forgotten. You see, God gives you the resources, the opportunities, everything you need to do good deeds. It's your responsibility to plant them, care for them and harvest them. You cultivate the opportunities God gives you in order to produce more crops. So when you invest what God gives you in His work, He'll provide you even more opportunities to give in His name. God stands ready to start this growing process in you. So get ready for a great harvest.

REFLECT: Giving is a mark of godliness. Giving to the poor is like planting seeds that will bear great fruits of blessing; not only to those in need but to you as well since God will always remember every good deed done in His name.

RESPOND: Ask God to give you the seeds – the opportunities – you need to sow good deeds. Ask Him to help you share His Word, love and mercy with others today.

Lord, bless the work I am doing in your name and may there be an abundant harvest of mercy in your name.

TO KNOW MORE:
2 Corinthians 9; Philippians 4.10-23 \\

Day 50 | *Worth*

PRAY: I want to be an example of your goodness to others, O Lord, and to live a holy and righteous life.

READ: Psalm 15 — How much are you worth? If you had to put a price on yourself, what would it be? There are a couple of different ways to think about this. If you were somehow able to break down the chemicals and compounds that make up your body and sell them on the open market, you might get a few hundred dollars. That's not bad money, but it certainly doesn't qualify you as a priceless artifact.

Except to God. You see, God appraises us on a much grander scale. He places a much higher value on people than we do. For reasons that are beyond our comprehension, we are incredibly valuable in His eyes. Every person with whom we come in contact is precious to God.

Isn't that great news. After all, who wouldn't want to be valuable to God? On the other hand, it places a great deal of responsibility on us to treat others with care and compassion. When we mistreat God's "valuables" – for instance, the poor and needy – in a sense, we are disrespecting Him. By thinking of others in this way, it helps "realign" our attitudes and we begin to see what really matters through God's eyes.

REFLECT: How would you feel if someone came into your home and started treating your most expensive possessions as though they were junk? If God says all human beings are valuable, who are we to disagree with Him? And, if God cares for His precious possessions, who are we to mistreat them?

RESPOND: Find ways to develop relationships outside your social circle.

Lord, give me eyes to see the needs of others and the courage and compassion to respond.

TO KNOW MORE: Psalm 15; Luke 15 \\

Day 51 | Sharing

PRAY: Help me to be generous with others out of the abundance you have given me.

READ: Exodus 3.16-17 — Have you ever wondered what it would be like to be a ruler? Imagine having hundreds of servants, extensive land holdings and exquisite castles throughout your realm. Think about the storehouses full of food and wealth, all at your fingertips!

Believe it or not, Christians are indeed wealthy beyond all measure. We tend to forget that everything we have comes from God. Just as the Israelites were promised a land "flowing with milk and honey", He has promised us all the time, energy, talent, money and possessions necessary to meet our spiritual and physical needs. And, by giving us free will, He has also made us rulers over a living, breathing kingdom—our very lives.

What you do with the abundance you have been given not only has eternal implications but will bring you great personal satisfaction each day. It's one of God's wonderful ironies that the more joy we can bring to others the happier and more satisfied we are with our own lives. Do yourself a favor and, in Christ's name, do something nice for someone today—you'll be amazed at how good you'll feel.

REFLECT: Do you freely share your gifts with others? Are you a generous master or thoughtless miser? God, who is the master over everything, has been more than generous with us. Shouldn't we be just as gracious to others? Remember, it's not as important how much you have as it is how you use what God has given you.

RESPOND: Think about the gifts God has given you. Are you a good singer? Do people turn to you when they need comfort? Can you help others with budgeting or finding a job? Try to use your gifts in ways that will glorify Christ and His Kingdom.

Lord, thank you for all you have given me. Help me to be equally generous with others.

TO KNOW MORE:
Exodus 3; Exodus 6.1-12; Deuteronomy 9 \\

Day 52 | *Willingness*

PRAY: Lord, I am truly sorry for my sins and pray that you will forgive me for not loving you more or treating my neighbour as well as I have myself.

READ: Leviticus 5.7 — Have you ever been offered something of value by a poor person? If you're like most people, you would resist taking it. How, you might say to yourself, can I take what this person surely can't afford?

In Leviticus 5, God spells out to the nation of Israel His requirements for atonement. In simple terms, atonement means "at-one-ment", or the act of bringing us back to companionship with God, in spite of our sins. In this chapter He describes the kind of sin offering that pleases Him—a female sheep or goat. But what about people who were so poor that they couldn't afford to bring an animal of such value? Were they unable to please God? God provided a way for the poor to present an offering by accepting animals of lesser value. Did that in any way diminish the effectiveness of the offering? Definitely not.

Some of the best hospitality you'll find anywhere in the world is in the poorest countries. Here warm and gracious families may not be able to serve the finest foods, but they will typically offer all that they have. And, you'll find the meal far better than the richest foods served in a household that shares only what it can easily do without. This is because you know immediately they are giving with their hearts.

REFLECT: The amount we give to God is important, whether it's money, possessions or abilities. But God has a special interest in our willingness to give something that will cost us, regardless of how much we actually have.

RESPOND: Don't carelessly treat your tithes and gifts to the Lord as a necessary and generally unpleasant commitment. Give joyfully and with prayerful thought as you give your best to further His work.

Lord, give me a willing heart and a desire to give my all to you without any hesitation and with great joy.

TO KNOW MORE:
Leviticus 5.7; 2 Samuel 24; Romans 5 \\

Day 53 | *Doubt*

PRAY: Fill me with confidence, O Lord, so that I can boldly share your message of salvation with others.

READ: Matthew 11.1-6 — When things don't go right and we start feeling down, it's easy to doubt that God is really in control. But don't be afraid of your doubts—just look in the Bible. You'll meet Doubting David, Doubting Peter, Doubting Moses and, of course, Doubting Thomas. There is no shortage of doubt in the Bible. So, if you've ever had this struggle, you're in good company. John the Baptist, as we find in Matthew 11, even had a few questions as to whether this man named Jesus really was the Son of God.

John was a wild guy. He lived out in the desert wearing a rough hair shirt, eating bugs, and preparing the way for the Messiah. He was bold. He was unorthodox. He attracted mobs of people with his clear, strong message of repentance. John baptized Jesus whom he recognized as the Messiah sent by God. But soon after, he was imprisoned when he got into trouble with Herod. As he sat in a lonely, dark prison, he started to doubt. He sent his disciples to ask Jesus if he was indeed the Messiah. Jesus answered with the words we find in today's passage. The evidence was all around—blind people who could see, lame who could walk, deaf who could hear, dead who were made alive. Yes, the Good News was being preached and put into action. And, indeed, it still is today.

REFLECT: There's nothing wrong with doubt . . . unless you get stuck in it and let it harden into unbelief. Consider all the Bible characters who doubted: Each one ultimately realized that God was who He said He was. So whenever you get worn down by the responsibilities you carry as a child of God, think of John in that prison cell. God will surely bless you when you overcome your uncertainties and stand strong in your faith.

RESPOND: If you've been feeling some doubts lately, let God know about it honestly. He already knows your heart so speak openly with Him about how you feel.

Lord, help me to be an encouragement to others and to effectively share your Good News of new life in Christ.

TO KNOW MORE: Matthew 11; John 20.24-31; Hebrews 11.1-16\\

Day 54 | *Happiness*

PRAY: Help me to be joyful in all things, O Lord.

READ: Psalm 100.1-5 — Here's one of the most serious questions you'll ever have to answer. What is the purpose of your life? Consider the question for a moment before you answer. God made us to worship him. It seems like a fairly simple purpose, –one that shouldn't be too hard to understand. So why is it so difficult for us to fulfill our purpose? Because many of us have convinced ourselves that we need other things in order to be happy.

"If I had more money, then I'd be happy." Wrong! All you need to be happy is the sense of fulfillment that comes from pursuing our purpose in life. The apostle Peter spoke of a "glorious, inexpressible joy" that overtakes us when we focus our desires and energies on God and place our trust in him. Throughout the centuries, people have tried everything under the un to find fulfillment in their lives–sex, money, possessions, family, careers, fame, drugs, and so on. But the simple fact is that we find fulfillment only by worshipping our Creator.

Look at the Psalmist's words in verse 3: First we acknowledge that "the Lord is God". Nothing in this world has greater power or significance than Him. Then we recognize that "He made us" and, in the process, gave us purpose for our existence. Finally we see His purpose, that we would be "His people, the sheep of His pasture" (v. 3). As our shepherd or caretaker, God will go to any lengths to ensure that those of us under his care are safe and content.

REFLECT: Praise God that he has created you with an important purpose for your life. Ask Him for help to fulfill that purpose.

RESPOND: Turn your attention away from your own desires and seek ways to help and meet the needs of others. You'll soon find true peace and happiness as your focus becomes less self-centred.

Lord, give me a contented heart so that I can worship you with more joy and serve others with greater purpose.

TO KNOW MORE:
Psalm 100; John 4.23-34; Revelation 5 \\

Day 55 | *Dishonesty*

PRAY: Lord, help me be truthful and honest in all my dealings with others.

READ: Jeremiah 5.26-31 — "If it seems too good to be true, it probably is". Unfortunately, people usually learn the truth of this statement by being conned. Con artists prey on the weak, the desperate, and the unsuspecting. Baiting their traps with extravagant promises, they draw in their victims.

Jeremiah's prophecy shares what God thinks about those who set traps. No one likes cheaters. In fact, every society has laws to protect citizens from being and taken advantage of. Thus we have contracts, full disclosure and "truth in advertising". It comes as no surprise, then, that God would have harsh words for those who get rich off the poor by cheating them and denying them their rights. What is shocking about this passage, however, is that these "wicked men" are members of the family. God calls them "my people" (v. 26). And He promises to punish them severely.

Those who claim God as Father should live like His children. This means obeying Him and caring for each other. Too often, however, there is very little discernible difference between those inside God's family and the rest of the world. They may look good on Sunday at church and then live for themselves during the rest of the week. For example, instead of taking care of the poor, they take advantage of them through shady business deals. God warns these people that they won't escape his wrath.

REFLECT: Consider the ways you take advantage of others to promote your own agenda. Do you exalt yourself by pushing down others? Do you enhance your status at someone else's expense? Determine to be part of God's solution, not the problem.

RESPOND: Confess those times you have done something unkind or dishonest to others so you would benefit.

Dear Lord, I want to live a life that reflects your goodness and integrity. Guide me in all my ways so that others will know that you are my heavenly Father.

TO KNOW MORE: Psalm 52; Ephesians 4.25-5.21 \\

Day 56 | *Judgment*

PRAY: Help me to be kind to others, Father, and to turn from harshly judging their actions.

READ: Romans 2.1-16 — It's not hard to walk down the street and look at various people with a judgmental attitude. That guy's on drugs. She isn't a good mother. They probably don't work and are on welfare. Well, if you've ever judged people like that—even if your opinions were correct—Paul the Apostle would like to have a word with you. Imagine the first Christians who listened as Paul's letter was read. After some opening words of encouragement, he jumped right in, talking about the sinfulness of humanity without God.

The people listening to these strong words about sinners were no doubt shaking their heads as they heard Paul's arguments. Paul read their minds: Some of you accuse others of doing wrong, but there is no excuse for what you do.

He was pointing out that they were doing many of the things they condemned in other people. The fact that they weren't being judged (yet, at least) was due solely to God's kindness, tolerance and patience with them. Christians can rejoice that Jesus paid the penalty for our sins. We can be assured of heaven. But we also know for sure that persistent sin leads only to great sorrow and personal tragedy.

REFLECT: God's judgment isn't based on who we are related to or how much money we have or how important we are in the community. Don't use these superficial things to assess a person's worth and decide that he or she is unworthy of your respect and kindness. We all stand equal before God and this is how we should view and treat those around us—regardless of their circumstances.

RESPOND: If you have been engaging in persistent sin—sin that you know can cause you and others harm—now is the time to get right with God. Confess your sin and ask Him for forgiveness.

Lord, forgive me of my sins so that I can serve you better and love others more effectively.

TO KNOW MORE: Romans 2.1-26; 1 John 1 \\

Day 57 | *Independence*

PRAY: Lord, help me to find complete and lasting freedom in you.

READ: Psalm 104.21-29 — Perhaps you spend a lot of time dreaming about becoming independent, not having to answer to anyone or live by your family's or employer's rules and regulations anymore. Independence is one of the most prized possessions in our society. But should it be? The author of Psalm 104 has a lot to say to people who believe they can handle life on their own.

Being overly dependent on someone else is usually viewed as weakness – and, in extreme cases, a mental illness. However, dependency on God is not a weakness; in fact, it's really nothing more than facing reality. God sustains all life every moment of the day. Apart from him nothing can exist.

If we really believe that every breath depends of God, shouldn't our lives reflect that belief? In fact, as extreme as it sounds, we should acknowledge our dependence on God in everything we do and say. So, instead of trying to accomplish things on our own, we should submit ourselves to God's agenda and allow him to carry it out through us.

REFLECT: By making ourselves dependent on God's provision, mercy and guidance we are free to turn our attention outward and to find ways to help others in their particular circumstances and needs. Use the freedom God has given you to bring relief into the lives of those bound by uncertainty and shackled by the cares of this world.

RESPOND: Ask God to make you aware of what He is doing in the lives of others around you. Notice the things that you can do to help and then make yourself available.

Lord, thank you for the freedom I have in you through Christ. Help me to bring your message of grace to a hurting world.

TO KNOW MORE:
Psalm 104; Ezekiel 37.1-14; John 15.5 \\

Day 58 | *Communication*

PRAY: Hear my prayer, O Lord, and help me to listen to your ever-present voice.

READ: Daniel 10.1-3 — Big events require preparation. We must pay attention to details if we want to enjoy a relatively stress-free life. In a similar way, we must pay attention to our preparation for meeting God. If we enter His presence casually or impatiently, how will we be ready to listen? Let's look at Daniel's life. His example shows us why he was ready to receive an important message from God.

One of the most amazing truths about God is that He desires to communicate with us. Not only does He want us to listen when He speaks, He also wants us to tell Him everything – our thoughts, fears, sins and hopes. The fact that God listens to us is especially important when we ask Him for help.

In order to communicate with God, to talk and listen to him, we don't have to follow some specific formula or ritual. What we do need to do is to set aside time to focus our minds on Him and His word. When we want to bring a specific need to the Lord in prayer, what are we willing to sacrifice out of our daily routine in order to focus all of our attention on asking God for help?

REFLECT: Our communication with the Lord is not limited to specifically scheduled quiet times. We have the opportunity to enjoy God's presence every day in many different ways. But just as we need focused time with any person with whom we want to have a relationship, so we need it with God. And there are times when that will take sacrificial preparation.

RESPOND: Ask God to help you strengthen the lines of communication between you and Him and between you and those who need to hear about the wonderful things He has done in your life.

Dear Lord, I pray for the discipline to develop an effective prayer life so I can walk according to Your will each day and share your Gospel message with others.

TO KNOW MORE: Daniel 9, 10 \\

Day 59 | *Goodness*

PRAY: Thank you for your daily kindness to me, O Lord. May I show the same mercy to those around me.

READ: Psalm 107.1-9 — Aslan, the lion in C. S. Lewis' classic children's novel The Lion, the Witch, and the Wardrobe, represents Christ. Lucy, a young girl, learns about Aslan from Mr. and Mrs. Beaver of the land of Narnia. Lucy is perplexed to hear of Aslan's fearsome nature. "Then he isn't safe"? Lucy asks Mr. Beaver. "Safe"? replies Mr. Beaver, "'Course he isn't safe. But he's good".

Psalm 107 offers some stunning examples of the goodness of God. This good God is the same fearsome Lord who destroyed the earth with a flood and sent horrible plagues on the land of Egypt. Throughout history God's holiness and judgment have struck fear in the hearts of men and women. Even God's angels caused people to tremble. It's no wonder that an angel's first words were often, "Fear not".

But according to this psalm, the redeemed – those whom God has brought into his family – can declare that God is good. Israel knew of God's goodness through his deeds. He brought the nation back together after it had been scattered by Assyrian and Babylonian conquerors. He rescued them from wandering in the desert and provided food and drink for them. He heard their cries for help and rescued them from their distress. He is unchangeable and what He did for His people then He will surely do for you today if you regularly call on His name.

REFLECT: Sometimes we may not recognize God's goodness. We may become perplexed by his awesome nature. We will never be able to understand God completely – at least not during our time on earth – because we are not God. But, regardless of our confusion, we can rest assured in the fact that God is good.

RESPOND: Ask God to help you and your family become instruments of His goodness to the poor and needy in your area.

Lord, show me ways that I can share your goodness with those who need a kind word and a compassionate shoulder to lean upon.

TO KNOW MORE: Psalm 107; Habakkuk 3 \\

Day 60 | Harmony

PRAY: Give me a spirit of cooperation, dear Lord, so that I can be a useful and vital part of your great Kingdom.

READ: Acts 6.1-7 — A 21-speed bike is an ideal picture of what working together is all about. Sprockets, derailleur's, shifters, control cables and chains work together hopefully in perfect unison. The result is a smooth transition uphill and down, one that gives endurance, fitness benefits and sustained power.

Sometimes, however, one part of the system gets out of alignment or breaks. When that happens, obviously the whole mechanism comes to an abrupt stop. That was what happened to the early church. From Scripture we learn about the church and how this body was intended to function smoothly as each person took a part. However, believers would encounter "abrupt stops" and would have to solve the problem in a creative and God-designed way.

First, they organized themselves. After agreeing on a plan, they divided the workload. At last, responsible people stepped up to the tasks at hand. A difficult process? Not really, unless one part of the body failed in its contribution. Note that rumblings, discontent, and complaining occur if we don't all carry our weight.

REFLECT: When we come together as Jesus instructed, He is glorified. And when we don't, we're distracted from our purpose. The mechanism, the organism we call the church, comes to an abrupt stop just like a busted bike. But when we share the work, God is glorified, and the number of believers greatly increases. Now that's a reward for teamwork!

RESPOND: If you can't identify your spiritual gifts, ask God to reveal them to you and pray for a servant's heart to use them for others.

Help me to find ways to successfully work in unison with fellow believers, Lord, so we can serve others more effectively.

TO KNOW MORE: Acts 6, 7 \\

Day 61 | *Unselfishness*

PRAY: God connect with me here, as I seek you in your Word.

READ: 2 Peter 1.14-21 — One of the greatest tenets of our faith is that the original manuscripts are inspired. The Scripture is "carried along by the Holy Spirit" or "God-breathed". Miraculously, the writers' personalities and uniqueness still came through. The Truth to be revealed was the driving force and all of this came from God and God alone. Could this be one of the greatest examples of unselfishness and committed love? These men, not developing their own agendas, willingly allowed themselves to be used for another's goal by the Holy Spirit. It was not one small act of sacrifice but they allowed the breath of God to push their pens.

This entire passage is a model of unselfishness for us, beginning with Peter's admission that he's about to die and his chief concern for those he leaves behind. He isn't concerned about their remembering him; instead, he desires that they not forget the inspired words – The Word – that God had used him to pen.

REFLECT: Peter takes or claims no glory for himself but constantly points toward the Lord he serves. Peter speaks of the confidence we have in Scripture because of the miraculous way it came about. God-breathed? Amazing! Yes, but nothing less than the fact that the Holy Spirit resides in you and me. He doesn't push your pen . . . but he does want to direct you in a life of unselfish love.

RESPOND: Picture the Holy Spirit's involvement in your life like a glove in which you need to insert each finger to be fully directed and used. Prayerfully ask: How much control do I give Him?

Lord, make me a willing and unselfish instrument of your will so that I can serve you and your Kingdom fully and more faithfully.

TO KNOW MORE:
Psalm 71.18; Isaiah 9.2; Romans 6.6 \\

Day 62 | *True Riches*

PRAY: God connect with me here, as I seek you in your Word.

READ: James 1.9-11 — How do you feel when you meet people who are very wealthy? Do you admire them? Are you jealous of what they possess – their clothes, their "toys," their cars? Do you hope you'll become their friend? How do you feel when you meet someone who's poor? Do you feel jealous then? The funny thing is, the Bible says the poor are the ones we should be jealous of, because they're the ones God has honoured! Want proof? Read today's Scripture.

James points out that the thing about wealth is that it's easy come, easy go. In the short term, if the stock market goes down a few points, a wealthy stockholder can lose millions of dollars, just like that. And in the long term – the eternally long term – wealth isn't even a factor because money doesn't exist in heaven. While poor people may be looked down on by a society that worships wealth, God raises them up and honors them. That's quite a contrast with the rich. James says they should be glad too, but for a different reason. Whether you're rich or poor, your attitude is what counts.

REFLECT: True wealth is found in growing your spiritual life, not your assets. God's more concerned with the eternal (our souls) than the temporary (our money and possessions). So no matter how much money you have in your bank account, keep your priorities straight. Know God. Serve Him.

RESPOND: Pray for the wealthy people you know. Ask God to reveal the truth about money and possessions to them and help them keep a proper perspective. Pray for the poor people you know. Ask God to meet every need they have.

Lord, I pray that I will never be jealous or resentful of what others have but will instead be grateful for all that you have generously given me.

TO KNOW MORE:
Deuteronomy 15.7; 1 Samuel 2.8; Proverbs 17.5 \\

Day 63 | *Falling Up*

PRAY: God connect with me here, as I seek you in your Word.

READ: Psalm 113.5-8 — Have you dropped anything lately? If so, you know that Murphy (the compiler of the infamous "Murphy's Laws") was right. If you drop a book, it will fall into a puddle. If you drop a bite of food, it will miss your napkin by less than a centimeter and end up in your lap. If you drop a tool while working on your car, it will roll to that exact spot where you can't reach it without crawling underneath through the grease.

In a spiritual sense, people slip or fall. The good news of Psalm 113 is that God can reach down, pick us up, and put us back where we belong. Our God is an awesome God. Nothing in the entire universe compares with Him. Yet God cares for his creatures. He looks down from on high and locates his children in trouble. The psalm tells us that he lifts the poor and sets them among princes. What does all this mean? In a spiritual sense, God can lift us from the depths of sin. In a physical sense, God can also rescue those on the edge. This psalm assures us that those who have fallen, who have slipped through the cracks of society, are not forgotten by God.

REFLECT: God wants to use you as His hands and feet to help pick up those who have fallen. The prayers you offer to God, the money you give to support a hungry child, the time you volunteer to serve in an inner-city mission; these are just a few of the ways God can use you to retrieve his precious creatures who have slipped or fallen.

RESPOND: Join the psalmist and praise the Lord for His greatness and love, Pray that every day both rich and poor will experience a fresh expression of God's love and come to a saving knowledge of Christ. Ask God also to show you new ways you can be His hands and feet to those who need to be picked up.

Lord, thank you for supporting me through both good and difficult times. May I give similar support and comfort to those in need.

TO KNOW MORE:
James 2.5; Luke 1.52-53; Job 5.15-16 \\

Day 64 | *Prosperity*

PRAY: God connect with me here, as I seek you in your Word.

READ: Proverbs 11.24-25 — What is the quickest way to prosper in our society? What is the best route to financial success? The first order of business is choosing the right profession. A career in technology might be a good move. Most doctors have bright financial prospects. Lawyers, for better or worse, are always in demand. After you've chosen a vocation, you'll need to come up with a financial strategy for your earnings. The stock market can pay big dividends, but it's risky. Mutual funds are safer but less likely to produce huge windfalls. You might also invest in anything from art to classic cars.

So in a nutshell, the quickest way to prosperity in our society today is choosing a well-paying career and then investing your money wisely. Right? Well, that may seem like a good plan, but the Bible offers an even quicker route to financial success in our reading today from Proverbs. To God, the true measure of prosperity is not how much a person has, but how generous that person is. It sounds odd doesn't it? The more we give away, the more we receive. But the key to understanding God's "balance sheet" is to look beyond the financial aspects of giving and receiving and to consider the eternal rewards that come from having a generous, giving heart.

REFLECT: The person who gives freely of his or her time, energy and money is going to impact a lot of lives and gain many friends. On the other hand, the stingy person who withholds money and who chooses not to share with others misses out on some tremendous opportunities for personal fulfillment and prosperity.

RESPOND: Ask the Lord to help you keep a proper perspective on prosperity and to encourage you to give freely of your time, energy and money.

Lord, I pray that you will instill in me a spirit of generosity and that I will always remember the source of my abundance.

TO KNOW MORE:
Proverbs 19.17; Luke 6.38; Ecclesiastes 11.1-2 \\

Day 65 | *Tribulations*

PRAY: God connect with me here, as I seek you in your Word.

READ: Job 1.20-22 — On the nightly news you watch footage of a town devastated by a hurricane. A few survivors speak to reporters in angry tones or seem bitter. Others project an image of a sad but quiet trust in God. Why the different reactions? Why do some people seem to lose their faith during times of intense trial, while others develop a stronger faith? The bigger question is: How do you react when life gets crazy?

The Old Testament book of Job tells the story of a wealthy man whose faith was severely tested. When Job's livestock and children were killed in freakish accidents, his reaction was remarkable. Notice that Job expressed great grief. But he also demonstrated deep trust in God. He bowed down, prayed and worshipped! How could he praise God in the midst of such tragedy? Apparently he understood God's sovereignty and that God is in complete control. He refused to accuse God of cruelty and never demanded answers. In your life, when the "roof caves in", how do you react? Do you yell at God or try to find a way to numb the pain? Or do you trust in the truth that God's ways are higher than yours?

REFLECT: It's important to remember that we can't control what happens to us, but we can control our responses to unfortunate circumstances. When hard times come, we can (and should) feel sad. We can (and should) be honest with God. Then by choosing to believe that God will somehow work everything together for good (Romans 8.28), we can endure. Like Job, it's possible for us to praise God, even from the pits!

RESPOND: Ask the Spirit of God to show you any "demanding" attitudes in your heart. Rather than blaming God for bad times and turning away from Him, why not express your trust that He is in control and turn to Him? Ask the Lord also to show you a hurting person today, someone you can encourage.

Lord, I pray for patience during difficult times and that I will always trust in your goodness and faithfulness .

TO KNOW MORE:
1 Thessalonians 5.18; Ephesians 5.20; James 1.17 \\

Day 66 | *Ignored*

PRAY: God connect with me here, as I seek you in your Word.

READ: Psalm 40.16-17 — Have you ever felt ignored? Do your peers at work ever discuss a group outing and leave you out of their plans? Has your family ever made you feel insecure and less than perfect? Read today's verses to find out about someone who is always thinking about those who feel ignored and rejected.

What confidence this passage expresses! It begins with the most important requirement for all believers: they must search for God. Those who want joy and gladness will not find it apart from Him. But if they search, they will find, and their joy will be complete and unshakable. Thus the poor person, who might be inclined to worry or curse his or her situation, waits with quiet confidence in God's goodness. That person may be ignored and despised, but he or she has a companion in God. Such favour is worth more than all the friendships in the world.

David is not telling us that God thinks only about the poor and needy; he reminds us, instead, that confidence in God enables us to put earthly troubles in perspective. No matter what happens, no matter who turns a cold shoulder, we have the friendship of our heavenly Father.

REFLECT: Remind yourself today of the great privilege of friendship God gave you when you came to Christ. Thank Him that you are no longer ignored. Then think about the needs of those who are ignored and rejected. Commit to pray for them. Take steps to ease their loneliness. Just as Jesus was known for befriending the friendless, we must be known by the kindness we show.

RESPOND: Thank God for the gift of his eternal friendship, then pray that you will be able to help someone who is lonely or ignored.

Lord, reveal to me those who need my friendship and let me be a light to them in your Name.

TO KNOW MORE:
Philippians 3.7-9; Psalm 105.3; Isaiah 65.13-14 \\

Day 67 | *Cliques*

PRAY: God connect with me here, as I seek you in your Word.

READ: Genesis 1.26-27 — Sometimes it seems like the entire world is made up of cliques: Upper class, middle class, lower class, baby boomers. Gen Xers, haves, have-nots, etc. In a society so intent on emphasizing differences, it can be tough to find common ground with other people. And yet, in the first chapter of the first book of the Bible, God makes it clear that everyone who draws breath on this planet shares one important characteristic: We're made in the image of God.

Most people learn at an early age that the world consists of "us" and "them". When one of us is in trouble—whether it's a friend, family member or neighbor—we'll usually do our best to help that person. When one of them is in trouble—a homeless person who lives in the park, an immigrant family struggling to support themselves without a steady income or a starving tribe in a foreign land—we're not as motivated to help. Why? Because we don't take their plight personally. We feel very little connection to them or their situation. We have nothing to gain by easing their hardships. Or so we think.

In reality, if we take God's words spoken at creation to heart, we will recognize that we're all created in God's image. When we choose to ignore the struggles and difficulties of our neighbours, no matter who they are, we slight the ones who bear the imprint of God's marvellous creation.

REFLECT: When we choose to get involved in the lives of those who are struggling, when we decide to focus on similarities rather than differences, we reflect not only God's image, but His grace as well.

RESPOND: Pray that you will focus more clearly on the similarities that you share with other people, especially those of a different culture or social position.

Lord, I pray that I can look past superficial differences and see others as created in your image, as people worthy to be loved and cared for.

TO KNOW MORE:
Colossians 1.15; Isaiah 43.7; Psalm 139.14 \\

Day 68 | *Depression*

PRAY: God connect with me here, as I seek you in your Word.

READ: 1 Kings 19.1-8 — It seems to be a law of nature and a fact of life that what goes up must come down. Often a mountaintop experience is followed by a trip through the valley of despair. Consider the case of Elijah. If anyone had a reason to celebrate a mountaintop experience it was this courageous prophet of God. Single-handedly he had stood against a tyrannical queen and hundreds of pagan prophets and triumphed over them all. His victory on Mount Carmel demonstrated God's power over his enemies in a way that shook Israel to its foundations. Yet where do we find Elijah after his stunning victory?

In today's passage we see that Elijah was caught in a wave of depression. Even after all he had seen and done, he declared that his life was no longer worth living. But God helped him by providing food and rest. Away from the noise and turmoil of Ahab's kingdom, he was able to regain his perspective and resume his faithful ministry.

REFLECT: We need to take the lesson from Elijah's life to heart. People who are constantly in motion need time apart from the turmoil to be with God. A constant schedule of work – even great work for God's Kingdom – can empty and drain us, leaving us depressed, restless and unsatisfied. We need to practice the habit of being still, listening to God's voice instead of talking; hearing instead of doing. If we do, we will find contentment in all circumstances.

RESPOND: Set aside five minutes and clear your mind of all distractions. Choose a favourite Bible verse and meditate on its meaning. Then ask God to help you think about and live out this verse throughout the day.

Lord, give me confidence, peace and rest for the responsibilities you have given me and the challenges I face each day.

TO KNOW MORE:
Psalm 34.10; Hebrews 1.14; Psalm 37.3 \\

Day 69 | *Living and Dying*

PRAY: God connect with me here, as I seek you in your Word.

READ: Mark 8:34-38 — When you decided to become a Christian and follow Christ, did you sacrifice or give up anything in your life—maybe a habit, a group of friends or an attitude? In the time you've been a Christian, have you ever faced any suffering or mistreatment because of your faith—perhaps taunting or derogatory jokes aimed your way? Nobody said being a Christian would be easy, right? In fact, Jesus Himself paints a rather stark portrait in Mark 8 of what it means to follow Him.

Jesus wanted his followers to understand one thing: Just as suffering, rejection and sacrifice were part of Jesus' life, they will also likely be part of the believer's life. Jesus gave a three part explanation as to what it means to follow Him. First, a person must deny himself—that is, shift his focus away from himself and toward Christ and his ministry. Second, a person must pick up his cross, demonstrating a willingness to suffer and die for the Lord's sake, if necessary. Third, a person must follow Christ, patterning his life, actions, and attitude after Jesus'.

REFLECT: Jesus' words make it clear that following Him is not a decision to be taken lightly. The possibility of actually dying for the Lord's sake underscores the seriousness of our faith. And yet it has been said that it is harder to live for the Lord than it is to die for Him. Anyone who has ever struggled to deny himself in order to minister to others knows how hard living for Christ can be. Placing the needs of someone else first—particularly those of the poor and "unlovable" of the world—goes completely against human nature. Yet that's what Christ calls us to do. So, are you willing to die for Christ, if necessary? More important, are you willing to live for Him?

RESPOND: Ask the Lord to help you maintain an "others first" attitude as you minister to people in your community and church.

Lord, I pray you will give me the courage to live for you and to die to my own selfish needs and desires.

TO KNOW MORE:
John 10.27; Galatians 5.24; Revelation 2.10 \\

Day 70 | *Friendship*

PRAY: God connect with me here, as I seek you in your Word.

READ: Proverbs 14.20-21 — "I just don't know who my real friends are anymore". How many times have you heard a celebrity say something like that? The pattern is inevitable: When a person becomes rich or famous, he or she is suddenly surrounded by a large group of friends, acquaintances and hangers-on. Everybody wants to be your buddy when you're on top.

When you're at the bottom, things are different. The poor and anonymous have very little trouble determining who their real friends are – they often don't have any friends. It seems cruel that on top of the economic frustrations that come with poverty, poor people have to suffer socially as well.

Why do you suppose so many of us feel uncomfortable about associating with the poor? Are we afraid that our reputations will suffer? Perhaps we avoid the poor in an effort to keep them anonymous. It's easy for us to ignore the plight of the needy if they're just a faceless group of people. If they're our friends, however, it's difficult for us to refuse to help them.

REFLECT: The book of Proverbs is quite clear on how we should treat the poor: Those who despise their neighbour sins but those who are kind to the needy are blessed. Showing kindness to the needy involves sharing food (Proverbs 22.9), lending money (Proverbs 28.8) and defending their rights (Proverbs 31.9) – all things that a good friend would do. Are you prepared to become a friend to the friendless? Are you prepared to show kindness to the needy?

RESPOND: Ask the Lord to create in you a heart a compassion for the needy and a desire to befriend the disadvantaged in your neighbourhood or community.

Lord, give me opportunities to be a friend to the friendless and a source of encouragement to those who are downhearted.

TO KNOW MORE:
Psalm 112.9; Proverbs 17.5; James 2.14-16 \\

Day 71 | *Legalism*

PRAY: God connect with me here, as I seek you in your Word.

READ: 1 Samuel 21.1-6 — Victor Hugo's Les Miserables tells the story of Jean Valjean, a man who is sentenced to hard labor after stealing a loaf of bread to feed his starving family. Even after his release, he is pursued by a cruel police official named Javert who will stop at nothing to keep Valjean under his power. Valjean, by his wits and courage, eventually overcomes his adversary.

Today's passage concerns another fugitive running from a vengeful pursuer. Like Valjean, David takes bread to survive his ordeal with the insanely jealous Saul. The loaves mentioned here – one representing each tribe – belonged to the priests and symbolized God's provision for Israel (Leviticus 24.5-9). In this story, David needs God's provision. He is running away from Saul, though he hides that secret from others (1 Samuel 21.2). Knowing his life is in danger, David asks for help. Despite God's regulations against it, Ahimelech gives David the holy bread for food because it was the only food available.

REFLECT: Jesus later cited this event to criticize the Pharisees for keeping religious customs while forsaking God. In Jesus' mind, saving a godly but starving David had been more important than keeping religious law. Healing someone was better than "not working" on the Sabbath. Jesus didn't condone lawbreaking but urged acting with a spirit of goodness that the law endorsed. Compassion matters more than tradition and customs to Jesus, and should, in turn, matter more to us.

RESPOND: Ask God for a compassionate heart toward people. Ask the Holy Spirit to reveal areas of spiritual pride or arrogance. Confess any ways you have made certain religious practices more important than caring for others.

Lord, show me how to be generous with my kindness and generosity toward others even when it conflicts with my comfort zone or the attitudes I've held my entire life.

TO KNOW MORE:
Mark 2.25-27; Luke 6.1-11; Matthew 12.3-4 \\

Day 72 | *Peacemaking*

PRAY: God connect with me here, as I seek you in your Word.

READ: Genesis 26.20-25 — "That's mine!" "No, it's mine!"

If you've ever been around children who fight over every toy, you know the frustration. After quickly intervening and making peace between them, you probably tried to teach the importance of "sharing" and "cooperation". But a few minutes later, they were at it again.

Some people never grow out of their selfishness. In fact, today's passage tells of jealous and spiteful grown men. Although resources were scarce in the land, God blessed Isaac with an abundance of crops and animals. This only enraged his jealous neighbors, who filled his wells with dirt and told him to leave. Then, after moving and digging a new well, the local shepherds claimed that well as their own. Instead of arguing or fighting, Isaac moved again, doing what was right and trusting God to provide for him and his family.

The natural human response is to claim what is rightfully ours and then to fight for it. Isaac's lesson, however, is that God has "room enough". That is, God will provide for our needs when we trust in Him and live the way he wants us to live.

REFLECT: Isaac had a heritage of faith. By remembering God's care for his father, Abraham, in the past, he was confident of God's care in the present. Each time Isaac responded with love and concern instead of anger toward his enemies, God met his needs. He'll do the same for us. What a great God we have!

RESPOND: Thank God for His continual provision for all your needs and confess any feelings of jealousy or resentment you may he harbouring.

Lord, help me to not look at others with jealousy and resentment and to always be thankful for your many blessings.

TO KNOW MORE:
Psalm 118.5; Luke 12.32; Hebrews 13.6 \\

Day 73 | *Neighbours*

PRAY: God connect with me here, as I seek you in your Word.

READ: Luke 10.25-37 — Who is your neighbour? The people who live next door? Okay . . . who else? Check out what Jesus says in today's reading. The man who asked the question was Jewish. The one who got beaten on the road was Jewish. Jewish people passionately hated the Samaritans (and the Samaritans returned the feeling). In today's story, one Jewish person after another walked past the hurting man. Only the despised Samaritan treated his "enemy" as a human being who needed help – a person worth loving and caring for.

A common and familiar summary of this parable is that the robbers beat the man up, the priest and Levite passed him up, but the Samaritan picked him up. The thief said, "What's yours is mine, I'll take it". The priest and Levite reasoned, "What's mine is mine, I'll keep it". But the Samaritan said, "What's mine is yours, we'll share it". How are we to interpret this morality tale? Jesus succinctly gives us the answer – "Go and do likewise".

REFLECT: Jesus' story gives us three truths to keep in mind when it comes to loving our neighbour: (1) Our neighbour is anyone who needs help, no matter their race, color, creed or social background. (2) We can always justify or rationalize not helping someone, but doing so is never right. (3) Loving our neighbour means acting in order to meet that person's need. Now, ask yourself again: Who is your neighbour?

RESPOND: Pray for your neighbours today. But don't stop with the people who live near you. Pray that as you come across anyone whose life is in turmoil, no matter who they are, God will work through you to meet their needs.

Lord, help me to see each person I encounter as a "neighbour" who is deserving of my kindness and mercy.

TO KNOW MORE:
Romans 13.9; 1 John 3.18; James 2.8 \\

Day 74 | *Responsibility*

PRAY: God connect with me here, as I seek you in your Word.

READ: Ecclesiastes 5.8-11 — More than a hundred years ago, a young woman named Hetty Green inherited a large fortune in property and investments. Yet she was determined to have more. Stingy and shrewd, she turned her sizable sum into an even greater fortune. Her appearance and manners matched her frugal ways. She wore faded and tattered clothes and traveled in a rundown carriage that had once been a henhouse. In her old age, she imposed her tightfistedness on others and criticized those who did not heed her advice. She supposedly died during an argument with a servant over a houseguest's spending habits.

The author of Ecclesiastes wrote about the trap of wealth thousands of years before Hetty Green was born. A greedy, never-enough attitude dwells deep in the human heart. Unfortunately, many act on that impulse and increase their wealth at someone else's expense. And more often than not, the victims are the poor and needy.

What can be done about this unfair situation? Plenty. We don't live in the same kind of society the writer of Ecclesiastes lived in. Our rulers are not sovereign kings who answer to no one but themselves; our rulers answer to us, the people. We have a say in what our leaders do. So when we see the poor and needy being abused, we have a right to do something about it.

REFLECT: God tells his people to take care of the less fortunate in society. Those of us who recognize that riches are meaningless compared to the needs of others must take action when we see the poor hurt.

RESPOND: There are many different ways to take action and help others with what we have, but it all starts with a right attitude toward riches.

Lord, show me where I can be of service to others and give me the courage to take action when I see injustice against those who are vulnerable.

TO KNOW MORE: Luke 22.15; 1 Timothy 6.10; Psalm 52.7 \\

Day 75 | *Kindness*

PRAY: God connect with me here, as I seek you in your Word.

READ: Ruth 2.1-10 — There are amazing and inspiring stories in every land and culture throughout history of showing kindness to strangers, sometimes at one's own peril and risk. In today's passage, kind Boaz makes Ruth (a Moabite) feel at home in Israel. Boaz's kindness to Ruth was surprising because Israel and Moab were enemies. Boaz was obviously a kind man – demonstrated in part by the way he blessed his workers.

Ruth is referred to as a Moabitess five times in the book of Ruth to repeatedly affirm her "otherness" – a negative in the eyes of Boaz's and Naomi's people. In addition, she was a gleaner which was an activity only the poorest members of this culture engaged in. Yet, none of this mattered to Boaz. As an honorable man of God, he ignored what others thought or said – and there were undoubtedly many raised eyebrows, snide comments and smirks when the subject of Ruth came up. His attitude is an example for us and a wonderful demonstration of how God expects us to treat the "gleaners" we see each day.

REFLECT: As believers we need to model Boaz's kindness. He not only helped Naomi and Ruth rise out of poverty, he also treated them respectfully. Boaz never looked down on them. In fact, he calls Ruth his "daughter" and eventually married her, giving her a real home. When we run into people different or less fortunate than us, we must treat them with dignity, just as Boaz treated Ruth.

RESPOND: Ask God to help you offer kindness to others, regardless of criticism.

Lord, I pray that I will faithfully be kind to others and will look for opportunities to share your love with those who need it most.

TO KNOW MORE:
Psalm 118.26; 2 Thessalonians 3.16; 2 Timothy 4.22 \\

Day 76 | *Repaid*

PRAY: God connect with me here, as I seek you in your Word.

READ: Luke 14.12-14 — If you were throwing a dinner party and could invite any ten people who ever lived, whom would you choose? Think of it–any ten people, famous or infamous. Depending on how creative you wanted to get, you could have some fun with your guest list.

Dinner parties in New Testament times usually had very specific guest lists. Reciprocity means doing something for another person and then expecting something of equal value in return. Jesus pointed out that it's no great sacrifice to invite someone to dinner when you know that you will be repaid for it later. A more generous and loving act would be to invite the poor, the crippled, the lame, and the blind–people who cannot repay the generosity.

The same concept holds true today. The rich and powerful are treated with great respect because people want their favor in the future. But, if a person is unable to care for him/herself, let alone repay a favor, then most people turn their backs on the person's hurts and needs. This is the kind of attitude Jesus is addressing. We must learn to help those who really need us–those who can't offer us anything in return.

REFLECT: True generosity is one-sided. It involves doing things for others simply because we care about them and because God expects us to–without any thought about what's in it for us. Eventually we will be rewarded for everything we do for the poor and needy. We may never see any evidence of this repayment in this world, but we can certainly expect it in heaven.

RESPOND: Ask God to make you aware of someone in your community to whom you can show some one-sided generosity. Ask if you can help them in any way, knowing that you'll get nothing in return.

Lord, I want to be a selfless giver–help me to see the needs of others and to share my time and attention in a way that will give them hope and dignity.

TO KNOW MORE: Proverbs 22.16; Matthew 5.46; James 2.1-6 \\

Day 77 | *Signature*

PRAY: God connect with me here, as I seek you in your Word.

READ: Isaiah 41.17-20 — You're listening to the radio in your car when you hear a song you've never heard before. You listen intently as you like what you hear and it's your favorite group and you recognize the guitar riffs, the lead singer's voice and the style of the lyrics. You can become so familiar with an artist that you can recognize his or her work instantly, even though you may never have heard the piece before. That's because all musicians have a "signature" – a style or trait that makes their craft stand out.

In the same way, as Isaiah tells us, we can recognize God's work through His great miracles. God's chosen people were wandering through the desert on the verge of dying from thirst. God used supernatural means and caused rivers to flow from barren mountains and springs to emerge from parched ground in the desert. God went to miraculous lengths to protect his people in the Old Testament. But does he still use supernatural means to help those who need him today? He does – through His people. The world often fails to notice these quiet wonders carried out by people who love God and take His commandment to love others with great seriousness. This is the mandate of love we have each been given.

REFLECT: We cannot begin to fathom the awesome power of God and the possibilities of that power as it relates to those who are suffering in the world. We can, however, be faithful to obey God's instructions to care for people in need whom we come in contact with, and trust Him to take action when He deems it necessary.

RESPOND: Spend some time in prayer, praising God for His awesome power and for the fact that He loves his people enough to help them in times of need.

Lord, I praise you for all that you've done for me, for my loved ones and for making provision for people around the world.

TO KNOW MORE:
Psalm 50.15; 2 Corinthians 12.9 \\

Day 78 | *Wants and Needs*

PRAY: God connect with me here, as I seek you in your Word.

READ: Numbers 11.4-10 — Mom, there's nothing to eat!" The young woman, puzzled by her nine-year-old's statement, walked into the kitchen and opened the refrigerator. Sliding open the cooler drawer, she saw several fresh apples and oranges, a bag of carrot sticks and strawberries. Looking in the pantry, she found crackers and fruit bars. "What do you mean?" she replied to her daughter. "We have plenty of food!" The girl wandered into the kitchen and made a face. "Not that kind of food!" she whined. "I mean cookies or potato chips!"

When the Israelites left Egypt for the desert wilderness, they needed food to sustain them. God took care of his people by sending manna, food from heaven, for them to eat every day. One day, however, the Israelites decided that they also wanted meat and vegetables in their diet. This request was met by anger from God.

The Israelites confused their needs with their wants. They needed God and his provision; they wanted more. Mistaking needs for wants is a common problem. In fact, need is one of the most misused words in the English language. "I need a new tablet PC." "I need a new car." "I need to live in a better neighbourhood." Perhaps the best way to tell the difference between a need and a want is to ask, "What will happen if I don't get it?"

REFLECT: The question we must regularly ask ourselves is this: Once our needs are met, should we be more interested in taking care of our wants or helping others meet their needs?

RESPOND: Ask God to help you distinguish between your wants and needs and to help you recognize the needs of others.

Lord, I pray that you will help me to distinguish between my wants and needs so that I'm not complaining about the lack of things I really can live without.

TO KNOW MORE:
Romans 13.14; Psalm 78.18-20; John 6.27 \\

Day 79 | *Community*

PRAY: God connect with me here, as I seek you in your Word.

READ: Acts 2.42-47 — Advertisers are brilliant at depicting a life-style that the world considers ideal. It seldom, if ever, includes satisfying the needs of more than an individual, a couple or a family. But today's verses are a revealing snapshot of what we're supposed to be about as a church and what our goals should be.

Early believers shared, worshipped and praised together. What a cause for rejoicing! Obviously, they were practicing what we must still do today. These early Christians made the decision to put aside their whims and desires so that others could be rich in the Lord, rather than striving to be materially rich while making others poor.

Does that mean we must literally be poor? No, of course not, but it does mean that we must choose to live a lifestyle that ultimately serves God rather than ourselves. No, it isn't easy. It will be a constant struggle. But note once again the result of their commitment: People were saved every day. In many ways, it comes down to a clear question and decision. What will I invest in? We must constantly evaluate whether our aspirations are for things or people.

REFLECT: Picture in your mind the latest technological marvel that you've been admiring. Now, consider the needs of certain families in your church. Helping someone else instead of acquiring another personal possession may be the greatest bargain you've ever experienced or enjoyed.

RESPOND: Consider what wants you have that are not in line with God's desires for your life. Confess these and ask God to challenge your heart.

Lord, I pray that you will challenge how I spend my money and time – help me to develop priorities that are pleasing to you.

TO KNOW MORE:
1 John 1.3; Romans 12.12; 2 Corinthians 8.14-15 \\

Day 80 | *Success*

PRAY: God connect with me here, as I seek you in your Word.

READ: Jeremiah 51.45-48 — Drive through neighbourhoods where many wealthy people live, and you'll see spacious and meticulously manicured yards. The ornate and large houses often look like palaces. Many of the homes have backyard swimming pools, and the driveways have luxury cars parked in them. Judging from the appearance of things, you may assume that the people living in these communities are very successful. But is success just based on what a person has?

Today's passage contains Jeremiah's message to another group of people who looked very successful on the outside: the Babylonians. They were the most affluent and powerful nation on earth. But were they really successful? Obviously God was not very happy with them. Even though they were successful in the eyes of the world, they were failures as far as God was concerned. That's because they valued wealth and possessions over faithfulness to God.

In contrast, Jeremiah was a total failure in the world's estimation. He had lived most of his life under the rule of evil kings who had no respect for God. He was rejected by his neighbours and his nation's leaders and was even tortured and threatened with death. He had no money or status. In the end however, Jeremiah and not the Babylonian kings received God's seal of success.

REFLECT: Earthly wealth disappears quickly, but eternal wealth lasts forever. Jeremiah made the right choice in being faithful to God although it cost him just about everything. Determine to be a success in God's eyes. He's the only one who really counts.

RESPOND: Ask God to help you desire his brand of success rather than the world's.

Lord, I pray that my vision for success will meet your biblical standards and that I will aspire to greatness in your eyes alone.

TO KNOW MORE:
Jeremiah 46.27; Luke 21.28; Luke 21.9-19 \\

Day 81 | *Underdogs*

PRAY: God connect with me here, as I seek you in your Word.

READ: Psalm 12.5-8 — Everybody loves to root for the underdog. There's something exciting about seeing the "little guy" prevail in the face of overwhelming odds. The higher those odds are, the harder we cheer. Many in the entertainment industry have built thriving careers on the conviction that audiences will flock to films where the strong and powerful are vanquished by the least likely of heroes or heroines.

But here's something you may not know: God also roots for underdogs. In fact, he does more than root for them. In today's reading from Psalms we find that God "will protect the oppressed, preserving them forever from this lying generation, even though the wicked strut about and evil is praised throughout the land."

God protects the weak and needy of the world in countless ways. The primary instruments He uses are His Christian servants. In fact, caring for and protecting the less fortunate are natural extensions of a Christian's relationship with God.

REFLECT: Caring for others can take many forms. It may involve physical protection – not necessarily from threatening people (although that may be the case sometimes), but from the elements. What can you do to make sure that the needs of your city's underdogs are met?

RESPOND: Ask God to help you understand your responsibility to the needy people in your area. Also ask Him to give you wisdom and courage when it is time for you to act on their behalf.

Lord, open my eyes to the needs of those around me – of the people who don't have an advocate or who are alone in a harsh and difficult world.

TO KNOW MORE:
Psalm 10.18; Psalm 74.21-22; 1 Peter 1.5 \\

Day 82 | Sincerity

PRAY: God connect with me here, as I seek you in your Word.

READ: Romans 12.9-18 — You know the type. In fact, a little too nice and friendly. You can't help but feel they have an ulterior motive and pretend to show concern. They may promise to pray for you about something but as soon as they leave you, you're certain they have totally forgotten about you. It's hard to feel close to people like that because they're not real. The things they do and say don't have much power when their words don't match their actions. As you read today's Scripture passage, keep in mind the difference between doing right, and really meaning it.

In verse 9 Paul reminds us to not "just pretend that you love others. Really love them". That's the key. Paul goes on from there with a whole list of ways to demonstrate the Christian walk. Notice the words Paul uses emphasize great enthusiasm. This is the core of the Christian life. If we love and serve someone as Christ has loved and served us, we will be living just the way He wants us to. That means loving, serving and reaching out to others sincerely and with an open heart and hands.

REFLECT: To love someone sincerely takes concentration and effort. It demands time, money and energy. It means helping without ulterior motive, giving without expecting anything back, and serving just because God wants us to. Does that sound too hard? It's not, if you trust God to give you the wisdom and guidance you need to do it.

RESPOND: Ask God for a genuine heart: one that longs to really love and honour people and stands up for what's right. Ask Him for an opportunity today to put your heart into action for someone else.

Lord, I pray that I will truly love others with a sincere and willing heart and that I can be a blessing to those you bring into my life.

TO KNOW MORE:
1 Timothy 1.5; 1 Peter 1.22; Hebrews 12.14 \\

Day 83 | *Trust*

PRAY: God connect with me here, as I seek you in your Word.

READ: Obadiah 1-9 — Are you sitting down? Then you're trusting that chair to keep you from falling. Do you have an alarm clock? Then you're trusting it to make sure you wake up. The only problem is that chairs can break and alarm clocks can fail to go off. So who or what is left? Read the first nine verses of Obadiah to find out.

Obadiah was a prophet from the nation of Judah. He was called by God to declare judgment on the nation of Edom. God was angry at the Edomites because they had rejoiced over the dismal fate of Israel and Judah. Edom was located just south of Judah. The capital at this time was Sela, a city the Edomites proudly felt couldn't be attacked. It was cut into rock cliffs and could only be approached through a narrow gap in a canyon. They trusted their high city to be safe, but God said they would fall from its heights. They also trusted in their own self-sufficiency, in their wealth, in their allies and in their own wise men. But every single thing the Edomites put their trust in would be totally destroyed by God. They had put their trust in the wrong things. Don't make the same mistake.

REFLECT: In prayer review your life before God. Ask yourself: whom do I trust? Are the people and things you get your security from keeping you from placing your total trust in God? Thank Him that He is totally trustworthy and that you can always rely on Him. Then commit to trusting in Him for all things.

RESPOND: Trust that God will give you wisdom as you reach out to others. Don't rely on your own preconceived ideas or personal prejudices but place your daily walk and ministry fully in His hands. He will never forsake you or steer you down a fruitless path.

Lord, I trust you with all that I have and I am grateful that you will never forsake me or ignore my pleas for your guidance and ever-present help.

TO KNOW MORE:
Proverbs 29.23; Proverbs 16.18; Psalm 33.10 \\

Day 84 | *Listening*

PRAY: God connect with me here, as I seek you in your Word.

READ: Psalm 22.24-28 — As Jesus hung on the cross, with the weight of the world's sins on His shoulders, He cried out, "My God, my God, why have you forsaken me?" At that moment Jesus was completely alone, abandoned even by His heavenly Father. Is it possible that there are people in the world today who feel similarly abandoned by God? Think of the African mother who watches three of her children die slowly and agonizingly of starvation because of a drought in her country. Is it possible that this woman might feel forsaken by God? More to the point, would she be justified in feeling that way?

What is God's attitude toward the suffering of His people on earth? What can we expect of Him? In the opening verse of today's passage we read, "For he has not ignored the suffering of the needy. He has not turned and walked away. He has listened to their cries for help." David's words in Psalm 22 make it clear that God cares about the suffering of the afflicted. He hears all cries for help, and he uses a variety of means to respond to those cries. As Christians, we must understand that we are among those "means," that we are instruments of God's grace, and that we have a responsibility to respond to the needs of others.

REFLECT: It's easy to dismiss others' suffering as being beyond our ability to help. Yet nothing is beyond God's ability. If we allow ourselves to be instruments of his healing, there is no limit to what can be accomplished. All it takes is a decision on our part to get involved.

RESPOND: Ask God to make you aware of ways in which He can use you to help alleviate suffering.

Lord, open my ears to the needs of others and give me a willing heart to answer their urgent pleas.

TO KNOW MORE:
Psalm 105.3-4; John 4.14; 1 Peter 2.9 \\

Day 85 | *Comfort*

PRAY: God connect with me here, as I seek you in your Word.

READ: 2 Corinthians 1.3-7 — Unfortunately, life is full of painful events, ranging from a paper cut to the loss of a loved one. At times like these, our faith can really grow. How do you respond when something bad happens to you? Do you get angry and sulk or withdraw in sadness or give up or press on? Paul suffered incredible difficulties and pains for his faith, and he offers a different way to deal with troubles in our reading today.

When troubles arise, the first thing to do is ask God for his comfort. That doesn't mean that the troubles will suddenly vanish. If that is so, people would turn to God as a pain reliever. Instead of popping a couple of aspirin, they'd shoot up a prayer. Our relationship with God is based on a desire to love and serve Him – not just a thing to do when we need help. Being comforted by God means getting the strength, the hope and the encouragement we need to get through our troubling situations. Similarly, when others are troubled, we should be able to give them the same comfort God has given us (v. 4).

REFLECT: Think about the opportunities you have to reach out to someone with God's comfort. What a privilege that can be. When someone comes to you hurting, lonely or frustrated because of their troubles, you can offer them understanding, acceptance and love in Jesus' name. You can be the channel for God's comfort in their lives. And there's no greater blessing than that.

RESPOND: If you're wrestling with troubles in your life, take a step back and look at the big picture with God in prayer. Ask Him to shower you with His comfort. Then ask Him to give you opportunities to share that comfort with others who are hurting too.

Lord, I pray that I can be a blessing to others and that I can share the peace that passes all understanding with those who need you the most.

TO KNOW MORE:
Psalm 32.7; John 14.26; 1 Thessalonians 5.11 \\

Day 86 | *Giving*

PRAY: God connect with me here, as I seek you in your Word.

READ: Malachi 3.6-12 — One of the touchiest and most confusing issues in all of Christianity is giving—specifically, how much Christians should give to the church and to other ministries. Some people say that "tithing" means giving ten percent of one's income. Other people say that tithing is the bare minimum and that Christians should give "offerings" on top of that. How much of an offering, you may ask? There is no agreed amount. Still others suggest that believers should simply give "what they can". But that doesn't really clarify anything, does it?

Do you see why giving is such a touchy issue? Too many unanswered questions and too many divided opinions. The only opinion that really matters, of course, is the Lord's. Based on His words In Malachi 3, we might conclude that if God were asked the question, "How much should a Christian give?" his answer would be, "More!"

This seems like an odd test, doesn't it? "Go ahead and give everything you can," the Lord dares. "See if I don't reward you beyond your wildest imagination". Quite simply, the more we give, the more we receive. God has an entire warehouse full of blessings that He's just waiting to pour out on those who are not afraid to give to Him and His ministry.

REFLECT: The more time, energy, and money we dedicate to the Lord and His work, the more blessings we can expect, in this world and in the next.

RESPOND: Thank God for the resources you have been blessed with and ask Him to help you give wisely and abundantly.

Lord, help me to be a cheerful giver and to share abundantly with those in need.

TO KNOW MORE:
Isaiah 55.6-7; James 4.8; Proverbs 3.9-10 \\

Day 87 | *Friends*

PRAY: God connect with me here, as I seek you in your Word.

READ: Galatians 2.1-5 — One of the basic tenets of the medical profession is "First do no harm." All medical caregivers – physicians, surgeons, nurses, emergency medical technicians, psychiatrists – are bound by this principle. The idea is that before any treatment is administered to a patient, the caregiver must determine to the best of his or her ability that the treatment will not injure or put the patient at risk.

Christian servants should adopt this principle. Before we do something to care for or protect a person in need, we should consider the implications of our actions. In our eagerness to minister, we may end up doing unintentional harm. The apostle Paul set up a system to safeguard his ministry. Paul guarded against losing his ministry focus by surrounding himself with people who would prevent him from going astray. He gave importance to companionship and fellowship through his friendships with Barnabas and Titus. This means that we need to find mature Christians who will be willing to serve as "sounding boards" and advisors to us. They will keep us from going astray and making hasty decisions or unwise plans.

REFLECT: Who are your friends? Can they be trusted to give you sound advice and that needed "second opinion"? Make it a point to surround yourself with mature and trustworthy friends.

RESPOND: Ask God to place people in your life who will further your ministry and challenge you to be your best.

Lord, bring people into my life who will encourage me in my Christian walk and who will be wise and godly advisors as I seek to serve you.

TO KNOW MORE:
1 Thessalonians 2.13; Psalm 51.12; 1 Peter 2.16 \\

Day 88 | *Dependency*

PRAY: God connect with me here, as I seek you in your Word.

READ: Matthew 6.10-13 — Guangzhou, China. Picture a bustling, crammed city with pedestrians, buses, motorcycles, bicycles and taxis—all jockeying for position. Does it sound like the city or town you live in? Not quite, for in Guangzhou there are no traffic laws or streetlights. Direction and U-turns are decided at will. We're talking a free-for-all, something like bumper cars on a grand scale. So when you climb into the front seat of a taxi, you learn quickly what it means to be totally dependent on that driver.

This image puts dependence in a whole new category. It's like what Jesus was trying to get across to His listeners when He first taught what we call "The Lord's Prayer". Because we've heard it so many times and have a tendency to repeat it, we've stripped this incredible prayer of the heart and depth of its meaning. To help restore this, picture your hands outstretched, palms up and open. In this position, we're vulnerable to Him, waiting, accepting, totally dependent on Him to fill, take away, lead and direct. Unfortunately, though, we're not always open to Him, we don't act or respond with this kind of posture. Instead, we have a tendency to wrestle with God, attempting to force Him to do what we want, our way, in our timing. We face Him with closed fists, ones already filled with our wants and desires.

REFLECT: Considering the messes we make of our lives, isn't it pathetic that we still insist on taking charge, attempting to do what we want? When we take a close look at what we've accomplished—as compared to God's plans for our lives—generally we realize we don't really want to be in charge after all. He knows what we need. He knows what's best for us. And He will provide.

RESPOND: Ask God to point out areas in which you're wrestling with Him. How are you attempting to drive your "taxi?"

Lord, I give my life fully to you and pray that you will guide me in all that I say and do.

TO KNOW MORE:
Psalm 40.8; Matthew 12.50; Hebrews 13.21 \\

Day 89 | Gifts

PRAY: God connect with me here, as I seek you in your Word.

READ: Ephesians 4.11-16 — A missionary in Africa was teaching an adult Bible class. During time for examination, he reminded them: Don't cheat! As soon as he handed out the exams, he found the pupils turned to one another sharing answers. The teacher was confounded that they ignored his instructions and violate such an important code of ethics. Finally, a national missionary came to his aid to explain the mystery. Don't cheat to them meant: Don't withhold valuable knowledge from one another!

In a way the students were merely exhibiting what Paul says in our reading today. Notice that Christ gave "gifts" to the church, and those gifts are given to apostles, prophets, evangelists, pastors and teachers – in other words, people just like us. Other gifts listed elsewhere in Scripture include hospitality, service and prayer. Each one is of infinite value and is absolutely necessary for the church to properly function. The design, fitted together by God, hinges on cooperation, commitment and contribution. So, if one withholds his or her gift, the church suffers. Each believer must do his or her part, or the church is cheated of that needed contribution.

REFLECT: The reward for fully committing to God's church – God's kingdom on earth – Paul tells us, is harmony and maturity. By growing together with others in Christ, we will not be deceived by wrong ideas. The church is indeed a living organism, formed of many parts to create a whole. Are you bringing your part to the living body with your God-given gifts?

RESPOND: Ask God to point out specific ways you can contribute to your local church. Prayerfully consider: Do I have a servant's heart?

Lord, thank you for the gifts you have given me. May I use them to your glory and in service to others.

TO KNOW MORE:
Ephesians 4.8; Acts 20.28; 1 Corinthians 12.7 \\

Day 90 | *Risk*

PRAY: God connect with me here, as I seek you in your Word.

READ: Matthew 25.14-30 — Have you ever gone whitewater rafting? If so, you know how nerve-wracking it is to negotiate your boat past giant rocks and over sudden drops. Veteran rafters know how falling into the river can result in serious injury. But, after you've braved your first trip down river, you also know how satisfying it is to make it safely to the takeout point. The feeling of accomplishment is worth all the risks. In today's passage, Jesus encourages us to take a big risk – to use all that we've been given for His glory.

Our talents, abilities, opportunities and gifts all come from God. He wants us to use what we've been given to forward His Kingdom. The issue is not what others have been given; the issue is being faithful with what we have. Serving God is risky business. It calls us to step out of our comfort zone and do things that are hard and sometimes a bit scary. However, if we are willing to give Him our all, we will eventually find fulfillment and joy we would never have known otherwise.

REFLECT: On a raging river, rafters put their faith in trained guides to take them safely through the perilous waters. How much more should we trust in God when stepping out into personally "uncharted territory" – whether it's volunteering at a shelter for families or joining your church's community outreach team. He has never failed those who keep their eyes on Him and He never will.

RESPOND: Confess any ways you have failed to use your gifts to glorify God. Commit yourself and all that you have to serving Him faithfully each day.

Lord, give me the courage to risk my all for you so that I can discover the joy that comes from being a faithful and fully committed follower.

TO KNOW MORE:
1 Corinthians 12.4; 1 Peter 4.9-11; Philemon 1.6-7 \\

Day 91 | *Eternity*

PRAY: God connect with me here, as I seek you in your Word.

READ: 1 Thessalonians 4.13-18 — Is there anything tougher than trying to comfort someone at a funeral? Often the best we can hope for in a situation like that is not to say something that causes even more pain. If you've ever lost a loved one, you probably know that people can say some inappropriate things when they're trying to "comfort" you.

The apostle Paul strongly encouraged Christians to comfort each other in the face of death. Paul explained a Christian's eternal destiny to the Thessalonians. Believers who died – or "have fallen asleep," as Paul put it – will be brought first to heaven by God as a result of Jesus' resurrection. Believers who are still alive when Christ returns will meet the Lord in the air on their way to heaven. Either way, all believers can look forward to spending eternity with the Lord. Those of us who try to comfort others with Paul's words need to keep this in mind. Grieving people may not always respond to our efforts to comfort them in the way we hope. If you're a person who wants to be able to provide real comfort to others, Paul's words in 1 Thessalonians 4 should be of great help to you.

REFLECT: Christ's resurrection opened the door for all believers to be resurrected, so death is certainly not the end. There's never been a grave dug that could hold the spirit of a believer. The trite saying still rings true: Christians who have died are in a much better place than we are.

RESPOND: Spend some time in prayer for people you know who have lost loved ones. Pray that in their mourning they will come to know (or be reminded) of God's victory over death.

Lord, help me to bring comfort to those who have lost a loved one and to have the appropriate words to give them the hope of eternity.

TO KNOW MORE:
2 Peter 3.4; 2 Corinthians 4.14; Isaiah 26.19 \\

Day 92 | *Rules*

PRAY: God connect with me here, as I seek you in your Word.

READ: Matthew 12.1-8 — "Rules were made to be broken". You may have heard somebody use this old saying. Some people just like to break the rules and get away with everything. Sometimes they get caught, but often they are not.

That doesn't seem fair, does it? God calls us to be obedient to His Word. His principles are always for our own good. But admit it, you've thought of breaking a few rules over time. In our reading today Jesus and His disciples broke some religious regulations . . . and got into trouble. It was the Sabbath–Saturday, the Jewish day of rest. Jesus and His disciples were walking through a wheat field grabbing at the heads and eating the grain. Some of the religious leaders caught the disciples in the act. They pointed out that it was against the Jewish law to "work" on the Sabbath.

Jesus answered them boldly. Of course the Sabbath is supposed to be kept holy. It's intended to be a time to set aside your work and worship God. The Pharisees kept the letter of the law but forgot the purpose of the law. Jesus reminds us of the real meaning behind the letter of the law–that God wants our honest, meaningful worship and obedience. Only when our hearts are right with God can we truly obey Him and do His will.

REFLECT: Jesus shook up the religious establishment of His time. Yet He never sinned. He never broke a single law of God. He was able to live a life of perfect obedience. Let Jesus be the Lord of your Sabbath and the Lord of every day of your life as you rely on Him for strength and direction.

RESPOND: Ask God to show you if and when you are just going through the motions of following the rules rather than obeying for the right reasons.

Lord, help me to be obedient to your Word with a joyful heart and a willing spirit.

TO KNOW MORE:
Mark 2 and Luke 6 \\

Day 93 | *Mercy*

PRAY: God connect with me here, as I seek you in your Word.

READ: Hosea 6.4-6 — "Give the gift that keeps on giving."
The idea is that the gift will continue to have value and impact as
time goes on. Prophet Hosea learned of another gift that keeps on
giving – the gift of mercy.

The Bible is filled with commandments that God expects us to
follow and instructions for pleasing Him. Hosea 6.6 explains
that God wants us to be merciful. Mercy is showing kindness,
compassion and love to someone who has no reason to expect
such treatment and who has nothing to offer in return. The Lord is
the ultimate gift-giver in this department. Because of sin, humans
are destined to spend eternity apart from God. But the Lord
showed mercy on us by sending His only Son to pay the penalty
for our sins, thus giving us an opportunity to spend eternity with
Him. No greater gift has ever been given.

Now this is where the "keeps on giving" part comes in. Because
we have received mercy from the Lord we have a responsibility to
show mercy to those who have hurt or offended us. Mercy does
not allow us to ignore the plight of someone who may have been
unkind to us. It calls us to show kindness, compassion and love.
Letting go of anger or our desire to settle a score takes time and
effort. We have received God's wonderful gift of mercy. It's only
natural that we should pass it on.

REFLECT: Mercy is not simply an attitude; it's a way of life. We
can't just "feel" mercy for another person; we have to show it in
our actions.

RESPOND: Spend some time praising the Lord for the mercy
He has shown to you. Then ask Him to help you show the same
type of mercy to others.

*Lord, I pray that I will be merciful to others in the same
way that you have shown infinite mercy to me.*

TO KNOW MORE:
Isaiah 5 and 2 Peter 2 \\

Day 94 | *Impossible*

PRAY: God connect with me here, as I seek you in your Word.

READ: Matthew 14.13-21 — Very often you may think: The task that lies before us is impossible. When you consider the many people who need help in this world, it's obvious that you cannot help all of them. How can we possibly feed all the hungry people? Help all the sick and hurting? Tell the world about Jesus Christ? It's overwhelming for sure. But think back to an "impossible" challenge that had the disciples shaking their heads with disbelief.

The people had been following Jesus, hungry for His word and His touch. Though He was tired and wanted some time alone, He had compassion on them and healed their sick. By evening, everyone had become hungry for food as well. Imagine the disciples' shock when Jesus said that they should feed them. There were only five loaves of bread and two fish. It was "impossible"! But Jesus multiplied it far beyond the need. Thousands ate and were filled. There were even twelve baskets of leftovers. Jesus had turned the impossible inside out. Today believers face a number of "impossible" tasks. But don't let yourself get overwhelmed by the immense need you see when you look at the big picture. Focus on the specific areas in which you can play your part as God guides you.

REFLECT: Remember, you follow the same Master the disciples did. He is all-powerful, all-knowing and all-loving. He is the Master of the impossible!

RESPOND: Pray God will remove the word "impossible" from your vocabulary as you trust Him more and more to do His amazing work in your life.

Lord, give me the courage to believe that you can accomplish the impossible through my efforts for your Kingdom.

TO KNOW MORE:
Mark 6 and John 6 \\

Day 95 | *Complacency*

PRAY: God connect with me here, as I seek you in your Word.

READ: Hosea 10.11-12 — Whatever the situation, it's nice to be content and comfortable.

Complacency has no part in the lives of God's people, as the Israelites discovered during the time of the prophet Hosea. Israel (referred to as "Ephraim" and "Jacob" in today's passage) had become complacent. Too often contentment and comfort lead to complacency and being self-satisfied. God compares the nation to a contented young cow that eats while it threshes grain. The Lord then warns that He will soon shake them from their complacency.

Why do you suppose God is so strongly against complacency? Perhaps the best explanation is that complacency is a problem of the heart. It indicates that we have become detached from God and His concerns. God has a tremendous plan for His people—a plan that requires work on our part. If God has blessed us with material possessions, we must not forget that those blessings are not merely for our own enjoyment; they're for the benefit of the entire Kingdom. We are commanded to use the blessings God has given us to help others. We must never forget or ignore that responsibility.

REFLECT: It's very, very easy to become complacent—often without even realizing it. That's why it's important to regularly check ourselves for signs of self-satisfaction.

RESPOND: Ask God to help rid any complacency in your life so that you can serve Him to your full potential.

Lord, I pray that you will show me areas of my life where I have become complacent and give me the desire to do your will with all my heart.

TO KNOW MORE:
Hosea 2 and John 15 \\

Day 96 | *Assumptions*

PRAY: God connect with me here, as I seek you in your Word.

READ: Matthew 16.21-26 — In the 1950s in Britain, physicians began writing prescriptions for a new drug called Thalidomide to reduce the severity of morning sickness. By the time scientists discovered that it was a direct harm to developing fetuses, more than 10,000 infants had been born with physical deformities. The drug was immediately recalled, but thousands of families had experienced profound trauma.

Many bad mistakes result from people with good intentions. Peter, who had been with Jesus, thought he had God figured out by this point. What was Peter thinking when he rebuked the Lord for talking about the suffering that lay ahead for Him? Maybe he had no idea what the Lord was talking about and just said the first thing that popped into his mind. Whatever the reason, Peter said the wrong thing. But Peter found out that he didn't know the situation as well as he thought.

Like Peter, we who have lived the Christian life a while may think we have God figured out. But if we are honest, we will begin to see a pattern: We are imposing our expectations on God. And as Jesus reminded His disciples, that is an attitude that is doomed to fail. We have to put aside selfish tendencies, whatever the cost, to follow Him.

REFLECT: What wrong ideas and bad attitudes are keeping you from hearing what God is saying today? Ask the Lord to give you the strength to take up your cross and follow Him.

RESPOND: Ask God to help you see things as He does. When you gave your heart to Him you also gave Him your trust that He knows best and that our assumptions, when not backed up by Scripture and fervent prayer, are misguided.

Lord, I pray that you will guide me in all of my actions and deeds so that I am living perfectly within your will.

TO KNOW MORE:
Luke 9 and Romans 12 \\

Day 97 | *Helpless*

PRAY: God connect with me here, as I seek you in your Word.

READ: Joel 1.16-20 — Prayers come in all shapes, sizes and varieties. Some, like public prayers in church, are well thought out and elegantly spoken. Others, like the Lord's Prayer or "Now I lay me down to sleep", are recited from memory. Still others are more urgent. In these prayers, people simply drop to their knees and cry, "Lord, help me!"

Prophet Joel offers an example of an urgent prayer. The situation outlined is that the people's food had been cut off. Herds of cattle and flocks of sheep were starving to death because they had no pastures in which to graze. The land was suffering from a drought so severe that entire streams dried up. The situation was so hopeless that Joel recognized there was only one thing to do – call on the Lord for help.

Joel understood that nothing is beyond God's capability. This is a principle we need to recognize today. Any calamity we face forces us to make a decision. Do we worry ourselves sick with the thought that we will be left shattered and hopeless? Or do we fall back on the promises of God and trust Him to lead us out of the darkness? We all encounter situations where we are powerless to help. We've all asked ourselves, "What can I do"? Sometimes our only option is prayer.

REFLECT: It is important to remember that God hears and answers our prayers – often when we don't even realize it. As a result, we are never helpless, no matter how hopeless a situation may seem.

RESPOND: Spend some time in prayer asking God to intervene in situations that seem beyond human control.

Lord, only you are able to control all things and so I place my concerns and difficulties in your hands, trusting in your provision and care.

TO KNOW MORE:
Jeremiah 1 and Acts 2 \\

Day 98 | *Creator*

PRAY: God connect with me here, as I seek you in your Word.

READ: Psalm 139.1-18 — The minute people lose sight of how awesome God is, they get off track in their thinking and actions. Question His goodness and you'll doubt. Doubt His power and you'll worry. Forget His mercy and you'll run from Him. Perhaps this explains why God included Psalm 139 in the Bible—to help us remember how awesome our Maker really is.

The first six verses of David's prayer celebrate God's omniscience—His knowledge of all things. God is fully aware of everything about us including our failures, our futures, even our unspoken thoughts. Nothing is secret with Him. But look at verses 13-18. This section depicts God's wondrous creation of a human being. David paints a word picture of a seamstress tenderly knitting every stitch so as to weave a beautiful garment. Imagine that—the God who knows everything, the God who is everywhere, is caring enough to make each individual into a unique masterpiece! This is how we should look at those around us—as wonderful creations who God loved so much that He sent His Son to die for the sins of the world.

REFLECT: It's our responsibility as believers to view others as loved by God and worthy of respect and mercy. God doesn't look at the poor and downtrodden, the unattractive or the poorly educated as beneath the rest of His creation and neither should we. We need to show the same compassion that our Heavenly Father has amply demonstrated to us.

RESPOND: Thank God that He loves you and cares so much about you. Confess any instances in which you have offended God in the past week by not showing compassion to others. Thank Him for His tenderness in the details, the fine needlework, of your life.

Lord, I pray that I can look past superficial differences and see others as created in your image; as people worthy to be loved and cared for.

TO KNOW MORE:
Psalm 17 and Revelation 2 \\

Day 99 | *Idols*

PRAY: God connect with me here, as I seek you in your Word.

READ: Matthew 19.21-22 — When was the last time you worshipped an idol? If you're like most people, when you hear the word idol, you probably think of celebrities or statues. As a result, you'll probably feel safe in saying, "Never!" Actually, an idol is anything in our lives that takes a higher priority than God. In the case of the rich young ruler, his idol was his wealth. He was unable to give up his riches, even if it meant receiving eternal life. He was trapped by his own idolatry.

Many things that become idols are not necessarily bad in and of themselves. Money is not only necessary in today's world, it can also be used to help others. Exercise is recommended for good health. Sports provide great opportunities for relaxation and fun. However, when these things begin to consume the majority of our time, energy and devotion we're in danger of committing idolatry. Wealth seems to be the most popular idol of all time. The story of the rich young ruler is a sad reminder of what happened when he placed too much emphasis on worldly possessions. This young man cared so much for his earthly riches that he couldn't see the treasure Jesus offered. The same danger faces anyone who places a high priority on money and possessions.

REFLECT: A person doesn't have to be rich to treat money as an idol. Take this test: If you are not following God with all your heart, discover what it is you lack in your life. Do you crave for what you lack? You may be surprised to find that what you crave for has become an idol blocking the path to following God. Determine to remove whatever is in the way so that you can serve God wholeheartedly.

RESPOND: Ask the Lord to help you identify any idols in your life and to give you the strength to rid yourself of them.

Lord, help me to identify and remove anything in my life that is a hindrance to living fully for you.

TO KNOW MORE:
Mark 10 and John 10 \\

Day 100 | *Security*

PRAY: God connect with me here, as I seek you in your Word.

READ: Amos 4.1-5 — If you were going to preach an effective sermon, how would you begin? With a joke? With an amazing story? How about by calling the women in your audience "big fat cows"? You cringe, but that's exactly what the prophet Amos did when he came riding into town. He wasn't worried about hurting feelings and bashed the Israelites for trusting more in their wealth and religious acts than they did in living godly lives. How did the women "crush the needy"? Probably by being stingy with food to poor slaves. Archaeological evidence confirms that Israel's Assyrian captors actually did hook prisoners through the nose, attach a rope, and tow them away. Israel's strong fortresses would not be able to protect them from this fate. Nor would her religious activities, done mainly for superficial, meaningless reasons.

Just like the Israelites, too often North American Christians rely on their vast wealth. It is odd that in a culture where food is so plentiful, eating disorders are also common. God's gifts, on the other hand, are taken for granted. Where is the gratitude? We can fall into the trap of thinking that religious activity done for God can replace spiritual intimacy with Him. God wants our hearts, not our empty actions.

REFLECT: Let the hard words of a straight-shooting prophet penetrate your heart today. You won't find ultimate security or self-worth eating a lot or a little, having a good time on the weekend or only going to church on Sunday. Look for your security in a God who loves you and wants you to love Him.

RESPOND: Pray that you will find your security in an intimate relationship with God. Ask Him to make you less worried about your own comfort and more sensitive to those in need.

Lord, I place my entire trust in you so that I can more effectively serve those around me and become less consumed with my own momentary desires.

TO KNOW MORE:
Psalm 22 and James 5 \\

Day 101 | *Impossibilities*

PRAY: God connect with me here, as I seek you in your Word.

READ: Matthew 19.23-24 — "There are two possibilities for winning the lottery: slim and none". Jesus came up with a pretty good expression when He was talking to His disciples about the possibility of rich people entering the kingdom of heaven. Unless you know of a species of microscopic camels (or a twenty foot needle), Jesus' point is obvious – it is difficult for a rich person to become part of the kingdom of heaven. This may not seem like much of a news flash to anyone who's read or heard about the wild, immoral lifestyles of the rich and famous in our society. However, for Jesus' disciples, this was a stunning idea.

During the time of Jesus' ministry, wealth was seen as a reward from God for spiritual faithfulness. Jesus called His disciples to surrender everything. Peter and Andrew left their fishing boat to follow Jesus. Zacchaeus promised to give away most of what he had and to repay generously those he had cheated. We too will discover true wealth when we put everything at God's disposal.

REFLECT: Many of us believe we are better than others simply because we have more money. Because of this, we often want to strike a deal with God. We'll accept His comfort, wisdom and guidance as long as our lives don't change too much; maybe not at all. But greatness comes from sacrifice – just look at the lives of the Apostles and the many godly saints that have followed them throughout history. They gave their all to serve God. The lesson of their lives: Don't hold on to what is impossible to keep and lose that which is eternal.

RESPOND: Spend some time praying for God to reveal anything you may be holding back. Ask for the strength to surrender everything.

Lord, help me to turn from my own sources of security and place my trust entirely in your generous provision.

TO KNOW MORE:
1 Corinthians 1 and 1 Timothy 6 \\

Day 102 | *Pride*

PRAY: God connect with me here, as I seek you in your Word.

READ: Psalm 140.1-13 — Few hurts in life can match those inflicted by a cruel tongue. A mean-spirited put-down in front of other workers; a taunting remark made at a dinner party to someone going through a difficult time. David knew the pain of a cutting remark. Proud people—whether individuals or groups or governments—think the best way to flex their muscles is to put others down. Proud people, to paraphrase C. S. Lewis, are always looking down on everything and everybody. Because of this, they can't see the God who is high above them.

David refused to give in to the temptation of pride. Instead of relying on himself and treating others unkindly, he put his trust in God. "I know the Lord will surely help", he exclaimed. While the proud were praising themselves and pursuing others with deadly words and force, David praised the Lord.

Have you ever felt discouraged, singled out or persecuted for being a Christian? Are you facing adversity or feeling helpless? Are you sensing you can't resolve a pressing problem? Know that you can call on the Lord. Say with David, "You are my God! Listen, O Lord, to my cries for mercy".

REFLECT: It's so easy to feel superior. Don't fall into the trap of pride and smug satisfaction. God has forgiven each of us for things we'd be embarrassed to reveal. Be thankful for His mercy, not condemning of others who would like the same compassion.

RESPOND: Confess any ways you've put others down because of pride. Ask God to keep you from having a cruel tongue at the expense of others. Give thanks, too, that God hears your prayers when you are going through difficult times.

Lord, thank you for your endless mercy toward me. I pray that my pride will not keep me from showing the same compassion to others.

TO KNOW MORE:
Psalm 43 and Habakkuk 1 \\

Day 103 | *Underfoot*

PRAY: God connect with me here, as I seek you in your Word.

READ: Amos 5.10-15 — In today's passage, God accused the Israelites of treating some people like dirt and walking all over them. And God's not very happy about it. Poor people have few resources and will find it very difficult to cope when they are being oppressed. They have no power in society, no influential friends in high places and no money to hire lawyers. Thus, they are vulnerable to being oppressed even further.

Unfortunately, some who are wealthy and powerful take advantage of those less fortunate and use them to maintain their opulence.

Justice is close to God's heart. He cares deeply that all people are treated with dignity and respect, regardless of their social standing. You can share God's passion for justice by doing good, especially by standing up for people who are treated unfairly.

REFLECT: On your way to work or the grocery store today, you probably stepped on grass, asphalt, litter and the floor mat of your car. As long as the way is safe, sturdy and somewhat clean, we usually give little thought to what's underfoot. In contrast, we feel the loss when we accidentally step on and break something of value. Yet nothing is more valuable than the world's population – men and women all created in the image of God. Remember we are called to care for His precious creation and treat everyone with kindness and dignity.

RESPOND: Pray for political and business leaders, especially Christians, to have the courage to do what they know is right when it comes to caring for the poor and the oppressed in our culture.

Lord, help me to not look at others with jealousy and resentment and to always be thankful for your many blessings.

TO KNOW MORE:
Ezekiel 32 and Micah 2 \\

Day 104 | *Infinity*

PRAY: God connect with me here, as I seek you in your Word.

READ: Psalm 146.3-10 — You've probably heard the adage "God helps those who help themselves". Maybe you've even thought that's a verse right out of God's Word. Not true. Actually, as Psalm 146 shows, the Bible teaches just the opposite: God helps those who in their helplessness call out to Him.

This passage contrasts human attitudes with God's nature. Verse 4 recalls that humans are mortal and could die at any time. In a moment all their plans can come to an end. We have very little control of what happens in the world, even while we live. On the other hand God created and regulates the entire universe. In addition to being the Creator, He is more faithful than a best friend. He "keeps every promise forever" (v. 6b).

Jesus helped people who could not help themselves. Today God is waiting and willing to help you. Acknowledge that you can't help yourself. He is infinitely patient and ever willing to listen.

REFLECT: Why would our infinite, all-powerful God care so much about finite and frail creatures? Why would He bother to "give justice to the oppressed and food to the hungry", "free the prisoners" and "open the eyes of the blind" (vv. 7-8)? This is a great mystery. What is clear is that God simply chooses to love us and show us mercy and grace. And He seems to have a special concern for those who are weak and powerless – an attitude we should share at all times.

RESPOND: Thank God for being your helper and friend. Share your needs with Him through faithful prayer, and listen for His comforting and assuring voice – a voice that is ever-present in His Word.

Lord, you are eternal and I am finite – Give me the wisdom to share all of my personal needs, as well as my concerns for others, with you.

TO KNOW MORE:
Psalm 103 and Psalm 105 \\

Day 105 | *Work Ethic*

PRAY: God connect with me here, as I seek you in your Word.

READ: Proverbs 6.6-11 — The book of Proverbs has a lot to say about the slothful. Humans are created by God to do work–it's part of our nature. Sometimes, though, work can be difficult and boring. This is when some people find work so distasteful that they choose not to do it. These are the irresponsible people the writer of Proverbs refers to; these are the "lazybones" who need to take a few lessons from the ant.

It's important, though, not to view everyone who is out of work or is homeless as being lazy. There are often circumstances involved that a person can't help. An injury, mental illness, job lay-offs–the reasons are many and the consequences are difficult to overcome. This is why Scripture makes it clear that those who are able to work should be eager and willing. They should also be compassionate to those who are unwillingly going through difficult times.

REFLECT: The Hebrew word used in today's passage for a lazy person is *asel* or sluggard. Not a pretty picture, is it? God is saying that He has no patience for those who refuse to accept the opportunities he or she is given. Be thankful for the responsibilities God has given you and strive to do the best that you can at all times. This not only honors God but gives others a solid reason to trust and have faith in you.

RESPOND: Like the ant, we should work hard when opportunities are available to not only meet our daily needs but also to prepare for any lean times that lie ahead. Yet, we should also prayerfully consider helping at community kitchens, donating to food banks and assisting with church outreach programs.

Lord, I am grateful for the many opportunities you have given me and I pray that you will show me opportunities where I can help those who cannot provide for themselves or their families.

TO KNOW MORE:
Psalm 12 and John 7 \\

Day 106 | *Charity*

PRAY: God connect with me here, as I seek you in your Word.

READ: Acts 11.27-30 — After watching a documentary or news report about unending war or a terrible famine you might ask yourself, "What can I do to help end all the suffering? I'm just one person." A lot of people feel overwhelmed like this when they see what shape the world is in. But God doesn't call us to alleviate all the world's suffering by ourselves. He calls us to start together, at where we are.

In today's passage, we see that the young church in Antioch sent "relief" to the mother-church in Jerusalem. Note that it was the Holy Spirit who prompted the believers to give. This reminds us of the importance of making sure that we are being led by God. One way to discern the Spirit's prodding is to talk about various needs with other prayerful Christians. The desire to help the poor in Jerusalem was apparently felt by the whole Antioch church (v. 29). Unity like this can be a confirmation of God's will. And when there is a sense that a particular project is "of God" people are motivated to give as much as they can. Nobody likes to give because they "have" to; they give because they "want" to!

REFLECT: The final step of the Christians in Antioch was to entrust their gifts to reliable carriers (v. 30). Barnabas and Saul (i.e., Paul) were men of complete integrity. If you decide to give money to a particular ministry or charity, make sure they really do what they say they will do. And if you're ever asked to carry a gift or message for someone, realize that others are trusting you to finish the job right.

RESPOND: Pray that the Spirit of God will lead you to give to the right causes. Thank God that you can make a difference as you work together with other believers.

Lord, show me where my tithes can do the most good and help me to find like-minded believers in my church so that together we can serve you more effectively.

TO KNOW MORE:
Psalm 22 and Romans 15 \\

Day 107 | *Burdened*

PRAY: God connect with me here, as I seek you in your Word.

READ: Galatians 6:3-5 — Paul knew the relief that comes when God lifts our burden of sin. He instructed Christians to imitate God's example by bearing each other's burdens. In the verses today, Paul explains that before we can be burden-bearers, we need to rid ourselves of conceit. The problem with conceit, which is believing that we're better than others, is that it causes us to be intolerant of other people's shortcomings. It's tough to carry others' burdens without having a proper attitude toward them.

The remedy for conceit is a thorough self-examination. Rather than comparing ourselves with other people and their ministries, we need to take an objective look at ourselves and our God-given gifts. This objective look will reveal not what we have accomplished but what God has accomplished through us. That's what we can take pride in—the work of God.

REFLECT: Carrying another person's burdens is a huge responsibility. It's a task that requires a proper attitude. Perhaps the best way to sum it up is to put it in physical terms. If we are going to respond to God's call to carry the burdens of the poor and needy, we need to make sure that we are in good enough spiritual shape to do some very heavy lifting.

RESPOND: Spend some time in prayer thanking the Lord for others whose help keep you from carrying your burdens alone.

Lord, I praise you for bringing believers into my life with whom I can share my needs and concerns—may I serve in the same way in their lives and the lives of others.

TO KNOW MORE:
Job 4 and Hebrews 12 \\

Day 108 | *Repentance*

PRAY: God connect with me here, as I seek you in your Word.

READ: Ezekiel 7.14-27 — For generations, the Israelites heard through the prophets all about God's promise of punishment if they didn't straighten up and return to Him. Here Ezekiel described again the certain desolation of Israel – the consequences of many years of willful disobedience. He let them know that when they cried out for mercy and made promises to repent it was too late and the time had come for the unrighteous to suffer and for the godly to be purified.

Just like a wise parent, God's patience is not limitless. He still expects His children to live obediently, maturely and wisely. If we don't, there will be consequences – perhaps not on the level the Israelites faced, but painful nonetheless.

REFLECT: Make sure your heart never hardens like the Israelites' hearts did. Be open to God's warnings about sin. Be diligent to seek His will. You don't have to experience what the Israelites did to "know that I am the LORD!"

RESPOND: Be honest with God about your walk with Him. What sins have you committed lately? What bad attitudes are you harbouring? Ask Him to give you the guidance and strength you need to live a righteous life.

Lord, forgive me of my sins and cleanse me of my unrighteous attitudes so that I can serve you more fully and faithfully each day.

TO KNOW MORE:
Isaiah 24 and Jeremiah 6 \\

Day 109 | *Certainty*

PRAY: God connect with me here, as I seek you in your Word.

READ: Acts 14.11-17 — In Acts 14 Paul and Barnabas were in Lystra, a city in Greece. When they healed a crippled man the people thought that Paul was the god Hermes in a human body and that Barnabas was the god Zeus. The two missionaries were stunned, but it also presented the perfect opportunity for them to share the Good News about the one true God (in contrast to the Greek belief in many gods).

As Paul explained, there had been times in history when God allowed people to go their own ways (v. 16) and believed all sorts of wrong things about Him. But to those honestly seeking the truth, the God of the Bible has never left Himself without a witness. There have always been reminders of His goodness.

Everyday life is full of hints about God's power and majesty. In Romans 1.20 Paul wrote the same thing – that from the time the world was created, people had seen the earth and sky and all that God made. They could clearly see His invisible qualities; His eternal power and divine nature. So they have no excuse whatsoever for not knowing God. It's undeniable.

REFLECT: God has placed within each and every soul a longing to know Him. God has left "winds of heaven" and "stuff of earth" (to again quote Rich Mullins) to evidence His handiwork. Indeed, everything points back to Him.

RESPOND: Ask God to make you more aware of His goodness and then thank Him for the wonders of His love.

Lord, may I be a witness to the wonders of your world to those who doubt or have lost hope.

TO KNOW MORE:
James 1 and Colossians 3 \\

Day 110 | *Righteousness*

PRAY: God connect with me here, as I seek you in your Word.

READ: Ezekiel 18.1-9 — The Israelites used the excuse that God was punishing them because of the sins of their ancestors. They said it wasn't their fault! True, generations of spiritual decay in Israel had made the situation incredibly bad. But in blaming their parents and grandparents, the Israelites didn't take any responsibility for their own behaviour and actions.

But Ezekiel the prophet set them straight. He explained that God judged each person individually, parent and child alike. Then he described a righteous person – one who does what is lawful and right. One who doesn't worship idols, but God alone. One who obeys God's laws regarding sex. One who deals honourably and justly in his or her business dealings. One who doesn't mistreat the poor but gives food to the hungry and provides clothes for people who need them. These actions have nothing to do with genetics or heredity – they are the result of being faithful to God and His Word.

REFLECT: Whether good or bad, each person receives God's fair treatment. We may suffer the effects of the sins committed by those who came before us, but God doesn't punish us for somebody else's actions. And we shouldn't use their behavior as an excuse for our misdeeds. Look to your Heavenly Father for guidance and live according to His perfect will.

RESPOND: Pray for yourself as an individual responsible to God. Ask Him to make you a more righteous and just person in every area of your life.

Lord, I pray that you will remind me daily that I am your child and have been created to live in harmony with your infallible Word.

TO KNOW MORE:
Psalm 19 and Romans 1 \\

Day 111 | *Healthy Living*

PRAY: God connect with me here, as I seek you in your Word.

READ: Daniel 1.11-20 — The category is Least Favorite Food. The nominees are spinach, cauliflower, broccoli and asparagus. Yes, in a fast-food world we often refer to some of our healthiest choices as being somehow undesirable. In biblical times, however, vegetables were much sought after for their nutritional content. In fact, in one instance, vegetables were actually an answer to prayer.

Daniel convinced an official to feed him and his friends nothing but vegetables and water for ten days. At the end of that period, the official compared Daniel and his friends with those who had eaten from the king's table. The faithful Hebrews finished the ten days looking healthier and better nourished than the other men.

God is concerned with our physical well-being—even down to the food we eat. When we shovel a constant stream of junk food down our throats, we are mistreating our bodies. And because our bodies are created by God, that's a serious offense. So while it's certainly important for us to make sure that the poor and needy are nourished, it is also important for us to maintain a healthy diet for ourselves.

REFLECT: If you find yourself in a compromising situation, turn to God for help. You may have to make sacrifices or face scorn from your peers because of your resolve, but He will bless you abundantly for your faithfulness.

RESPOND: Self-control and unyielding faith are two of the lessons we can gain from Daniel's life. If you adhere to these guiding principles then you will discover the peace and certainty that come from obeying God's rules for living.

Lord, I pray that you will give me a desire for moderation and that I will refrain from temporary pleasures that harm the body and consume energy that could be used for a greater purpose.

TO KNOW MORE:
Leviticus 11 and 2 Chronicles 36 \\

Day 112 | *Giving and Receiving*

PRAY: God connect with me here, as I seek you in your Word.

READ: Acts 20.33-35 — We've all given something special to someone – a parent, a spouse, a child, a friend. Think about how that experience made you feel and then read today's passage. Paul, meeting with the leaders of the church at Ephesus, reminded them of his own attitude regarding giving and receiving. A missionary, chosen and approved by God, Paul refused to take their money. He gladly worked extra hard for funds to give to them as he deeply loved the Ephesian Christians (a simple reading of his letter to the Ephesians will confirm this).

This explains why we feel so good when we give a gift to a friend. We love our friends, and it is the very nature of love to "give" (see John 3:16). "Love" that only takes is not love. According to Paul, Jesus did not say "It is better to give . . ."; He said, "It is more blessed to give …" (v. 35b). Giving pleases God, not because God needs our gifts, but because our giving shows God we love and value Him. We need to be generous as Paul was, to anyone around us who has a need. The right gift offered with the right attitude results in tremendous blessing: God is honoured; others are helped; and we find unearthly joy!

REFLECT: How we handle money is always an accurate monitor of our spiritual health. Giving helps focus our minds on God as the source of all the good things in our lives. And, amazingly enough, when we give we are blessed.

RESPOND: Thank God for the many blessings He has given you. Pray about the ways you can give these gifts (time, talents, prayer support) back to others in His name.

Lord, help me to be a cheerful and creative giver – using the gifts you have given me in service to others.

TO KNOW MORE:
Genesis 48 and 1 Thessalonians 5 \\

Day 113 | *Listening*

PRAY: God connect with me here, as I seek you in your Word.

READ: Proverbs 21.13 — Have you ever wished you could turn down the volume on your ears whenever someone is saying something you don't want to hear? (A teacher of deaf children once said that her students used to turn down their hearing aids when she gave an assignment they didn't want to do.)

Unfortunately, humans tend to tune out God and ignore the cares of needy people. But what is the consequence of this action? Today's verse seems to indicate that how we treat the poor will determine how we will be treated. The challenge is to open our ears and listen – to be sensitive to people in need. Because such compassion requires time and because our lives already seem filled with activities and interests, it may seem impossible to slow down long enough to listen. But helping the poor is a priority with God, so it needs to be a priority with us.

REFLECT: Beyond hearing their cries, the real challenge is to help the poor. We need to follow through with loving actions. Remember, God hears our cries and reaches out to us when we are spiritually destitute. He hears every prayer and is always ready to help when we ask. By reflecting God's love, we should be willing to do the same for others.

RESPOND: Ask God to open your ears to the cries of the poor and to show you ways you can respond to their needs.

Lord, I pray that I will not turn my back on the needs of those around me but will be ever attentive to their silent cries.

TO KNOW MORE:
Psalm 74 and Nehemiah 1 \\

Day 114 | *Freedom*

PRAY: God connect with me here, as I seek you in your Word.

READ: Romans 7.1-6 — The Jewish people in Paul's time had to live under a system that was demanding. They had to obey a long list of laws, rules and regulations in order to be right with God. Paul used the illustration of marriage to explain our relationship to the law of God. When two people were married, they were subject to the laws of marriage. But if one of them died, the other would be free from those laws and could remarry. In the same way, Christians today are free from the power of the law. We have a new way of living.

Some people try to keep a set of rules – in order to gain acceptance by God. But the only thing they get for their troubles is frustration. People simply can't make it to God on their own. By dying on the cross, Jesus opened the way to God. He makes believers perfect in God's sight. And now, rather than trying to follow impossible rules, we can live in the power of God's Spirit.

REFLECT: We can become more and more like Jesus by living for Him every day. Thank God for freedom from the power of the law. Praise Him that he has given you freedom to live, freedom to serve and freedom to reach out to others.

RESPOND: Ask God to give you opportunities to exercise your freedom in the power of the Spirit today.

Lord, thank you for sending your Son to die for my sins so that I can enjoy the freedom of serving you apart from the constraints of legalism and judgment.

TO KNOW MORE:
Proverbs 6 and 1 Corinthians 9 \\

Day 115 | *Champion*

PRAY: God connect with me here, as I seek you in your Word.

READ: Proverbs 22.16-23 — According to legend, in the year 1160; a baby boy was born to a woodsman and his wife. Over the years he became quite proficient with a bow. One day, the boy suddenly became an orphan. That's when he chose his life's goal: steal from the rich and give to the poor. You've heard of Robin Hood. Even today, he enjoys a legendary reputation as a defender of the oppressed.

In today's passage we learn about another defender of the poor. He is real and still at work and isn't a legend. Verse 16 promises that a person who gets ahead by oppressing the poor will end up in poverty: spiritual poverty. Verse 22 commands, "Do not exploit the poor because they are poor and do not crush the needy in court." Why? Verse 23 has the answer: ". . . for the LORD will take up their case and will exact life for life." From these three verses, it is plain that God highly regards the poor. It is not enough to promise not to hurt or take advantage of them; God wants us to go a step further and defend them as well.

REFLECT: There is no greater honour than helping those who are unable to afford shelter, feed their family or defend themselves against unfair oppressors. Our attitude toward the poor should reflect God's mercy. After all, it's because of His compassion toward us that we have the joy of eternal life awaiting us in heaven.

RESPOND: Pray for opportunities to become a defender of the poor.

Lord, open my ears to the needs of others and give me a willing heart to answer their urgent pleas.

TO KNOW MORE:
Ecclesiastes 7 and James 2 \\

Day 116 | *Preparation*

PRAY: God connect with me here, as I seek you in your Word.

READ: Daniel 10.1-3 — We must pay attention to our preparation for meeting God. If we enter His presence casually or impatiently, how will we be ready to listen? Let's look at Daniel's life. His example shows us he was ready to receive an important message from God.

One of the most amazing truths about God is that He desires to communicate with us. Not only does He want us to listen when He speaks, He also wants us to tell Him everything – our thoughts, fears, sins and hopes. The fact that God listens to us is especially important when we ask Him for help.

In order to communicate with God we don't have to follow some specific formula or ritual. What we need to do is set aside time to focus our minds on Him and His Word. Our human problems can give us opportunities to:

- Remember that Christ suffered for us.

- Stay humble and dependent on God.

- Look beyond life on earth and count on life in heaven.

- Grow in our faith as we trust God more.

- Identify with others and comfort them in Christ's name.

- See God's power at work in our lives.

REFLECT: Think of your problems as growth opportunities. Look beyond them to what waits for you, a child of God, in heaven forever.

RESPOND: Thank God for the gift of eternal life. Ask Him to help you keep heaven on your mind as you live each day for Him on earth.

Lord, prepare my heart so that my prayer life will be a time of spiritual refreshment and renewal.

TO KNOW MORE:
Nahum 2 and 1 Corinthians 9 \\

Day 117 | *Restoration*

PRAY: God connect with me here, as I seek you in your Word.

READ: Ezekiel 47.1-12 — Concern about pollution, global warming and rain forest destruction grabs headlines these days. Yet we hear relatively little about the spiritual pollution that threatens countless lives. Every day, our culture suffers the consequences of our sinful actions.

Thousands of years ago, Israel witnessed the slow, steady destruction of their own land caused by generations of sinful behavior. God promised a stunning restoration of the land. After Jerusalem fell, Ezekiel offered the people a message of hope. He explained that God is holy, but Jerusalem and its Temple had been defiled. The nation needed to be cleansed from years of disobedience to God. So God sent the Israelites into captivity in order to purify the land. In a vision, Ezekiel returns to the renewed nation. He watches the fresh, lively stream flowing and healing the land, making the Dead Sea pure and fresh. This is a beautiful picture of God's healing touch. And it will come true when Jesus returns.

REFLECT: The same way that God heals and restores the land, he restores individuals. Yes, even those who have experienced total degradation. When God unleashes his healing power, dry, dusty hearts bubble up with the Spirit of God. Fruit grows abundantly and there is lush and beautiful growth.

RESPOND: Pray that healthy spiritual fruit will flourish in your life.

Lord, I pray that you will transform me into your image so that my life will be a testimony to your restoring power.

TO KNOW MORE:
Colossians 1 and Revelation 22 \\

Day 118 | *Faithfulness*

PRAY: God connect with me here, as I seek you in your Word.

READ: 2 Corinthians 6.3-10 — How would you respond if your life was marked by one hardship and calamity after another? What would you do if you were beaten, put in jail, attacked by angry mobs, forced to go without sleep and food—all because of your faith in Christ? Would you quit living for Christ? Before you answer, read how Paul responded to these very circumstances.

To begin with, he never gave up. Despite horrifying circumstances and trouble on top of trouble, his attitude never wavered. He knew he was doing right. He knew the One he believed and followed day by day, wanting to share with others. The same power that gave Paul the strength to stand up and do right dwells within you. Don't let tough circumstances affect the way you live and believe. God is able and ready to give you all the strength you need to deal with life's problems. Refuse to compromise what you believe in and how you live. Then you, like Paul, can lead a victorious and faithful life.

REFLECT: Paul remained faithful to God whether people praised him or abused him. He remained joyful and content in the toughest of circumstances. Even though he was poor, he was able to give spiritual riches to others. "We own nothing, and yet we have everything" (v. 10). Can you say that too?

RESPOND: In many places around the world, Christians are attacked, humiliated and mistreated because of their faith.

Pray that God will enable them to stand strong in the face of such trials. Ask Him, too, for the strength to stand firm regardless of your circumstances.

Lord, I pray for the resolve to remain faithful in all situations and I pray, especially, for those who are persecuted because of their love for you.

TO KNOW MORE:
Isaiah 53 and Romans 14 \\

Day 119 | *Investments*

PRAY: God connect with me here, as I seek you in your Word.

READ: Proverbs 22.2-9 — Those who frequent casinos, buy dozens of lottery tickets weekly or bet on sporting events all hope for the same thing: easy money. Put a little in, get a whole lot more back. And sometimes, people do. But, of course, this rarely happens. Usually a good return requires planning, careful investments and patience. Of course this formula is true in all aspects of life, including one's spiritual growth.

Solomon, no stranger to wealth, offered his own advice on resource management in Proverbs 22. Today's reading speaks to us about the investment we make in other people. God blesses those who are generous with true riches such as the joy that comes from helping another, the peace that comes from obeying God and eternal rewards that we cannot begin to fathom. Such rewards are not always immediate. When he promises blessings, we can surely expect it. And that's an investment strategy that has unlimited returns.

REFLECT: Generosity is not just a good feeling. We can't call ourselves generous if we merely sympathize with the plight of the poor. Generous people are sacrificing people. They surrender convenience, comfort and luxury so that others will thrive. But if we are willing to take the narrow path, we will find greater rewards than we could ever achieve in a headlong rush for the good life.

RESPOND: Pray for missionary families from your church today – those who have invested their lives in sharing the Good News with others.

Lord, I pray for (names) who are faithfully serving your Kingdom – bless, encourage and protect them this day and may their efforts yield great returns.

TO KNOW MORE:
Psalm 112 and Luke 16 \\

Day 120 | *Ripples*

PRAY: God connect with me here, as I seek you in your Word.

READ: 2 Corinthians 9.11-15 — One small movement, one slight ripple, has the potential to produce a tremendous impact. Paul emphasized this principle in his second letter to the Corinthians. Paul wanted the Corinthians to recognize the enormous impact their generosity was producing. Not only did their support meet the immediate needs of the people in Jerusalem, it resulted in widespread prayer and praise being offered to God. The impact of such prayer and praise, in turn, was immeasurable.

The same principle holds true today. Befriending an immigrant family in your neighbourhood and helping them adjust to life in this country may not seem like a big deal. Sending a portion of your monthly income to support a child overseas may seem like a small sacrifice. Organizing a coat collection drive for the homeless in your community seems hardly worth mentioning. But a tiny ripple can eventually produce a tremendous impact.

REFLECT: Impacting a person's life in Christ's name will create tiny ripples that can make a big difference in hundreds of lives someday.

RESPOND: Ask God to show you where and how you can increase your giving and ministry outreach so that countless people may benefit.

Lord, I pray that you will multiply my efforts so that many will be served in your name, both now and in the future.

TO KNOW MORE:
Proverbs 3 and 1 Timothy 6 \\

Day 121 | *Tithing*

PRAY: God connect with me here, as I seek you in your Word.

READ: 2 Corinthians 8.1-15 — Have you ever given someone a gift just because you care? It's a gift of love with no strings attached. You love God, right? So how do you give Him gifts of love? Paul complimented the believers in the city of Corinth for their great faith, strong teaching and beautiful service to one another but also wanted them to "excel in the gracious ministry of giving" because they were missing out on a great blessing. Paul gave general guidelines we would do well to follow:

- Give in response to God's love, not to get something in return.

- Give whatever you can according to how much you have.

- Give sacrificially but responsibly.

- If you give to others in need, they will help you out when you're in need. In this way, Paul said, everyone's needs would be met.

Sharing the blessings God has given us with others is a wonderful way to demonstrate our love for God and an essential way to truly enjoy our full membership in His earthly Kingdom.

REFLECT: Giving to God can be a real blessing—especially for the giver. But there's only one way to find out! Ask God to guide you in the matter of giving. Supporting your local church should come first, but also be open to ministries and organizations that can use your one-time or ongoing gifts.

RESPOND: Prayerfully seek God's guidance about your tithes. He will reveal where your charitable giving can help to meet the greatest need.

Lord, create in me a generous spirit so that I can be of service to others and can show you my thankfulness for your great and unending love.

TO KNOW MORE:
Ephesians 3 and 1 Thessalonians 3 \\

Day 122 | *Trustworthy*

PRAY: God connect with me here, as I seek you in your Word.

READ: Habakkuk 3.1-18 — Today's reading from the prophet Habakkuk, written as a part of the public worship services of ancient Israel, reflects the foolishness of the attitude, "What have you done for me lately"? when it comes to relationship with God.

This prayer was composed as a song set to the kind of music with which the psalm was to be accompanied. It was to be sung triumphantly in great excitement. Though the prophecy given is dark because it involves the judgment and destruction of Judah, the prophet is not discouraged for he knows that ultimately Israel will be exalted and Jehovah's glory will fill the earth.

In reflecting upon the majesty of God and what He will do in the future, the prophet turns his eyes to the promises God has kept in the past. Habakkuk knew that not only does God dwell in the eternal present, He is also perfectly loving and trustworthy. As we think about our daily needs–it's important to remember that God will never fail or forsake His people. He has been faithful for thousands of years.

REFLECT: "I don't know what the future holds but I do know who holds the future." This is the attitude God wants us to have. We shouldn't worry about tomorrow when we have the assurance that tomorrow has already been taken care of by our Creator.

RESPOND: Ask God to give you the faith to walk boldly and confidently through life. Pray that He will give you opportunities to share His merciful kindness with others.

Lord, help me to remember your faithfulness when I face difficult times and let me be a witness to your love when I encounter those in physical, spiritual or emotional need.

TO KNOW MORE:
Psalm 7 and Psalm 66 \\

Day 123 | *Justice*

PRAY: God connect with me here, as I seek you in your Word.

READ: Job 24.1-8 — In many fairy tales, poor or cruelly treated people end up "happily ever after." Adults and children alike love such rags-to-riches tales. But do fairy tales bear any resemblance to real life? In today's passage, Job wonders why poor people endure misery without relief. This passage points out that robbery spreads like an epidemic (vv. 2-3). The poor are hungry (v. 5), naked (v. 7) and homeless (v. 8). "Why doesn't the Almighty open the court and bring judgment? Why must the godly wait for him in vain?" Job asks (v. 1). While answers may be beyond us, hidden in God's ultimate purposes, we can know something about His will from readings over the past few weeks. Our readings have also shown that God blesses those who trust Him. Faith is trust in God.

In the Bible, poor people and widows demonstrate remarkable faith. The widow who feeds Elijah with the last of her flour is rewarded with a bottomless jar until the drought ends (1 Kings 17:8-16). Jesus blesses the widow who gives her final coins as a temple offering (Luke 21:1-4). In ancient times and today, many poor people have strong faith because, in their povert, they understand what it means to be needy. Jesus specifically promises to bless the poor and to fulfill their needs (Luke 6:20).

REFLECT: God tackles Job's second complaint in the final verses of chapter 24. He promises to rescue the poor in His own time (v. 21ff). God's promises are more dependable than even the happiest fairy tale. Whether we help the poor frequently or pray for God's justice in the world, our mission is to watch and act as God directs.

RESPOND: Pray for God's justice to prevail in the world and that Christians will be vehicles of His work. Pray for patience to wait and trust in God's good promises.

Lord, I pray for justice and mercy – both for myself and for others facing hardships around the world.

TO KNOW MORE:
Psalm 9 and 1 Thessalonians 5 \\

Day 124 | *Perspectives*

PRAY: God connect with me here, as I seek you in your Word.

READ: 1 John 2.3-8 — That church down the street from yours is a little different, isn't it? They may not have it right. In fact, they can really be messing some people up. The church two blocks away is too emotional. The one your sister goes to is too rigid. This other one is too liberal. And the one across town is just way too boring.

Do you ever have thoughts like this? You may not even realize that you have such thoughts. So think about it. Then read what John has to say about such an attitude. If we really love God, then we'll follow His way of life. "Those who say they live in God should live their lives as Christ did" (v. 6). Sacrificially and lovingly.

This kind of love has no room for judging others. If you say you're a Christian but reject another Christian, you're revealing your own ignorance and lack of true faith. Is John saying that if you dislike someone you aren't a Christian? No. Other Christians may be hard to get along with. That's just a fact of life. But that doesn't mean you can ignore them, say negative things about them or treat them as enemies.

REFLECT: Christian love isn't a feeling. It's a choice. You can choose to be concerned about someone else and treat them with respect without feeling affectionate toward them. When you make that choice, God will honour it and help you show real love.

RESPOND: Confess to God any judgmental attitudes you've had about your brothers and sisters in Christ. Ask Him to guide you as you walk in the light, that you will be able to love others as Jesus has loved you.

Lord, forgive me for any judgmental attitudes I hold and fill me with love for those around me — regardless of whether I agree with their religious views or not.

TO KNOW MORE:
Psalm 119 and John 14 \\

Day 125 | *Attitudes*

PRAY: God connect with me here, as I seek you in your Word.

READ: Revelation 2.1-6 — Have you ever seen someone who was just "going through the motions?" You may have even suffered from this lack of motivation yourself. It's usually pretty easy to spot these people and their lack of enthusiasm, passion and excitement. In the book of Revelation, the Lord confronted a church that had lost its motivation and passion.

Unlike other churches, the people in Ephesus had refused to tolerate wicked men and false teachers. They had endured hardships without growing weary. In fact, as far as we can tell, the church lacked only one thing—love—something extremely important—its motivation for good works. God is interested in our work, but He is more interested in our motivation for doing it. Work that is done grudgingly or with a grumbling attitude is unacceptable to Him. We should commit ourselves to helping others because we love God and His people.

REFLECT: God doesn't expect us always to be "up" and excited about our work. For imperfect humans who go through mood swings and bad days, that would be hard to do. However, God does expect us to hold on to our "first love"(v.4). The only way to keep that first love is to set aside time to pray, to read His Word and to think about Jesus, who saved us and sustains us every day. If we're burned out or just going through the motions, it's a sign that we need to return to our first love.

RESPOND: Ask the Lord to honestly evaluate the motivation behind your actions. If you believe that you've lost your first love, ask Him to help you rekindle that old flame. Be honest. He wants you to turn back!

Lord, help me to serve you with a generous and grateful heart.

TO KNOW MORE:
1 John 4 and Hebrews 6 \\

Day 126 | *Salvation*

PRAY: God connect with me here, as I seek you in your Word.

READ: John 3.16-21 — When you were in school did you ever use study guides that encapsulated plot summaries to give you a sense of a novel's meaning before wading into its pages? These handy and popular synopses are invaluable, time-saving tools for procrastinators, the befuddled and the lazy!

The entire message of the Gospel can be found in John 3:16. Here the love of God is clearly shown: The source of love is God. The extent of His love is the world. The sacrifice He gave for love was His only Son. And the result of this love is that whoever believes in Him will have eternal life. Condemnation is reserved only for those who reject Christ and the salvation He freely offers. Yet, sadly, the light of Christ is rejected by a world darkened in sin. Many turn from the light of Christ's love because they don't want to commit to Him or they'd rather go their own way. By embracing the saving light of Jesus we show that our works are blessed by God and that we are in happy obedience to His will.

REFLECT: God has made salvation so easy that many feel they must do something else – spend a certain amount of time each day doing good works or commit to an array of rules established by others – to earn His favour. This isn't true. It sounds impossible, it seems too good to be true, but all that is required of us is to believe and trust that the sacrifice Jesus made on the cross is all sufficient for our salvation. If you haven't made this decision yet, turn to Him in prayer today. In less than a minute your life will be changed – forever!

RESPOND: Ask God to give you opportunities to share the Gospel message with others. Your witness will transform both individuals and families.

Lord, thank you for sending your Son to die for my sins so that I might have eternal life – may this be a message I freely and enthusiastically offer to those around me.

TO KNOW MORE:
Romans 5 and Ephesians 2 \\

Day 127 | *Haven*

PRAY: God connect with me here, as I seek you in your Word.

READ: Genesis 7.1-23 — Do you have a safety plan for your family in case of a natural disaster? Depending on where you live and the time of year this could include everything from a blizzard that leaves you snowbound for days or a tornado that suddenly whips up, destroying nearly everything in its path.

In today's reading we find God inviting faithful Noah and his family, along with creatures of all types, to enter a place of absolute safety – the sturdy, waterproof ark. Have you ever thought about the reason why God allowed an entire week to pass before the deluge while Noah, his family and the animals silently waited in the ark? Doubtless, this was done to give the world an opportunity to repent and join those who had found safety (salvation) – like a calm before the storm. And yet Noah's contemporaries continued their lives of reckless disregard toward the commandments of God.

Don't ignore the soft whisper of the Holy Spirit when he directs you to turn from the things you know are wrong. God is always faithful to those who obey Him and, while He doesn't always keep us from trouble, He will never stop loving us or caring for our needs.

REFLECT: As believers, we are able to find our spiritual refuge in Christ, the only true source of salvation. It's important to be a confident witness – one who isn't afraid of either the future or the vagaries of everyday life – to affirm to those around you that peace can only be found by clinging to the solid rock of Jesus.

RESPOND: Commit to living a victorious Christian life so that others will see your Father in heaven and want to join you in your positive, daily walk with Him.

Lord, you are my refuge and my security – may I show to others the joy and peace you have given me by both my actions and my words.

TO KNOW MORE:
Psalm 33 and Hebrews 11 \\

Day 128 | *Fasting*

PRAY: God connect with me here, as I seek you in your Word.

READ: 2 Chronicles 20.2-17 — In an earlier devotional, we talked about fasting. Yes, it seems old-fashioned and even a bit odd not to eat for a day or two. Should we fast? Well, read today's story to see how fasting played a role in an amazing answer to prayer.

What caused Jehoshaphat and his people to fast? They learned that they were about to be attacked by a large army. The king's response was immediate. He sought God's guidance. He also ordered the people of Judah to observe a fast. They were forced to depend on God–and their hunger reminded them of that dependence. These spiritual warriors accomplished more than any army with swords and spears, for the Scripture tells us that the soldiers of Moab and Ammon turned on each other. The end result of Judah's obedience was a spectacular victory over the enemy. Why? Because the people of Judah diligently sought God. Imagine what you can do if you put aside distractions–even necessary ones like eating–to spend earnest time in prayer and Bible reading. You, too, will soon realize "spectacular victories" in your own life!

REFLECT: When you need clarity about a decision or you realize you need to be spiritually cleansed from sin, consider fasting. Avoid food for a day, and spend the time you'd normally use eating in prayer instead. Focus on God. Read His Word. Seek His guidance. Let your hunger remind you of your spiritual hunger for Him.

RESPOND: As you spend lime in fasting and prayer, ask God to show you sins to confess, attitudes to improve, decisions to make, people to forgive, painful memories to let go of and callings to obey. Be sure to spend a good amount of time in quiet solitude and listen carefully to your loving Father.

Lord, I pray that you will refresh my spirit as I turn all of my thoughts toward you–give me a renewed love for your Word and an eagerness to serve others in your name.

TO KNOW MORE:
Esther 4 and Psalm 56 \\

Day 129 | *Mercy*

PRAY: God connect with me here, as I seek you in your Word.

READ: 2 Samuel 24.14 — One of the first things many children learn about God is that "He's got the whole world in His hands." If you went to Sunday school or vacation Bible school as a kid, you probably sang (or at least heard) this song. If so, did you ever wonder what it means? Maybe you pictured God holding the earth in His outstretched hands, cupping it like an egg. Or maybe you envisioned him spinning the earth on His index finger like a celestial Harlem Globetrotter. Or maybe you were bright enough as a kid to understand that the song refers to the fact that God takes care of the earth and everyone in it. This is a principle King David understood very well. David had sinned against God by ordering an unauthorized census of Israel's army. When David repented of his sin, God gave him a choice of three punishments: three years of famine, three years of being pursued by enemies or three days of plague in the land. David knew that God, even in his anger, would be more merciful than humans would be, so he chose the plague. David was confident of the Lord's mercy because he had personally experienced it many times before.

How about you? Do you have as much faith in God's mercy as David had? Do you see evidence of God's mercy in your life or in the world around you? In what ways does God make His mercy known to you?

REFLECT: Do you think God could use you as an instrument of His mercy? In other words, could you use your time, resources and talents for others on behalf of the Lord? Prayerfully consider your answers.

RESPOND: Ask the Lord to make you an instrument of His mercy. Ask Him to prepare your heart and spirit so that you can make a difference in someone else's life.

Lord, I pray that I can be a blessing to someone today in your name.

TO KNOW MORE:
Proverbs 29 and James 1 \\

Day 130 | *Thankfulness*

PRAY: God connect with me here, as I seek you in your Word.

READ: Psalm 92.1-4 — If you had to come up with a slogan or saying that captures most people's attitude in society today, what would it be? Here's a suggestion: "It's my right." It's actually hard to find true thankfulness in people. Sure, we say thanks when someone does something nice for us, but are we really thankful? Many people believe that they are entitled to everything good that happens to them and, therefore, see no need to be thankful. After all, they think, I'm entitled to it.

In contrast, the writer of Psalm 92 displays a much different type of attitude. Have you ever been so overwhelmed by an emotion or feeling that you just had to blurt it out—regardless of the consequences? That's kind of what David does in this passage. He's got this feeling building up inside of him until he just can't keep it in any longer: "I sing for joy because of what you have done."

Not only is David thankful for what God has done, he also reveals a genuine passion for God. A truly grateful person recognizes that we have no right to expect anything from God—or from anybody else, for that matter.

REFLECT: Sometimes it's difficult to maintain an attitude of thanksgiving. But as hard as it may be to believe, even in times of great hardship we can legitimately give thanks to God. That's because no matter how bad things are, the fact remains that God loves us, that He is always present with us and that He has provided a glorious future with Him forever.

RESPOND: Make a list of the things for which you are thankful and pray through them, offering back to God a sacrifice of praise and thanksgiving.

Lord, I am so grateful for all that you have done for me and I ask that you will continue to bless me with your infinite love and mercy.

TO KNOW MORE:
Psalm 107 and Ephesians 5 \\

Day 131 | *Busyness*

PRAY: God connect with me here, as I seek you in your Word.

READ: 2 Chronicles 35.1-6 — Have you ever gotten off track with God? It's easy to let some things slide, like attending church, reading the Bible every day or praying whenever you can. It's easy to let other activities take up your time so that you no longer do what is most important. As a result, your heart becomes cold and your life becomes meaningless.

It's surprising to learn that the people of Judah had forgotten Passover during the reign of King Josiah. After all, it was the most important celebration in the life of the nation. Passover looked back to the time when God freed His people from bondage in Egypt. But centuries of disobedience and false religion took their toll on the land, and soon everything the people were supposed to hold dear was buried beneath the rubble. Like the ancient Israelites, we can become too busy sometimes with the things of this world to practice and embrace what really matters in life.

REFLECT: Judah's lesson came too late. Despite Josiah's good intentions, his country fell into its bad habits soon after the king died. Not long after that, Judah was taken into captivity. Don't let your heart be captured by the false things of this world. Remember what the Lord has done for you, and keep your will open to Him.

RESPOND: If you've gotten off track in your walk with God, make it a matter of serious prayer. Confess your sins, accept His cleansing and commit your heart to renewed, refreshed obedience to the things He is calling you to do.

Lord, I surrender my thoughts and actions to you and pray that I will always remember to place you first in my life.

TO KNOW MORE:
Psalm 135 and 2 Corinthians 4 \\

Day 132 | *Abundance*

PRAY: God connect with me here, as I seek you in your Word.

READ: Ezra 2.68-69 — Imagine that an army captured your town and shipped everyone to a foreign country. For fifty years, your people lived as slaves under an oppressive government that didn't allow you to fully practice your faith. Now you can understand how the Israelites felt during their half-century of exile in Babylon. But when King Cyrus of Persia conquered the Babylonians and ordered the return of all exiled peoples – including the Israelites – to their native lands, the people of Israel were able to reinstate their God. What a breath of fresh air! What an occasion to rejoice!

At this critical moment, God stirred the hearts of the priests and Levites and the leaders of the tribes of Judah and Benjamin to return to Jerusalem to rebuild the Temple of the Lord. Each family head gave as much as he could for the rebuilding of the Temple, and some gave generously. They willingly gave beyond what they could actually afford. Before the Israelites returned home, something quite remarkable occurred. Their foreign neighbors, in extravagant measure, gave them gifts, including silver and gold and supplies for their journey. So it seemed only fitting that they give back to God the unexpected blessing they had received from others.

REFLECT: Giving back to God honours Him because it acknowledges that He is the initiator of all good things. Even our love for Him is an offering of what He has given us. 1 John 4:19 says that "we love each other as a result of His loving us first." When we're inclined to hold back, to say that we don't have enough to give, we need to come back to the reality that God has given richly to us and wants us to follow His example.

RESPOND: Ask God to stir you to richly give of what He has given you.

Lord, thank you for the abundance you have given me and I pray that you will take my tithes and use them to further your Kingdom on earth.

TO KNOW MORE:
Luke 21 and 2 Corinthians 8 \\

Day 133 | *Courage*

PRAY: God connect with me here, as I seek you in your Word.

READ: Nehemiah 5.1-8 — The world is full of leaders who take advantage of the poor. Many years ago, the Marcos family ruled the Philippines and lived in splendour at the expense of their fellow citizens, who suffered in abject poverty. One man, Benigno Aquino, stood up and said, "This is not right!" His tireless campaign for justice eventually led to his murder by Marcos' henchmen. But three years later, a pro-democracy movement led by Aquino's widow toppled Marcos from power.

Nehemiah, who lived near the end of the Old Testament era, took a similar stand as he reprimanded some of his own people for exploiting the poor. Nehemiah first silenced the accused with a question: How many times will we have to buy back the people you sell into slavery? Seeing that they were starting to feel shame, Nehemiah fearlessly got right to the point: "What you are doing is not right!" (v. 9). He then demanded that the poor be reimbursed for all that they had lost. Nehemiah also made the rich take a vow to no longer take advantage of their neighbors.

Not everyone is called to lead a resistance against an unjust government, but we can speak out against the injustice we encounter in day-to-day life.

REFLECT: We can follow Nehemiah's example of confronting people with the consequence of their action by forthrightly declaring that it is wrong, and by calling for justice.

RESPOND: Pray that God will give you the courage to speak out against injustice.

Lord, I pray that you will give me resolve of my convictions to stand firm against those who oppress the poor and powerless.

TO KNOW MORE:
1 Corinthians 6 and James 5 \\

Day 134 | *True Wealth*

PRAY: God connect with me here, as I seek you in your Word.

READ: Luke 16.19-31 — Have you ever seen the bumper stickers that read, "He who dies with the most toys wins" or "Hearses don't have luggage racks?" These opposite views of the value of money and possessions are powerfully illustrated in Jesus' parable of the rich man and Lazarus in the Gospel of Luke. The rich man had it made in this world, wearing expensive clothes, eating the best foods and living in luxury. Lazarus, on the other hand, lived a life of misery. He was so desperate for food that the crumbs from the rich man's table looked good to him. He had nothing.

When the two men died, however, their situations changed drastically. Lazarus was carried away by angels. The rich man found himself in hell, the place of eternal torture. Can you imagine the horror the rich man must have felt when he realized that his riches could do him no good anymore? This story should stand as a strong warning to anyone who allows material possessions to rule their lives. "Things" will vanish like smoke when our lives end. When we stand before God, we will have to answer for the things we have done and the priorities we have set in this life.

REFLECT: Make a list of your priorities then evaluate what you've written. If worldly pleasures outrank the things God considers important then prayerfully consider how you can re-prioritize your life according to His will and His Word.

RESPOND: Ask God to give you an eternal perspective on wealth by helping you recognize the importance of using material possessions in ways that honour Him.

Lord, help me to value the things you value and seek after spiritual, rather than material, riches.

TO KNOW MORE:
Psalm 73 and James 2 \\

Day 135 | *Justice*

PRAY: God connect with me here, as I seek you in your Word.

READ: Psalm 82.1-8 — In today's reading we find that court is in session in heaven. The rulers of this world are on trial, and God is the judge. He wants to know one thing: How well did the rulers and judges treat the poor and oppressed of this world? God wants to know what they have done to help the neglected and needy.

The psalm writer makes an interesting statement regarding the influence of powerful judges and rulers. He says that because they walk about in darkness, the world is shaken to the core (v. 5). Did you notice that? Mistreatment of the poor and oppressed can have a worldwide impact!

God's final warning to the judges and rulers in this passage should also serve as a wake-up call to us. Though these people may have great power in our lifetime, God says that in death they are only humans. One day they, like all people, will stand before God with their titles and authority stripped away, facing their Creator as ordinary men and women.

REFLECT: What will you be able to say to the Creator on that day about your treatment of the poor and neglected people in society?

RESPOND: Pray that our nation's judges and politicians will apply wisdom and compassion in their decisions.

Lord, I pray for our leaders that they will rule with compassion and I ask that you will give them a heart of mercy toward the oppressed.

TO KNOW MORE:
Psalm 58 and Galatians 2 \\

Day 136 | *Curiosity*

PRAY: God connect with me here, as I seek you in your Word.

READ: Luke 19.1-10 — People are innately curious. What else can explain the way we slow down to stare at car wrecks? Why else would so many buy tabloid newspapers? You've heard the saying, "Curiosity killed the cat." Maybe today's reading should be headlined "Curiosity saved the tax collector."

Imagine being Zacchaeus. You have heard all about the miracle working carpenter from Nazareth and got word He was coming to your town. Something–curiosity, desire, emptiness–drew you to go see for yourself. Then it happened. Jesus stopped and spoke to you. You were so shocked, you almost fell out of the tree! He invited himself to your home. Everyone was watching and whispering. As you climbed down and walked away with the Teacher, you felt a cataclysmic change take place in your heart. In that moment, you were engulfed by love. Despite being short and insecure, dishonest and despised, Jesus had accepted you completely and unconditionally. You know at last you're free. Zacchaeus' story reminds us of a simple truth: Jesus accepts you just as he accepted a despised tax collector.

REFLECT: Let the fact that Jesus loved even the most despised men and women of His day inspire you to respond with the same level of kindness and joy to others you meet.

RESPOND: Thank the Lord for accepting you unconditionally. Confess any ways–like Zacchaeus–in which you have tried to find security in something (such as money or power) other than God's love.

Lord, I pray that I will show others the same love and kindness you have faithfully and repeatedly demonstrated to me.

TO KNOW MORE:
Genesis 18 and Psalm 101 \\

Day 137 | *Fame*

PRAY: God connect with me here, as I seek you in your Word.

READ: Jeremiah 9.23-24 — Some people act as though name-dropping is a professional sport. They met a popular actress at the mall, saw a famous author on the beach, sat near a well-known athlete on the plane. Evidently they feel important by associating themselves with celebrities.

The same thing happens in everyday relationships. People like to associate with those who have achieved a measure of stardom or status. They want to be part of the in-crowd. Read today's passage to see who is really worthwhile to know. But God points out that even those who are wise, powerful and wealthy have nothing to brag about. All of their popularity and status is meaningless when compared to our awesome Lord. In this passage God is saying, "The only One worth knowing is ME!" And when we get to know the Lord, we realize that He alone is just, righteous, loving and faithful. Now that's a name worth "dropping."

REFLECT: Where do you find your identity and your self-worth? If it's from your friends, a clique or the business you work for then think again. Only God is just, righteous and loving and everything of true worth comes from Him.

RESPOND: Instead of worrying about status and popularity, focus on knowing the Lord.

Lord, help me to value you above all others and to seek your wisdom rather than the musings of the rich and famous.

TO KNOW MORE:
Psalm 49 and Proverbs 11 \\

Day 138 | *Happiness*

PRAY: God connect with me here, as I seek you in your Word.

READ: Psalm 78.14-22 — Imagine being rescued from a horrendous situation and released into total freedom. And imagine getting frustrated by it, even angry at God. Imagine complaining bitterly about this kind of treatment. That doesn't make much sense, does it? It's amazing to read of the awesome exploits of God on behalf of the Israelites and then to read of their thanklessness, their bitterness, their unceasing desire for more than what they were getting. Instead of fully trusting the God who rescued them to take them through it His way, they blamed Him for every problem they encountered.

Yet, when we get overwhelmed by the needs and responsibilities of life, isn't it easy for us to blame God? Don't we get upset and even bitter when God doesn't do things exactly the way we think He should for us? The truth is, deep down, we're really not so different from the Israelites. Our hearts can become just as hardened as theirs if we're not careful. Regularly examining our lives in the light of God's Word will keep us from believing the lies we tell ourselves.

REFLECT: If you are unhappy, frightened, worried or believe that God is not doing enough to rescue you from dire circumstances, then take a deep breath and share your feelings of despair with Him. He is always patient with His children and will give you "the peace that passes all understanding" if you will be open and honest with Him.

RESPOND: Confess to God any areas of your life where you've been harbouring grudges against Him and bad attitudes that keep you from fully enjoying and experiencing the gushing, streaming waters of His blessings.

Lord, forgive me for my complaints against you and fill me with confidence that you see my situation and are willing and able to meet my needs in your perfect timing and according to your perfect will.

TO KNOW MORE:
Psalm 106 and Hebrews 3 \\

Day 139 | *Confession*

PRAY: God connect with me here, as I seek you in your Word.

READ: Isaiah 22.12-14 — In today's passage, Israel celebrates even though the Lord commands all the Israelites to mourn. Jerusalem was told to mourn because its sin had offended a holy God. In the biblical way of thinking, full realization of sin should lead to sadness and, perhaps, weeping. David wept when he confessed his affair with Bathsheba (2 Samuel 12.13-23). The Jewish remnant wept when they heard God's law, understood it and realized how far from it they had strayed (Nehemiah 8.9).

But in Isaiah 22; Jerusalem was one big party. Contrast this behaviour with the record of the Ninevites when Jonah finally preached God's message of repentance to them (Jonah 3.6-9). On the verge of destruction, Nineveh recognized its sins and repented; but here Jerusalem did not.

God is not calling us to live sad or guilt-ridden lives. True confession doesn't leave stains of self-hatred but enables us to experience a new sense of God's forgiveness. When we confess, we admit a need: a need not just for peace and comfort but, ultimately, for forgiveness.

REFLECT: An honest cry from the heart is always good. When you have confessed your sins to God, learn to let go of nagging guilt feelings and remember Christ's firm yet gentle words: God blesses those who mourn, for they will be comforted (Matthew 5.4).

RESPOND: Ask God to soften your heart so you can feel genuine sorrow when you disobey. If you are aware of areas in which you have violated His commands, confess those wrong actions or attitudes. Claim the forgiveness that is available in Christ.

Lord, forgive me of my sins, cleanse me of my unrighteousness and give me a heart that yearns for holiness.

TO KNOW MORE:
Ecclesiastes 3 and James 4 \\

Day 140 | *Provisions*

PRAY: God connect with me here, as I seek you in your Word.

READ: Mark 6.7-9 — When Jesus sent his disciples out to tell others about Him, He gave a whole new meaning to the phrase "traveling lightly." He instructed His disciples to take only the barest of essentials with them. Let's look at the contents of the disciples' traveling kit: A staff (or walking stick) and a pair of sandals – that's all the disciples needed to take with them on their journeys. It was not necessary for them to bring food, money or even a blanket, because all of these would be provided for them.

How do you suppose the disciples felt as they embarked on their trips? Do you think they felt "naked" traveling with so little? Do you think they were at all apprehensive about where they were going to stay or how they were going to find food? It's hard to say, but we do know they were taken care of.

If you had to make a list of the things necessary in order for you to go out and minister in your community, what would you include on it? Do you need some sort of transportation? Do you need someone to accompany you like the disciples did? Do you need money? Do you need a Bible? The Lord knows all our needs, and can and does supply us with everything necessary to serve Him.

REFLECT: We don't need a lot to serve the Lord. In fact, all it really takes is the willingness to go where He sends us and to walk through the doors He opens for us in order to minister to others. So if you're waiting for a better time, more education or more money in the bank, stop! God can use you as you are right now.

RESPOND: Ask God to help you discern between your needs and wants as they relate to ministry. Ask Him to supply everything you need in order to minister to others.

Lord, I want to serve you by ministering to others and I pray you will supply everything necessary to fulfill the mission you've set before me.

TO KNOW MORE:
Luke 9 and Acts 12 \\

Day 141 | *Bullies*

PRAY: God connect with me here, as I seek you in your Word.

READ: Isaiah 3.13-15 — Every playground has its share of bullies and all of them have one thing in common: they love to take advantage of those who are smaller and weaker. Bullies can make life miserable. There is no age limit for bullies. In fact, some of the meanest bullies are adults. They take advantage of the weak and thrive on other people's misery. God has some strong words for these bullies. Let's see what He has to say in today's reading. Notice the words used to describe what these people did. It's not a coincidence that the Lord used such violent imagery. Even though these bullies weren't putting a physical squeeze on the poor, they were doing severe damage nonetheless.

Who are the bullies? Often they're people in positions of power who use their influence to take advantage of others – particularly those who are weaker than they are. They may be politicians who use their office and clout to help themselves get richer while turning their backs on the people who need help the most. However, these bullies will not prevail. One day they will have to give an account for the injustices they have created. What's more, they will realize too late that the people they oppressed are often the ones who have attained true riches.

REFLECT: While we Christians have a responsibility to do everything we can in this world to relieve the suffering of those who are oppressed, we can also look forward to God's final judgment on the oppressors.

RESPOND: Ask God to give you the strength, wisdom and courage to stand up to bullies who use their position and power to oppress the poor.

Lord, I pray that you will show me where I can be of comfort and aid to those who are mistreated due to social position, age, illnesses or other situations and conditions that leave them vulnerable.

TO KNOW MORE:
Psalm 12 and Proverbs 22 \\

Day 142 | *Devotion*

PRAY: God connect with me here, as I seek you in your Word.

READ: Matthew 26.6-13 — Matthew did not mention the name of the woman who poured the fragrance on Jesus, but John identified her as Mary, the sister of Martha and Lazarus. In other passages, we learn of Mary's utter devotion to Jesus (Luke 10.38-42). So her perfuming incident should come as no surprise. But Matthew reported that the disciples were "indignant" (v. 8).

They accused Mary of wastefulness: "She could have sold it for a fortune and given the money to the poor" (v. 9). Isn't it sad that the disciples got so hung up on the extravagance of the gesture that they missed the love that prompted it? Perhaps they really were concerned about the poor. Maybe they didn't understand Mary's love. Or possibly, they just felt guilty because they had never demonstrated such affection. Whatever the reason, the disciples learned a great lesson about worship from this incident. Mary offered the very best gift she had. It was costly. Based on historical and archaeological evidence, scholars are fairly certain that Mary had to break the jar to release the fragrant ointment inside. This meant she couldn't have saved any of the perfume for another occasion. She used it all on Jesus, and from the sound of the passage, she did so gladly.

REFLECT: Worship is all about declaring the worth of the Lord. He alone deserves our attention, our allegiance, our affection and our resources. And when our worship stems from a heart full of love and gratitude, it produces a pleasing aroma, whether it involves perfume or not!

RESPOND: Confess any instances in which you, like the disciples, have held back in your devotion to God. Pray that your worship of Jesus and service to Him will be pleasing as the sweetest perfume.

Lord, I joyfully worship and adore you for you alone are my loving Redeemer.

TO KNOW MORE:
Luke 7 and John 12 \\

Day 143 | *Witnessing*

PRAY: God connect with me here, as I seek you in your Word.

READ: Romans 9.1-5 — There are many needy people around you. You see them in news photos and on the Internet. You walk past them on the street. The hurting. The spiritually hungry. People without Christ. They may be rich or poor. But they are lost in a world of sin and despair. And that's a real shame.

Paul was raised a good Jew, became influential in the synagogues and was a leader. Then one day, on the road to Damascus, Jesus intervened. Paul became a new man, an apostle full of zeal for the Lord. But he was still Jewish. So his heart was "filled with bitter sorrow and unending grief" (v. 2) for his people. They were lost, blind to the light of Christ. And they were destined for eternal destruction. Paul emphatically declared that he "would be willing to be forever cursed, cut off from Christ, if that would save them" (v. 3). That would be the ultimate sacrifice, to set aside eternity with Jesus if that would help other people experience Him for themselves. Paul showed to these people a depth of love and concern that was totally selfless. Like Jesus, Paul was willing to sacrifice everything dear to him so others could be saved.

REFLECT: With Paul's example in mind, ask yourself: How concerned am I about people who don't know Jesus? Am I willing to sacrifice my time, my money, my efforts to introduce them to the Lord of eternity?

RESPOND: Ask God to give you a heart willing to make sacrifices in order to reach out to others in Jesus' name. Remember to pray for your friends and family members who don't know Jesus yet.

Lord, I pray that I will not turn my back on the unsaved around me but will be ever attentive to their need for you.

TO KNOW MORE:
1 Timothy 2 and Philippians 3 \\

Day 144 | *Fair Play*

PRAY: God connect with me here, as I seek you in your Word.

READ: Isaiah 10.1-5 — Have you ever taken advantage of someone who doesn't know how a game is played? Such trickery may be "no big deal" in a game. You may get away with it and even win. But in real life when the rich or powerful abuse the poor and weak, God gets angry and He comes to the defense of the afflicted.

A major Bible theme (emphasized again in today's passage) is that God cares deeply for the helpless. He becomes angry when the poor are mistreated, exploited or ignored. This passage condemns those who twist justice by maligning the poor. God asks some sobering questions in verse 3 of this passage: "What will you do when I send desolation upon you? Where will your treasures be safe?" The implicit answer to this question is: They won't be safe. History shows that God stripped Israel of her treasure—her special blessings and position. God vented anger against people who cared more about living comfortably than about living holy lives before Him. He never stopped loving Israel, but He disciplined His wayward people. He will do the same thing to those who mistreat the poor today. They will have to contend with the anger of God.

REFLECT: Consider how Jesus reacted when He saw instances of injustice. He criticized Israel's religious leaders for completely forgetting about evenhandedness, hoarding things and ignoring the needy (Luke 11.37-43). The scribes and Pharisees were too busy worrying about all their regulations and traditions to care about the less fortunate. They forgot, as did the leaders in Isaiah's time, that God valued caring for the poor and treating people right far more than He's concerned about rule-keeping. Today, as in ancient times, He wants to see changed hearts that love and treat the poor with dignity and justice.

RESPOND: Confess any instances you have ignored the poor or acted selfishly rather than compassionately toward those in need.

Lord, help me to treat all people with kindness and mercy and let them see your love through my words and actions.

TO KNOW MORE: Psalm 94 and Matthew 23 \\

Day 145 | *Rules*

PRAY: God connect with me here, as I seek you in your Word.

READ: Mark 2.15-17 — Pity the poor Pharisees of Jesus' day. These men were so obsessed with making sure that every aspect of the law was followed that they began creating their own laws within the law. This situation escalated until the Jewish people were faced with a system of rules that was impossible to keep. So the law became a source of frustration to the people. The Pharisees took pride in their self-determined righteousness and lorded their piety over the "common" Jews.

Then Jesus came and challenged their authority. Look at the way he cut through their indignation in Mark 2. The Pharisees were looking to discredit Jesus, lest people began to follow his teachings rather than theirs. So when Jesus entered Levi's house, the Pharisees made a big deal of His eating with unclean sinners.

Jesus replied in this way: You Pharisees claim to be righteous and to have no need for repentance. These tax collectors and admitted sinners, on the other hand, realize their need for repentance. So who do you think I'm going to spend my time with? Not surprisingly, the Pharisees had no response to Jesus' explanation.

REFLECT: As followers of Christ, we have a similar responsibility to the outcasts of society: the poor, the lower class, the ignored. Jesus was not above mingling with and ministering to such people, even going so far as visiting them in their homes. Should we then be any different? Are we above ministering to these people in need? The answer is a resounding "No!"

RESPOND: Thank the Lord for His example of ministering to outcasts. Then ask Him to strengthen your resolve in ministering to those who are ignored or condemned by society today.

Lord, forgive me when I create unnecessary rules that add to your Word and give me a heart of compassion for those who truly need to see your love through my actions.

TO KNOW MORE:
Luke 19 and Hebrews 12 \\

Day 146 | Good Times

PRAY: God connect with me here, as I seek you in your Word.

READ: Romans 8.28-39 — Your boss yells at you. You fight with your spouse. Someone cuts you off in traffic and then curses at you. Worse, a loved one is terminally ill, or your house is destroyed by a natural disaster. When terrible things happen, it's natural to think that God does not love you. But today's passage claims the opposite.

Let's pick out the highlights from Paul's letter to the Romans:

- Even negative circumstances ultimately are a blessing for those who "love God and are called according to His purpose for them".

- God is the all-powerful King of the universe. He will give us everything we need to be victorious in life.

Not a bad list to reflect on when you're hoping to turn around an otherwise unfortunate day!

REFLECT: God's love for you is beyond measure. Even in the midst of bad times, you can hold on to that truth, because God is doing something wonderful in your life.

RESPOND: If you're struggling with something bad that's happened to you lately, ask God to let His truths transform your thinking and build your faith.

Lord, help me in the midst of my trials to never forget that you are always present in my life and that your love will never change under any circumstances.

TO KNOW MORE:
Psalm 69 and 1 Peter 1 \\

Day 147 | *True Love*

PRAY: God connect with me here, as I seek you in your Word.

READ: 1 Corinthians 13.4-13 — Let's start off with a quick multiple-choice quiz:

- What is your favorite primary color?
- Which hockey team do you cheer for?
- Is faith, hope or love the greatest virtue?

The first two questions call for opinions, so obviously there are no right or wrong answers (unless you picked a team based in the hottest part of the United States). Paul answered the third question in the last verse of 1 Corinthians 13. In this one chapter of the Bible, the apostle gave us the most complete description of true love ever.

This isn't the hearts-and-flowers kind of love you might read about in a greeting card. Love like this takes a lot of work and sacrifice to achieve. It's a love that comes only from God but is the love that Christians are instructed to show one another. More than a feeling, this love is an action.

REFLECT: How do we start to show love for those around us? Paul spelt things out rather clearly in his description in verses 4-7. We can show patience by not losing our temper when other people do things we don't agree with. We can show kindness by doing small things to help a person in need. We can avoid envy by learning to be truly happy when good things happen to others. We can avoid boasting simply by keeping our mouths shut. These are just some ideas to get you started. If you put your mind to it, you'll probably be able to come up with dozens of other ways to show love to those around you.

RESPOND: Ask God to help you demonstrate true love – the kind Paul described in 1 Corinthians 13.

Lord, I pray that you will fill me with love for others that is kind, charitable and has no qualifications whatsoever.

TO KNOW MORE:
2 Corinthians 6 and 2 Peter 1 \\

Day 148 | *Temptation*

PRAY: God connect with me here, as I seek you in your Word.

READ: Matthew 4.1-4 — Food is a source of temptation for a large percentage of humans. Bulimics and chronic overeaters are constantly tempted to consume unhealthy amounts of food. People with high blood pressure or heart conditions are often tempted to eat what is to them "off-limits" foods high in fat and sodium. Serious dieters have been known to empty their refrigerators, pantries and cabinets completely to keep from being tempted to eat. Even so-called moderate eaters are often tempted to grab a bite at a fast-food restaurant rather than eating a more healthy meal at home.

It's probably safe to say, however, that no one has ever faced a food temptation quite like the one Jesus experienced in Matthew 4. Satan was trying to get Jesus to use His supernatural powers for His own benefit. Knowing that Jesus hadn't eaten in forty days, Satan chose a basic human need to undermine Jesus' work. Hungry as He was, Jesus chose spiritual nourishment over physical sustenance. As the Son of God, Jesus had the power to turn the stones into bread, as Satan suggested. The evil one knew this and urged him on. Yet, Jesus refused to yield to His human needs. He refused to satisfy His hunger apart from God's will. The point Jesus made to Satan is still valid today: Humans do not live on food alone, but by spiritual nourishment from God.

REFLECT: To stay fit in God's Kingdom, we must thrive on constant study in His Word.

RESPOND: Ask the Lord to give you strength and to help you rely on His Word as you face temptations in your daily life.

Lord, I pray that you will feed me with true spiritual food that can only come from the wisdom found in your holy Word.

TO KNOW MORE:
Romans 8 and Hebrews 2 \\

Day 149 | *Greatness*

PRAY: God connect with me here, as I seek you in your Word.

READ: Jeremiah 22.15-17 — The Nobel Peace Prize is one of the world's most prestigious awards. It is given annually to people who distinguish themselves in the areas of physics, chemistry, medicine, literature and the pursuit of peace. Some might say that it is a sign of true greatness to be awarded one of these prizes.

To find out what God thinks about true greatness, read today's passage. In 1979, one of the Nobel prizes was awarded to a poor woman living in the slums of a huge city. Known for her ministry among lepers and street people, she spent her adult life working with the poorest of the poor. Her name was Mother Teresa. Indeed, she exemplified true greatness, according to God's definition.

Jeremiah presented a similar picture of greatness in the words written about King Josiah: "He was just and right in all his dealings…He made sure that justice and help were given to the poor and needy" (v. 15, 16). You may be thinking, "I'm not Mother Teresa, so what does God expect me to do?" Look again at what Jeremiah wrote. The actions and qualities of true greatness are possible for anyone, with God's help.

REFLECT: Can you be just in your dealings with your friends and family? Can you give help to the poor and needy? Sure you can. You can make a difference. Look for opportunities to win "God's peace prize."

RESPOND: Ask God to help you be just and fair in all areas of your life.

Lord, I pray that you will give me opportunities to achieve "greatness" in your eyes as I live a life of service to you and your Kingdom.

TO KNOW MORE:
Psalm 72 and Titus 2 \\

Day 150 | *Missions*

PRAY: God connect with me here, as I seek you in your Word.

READ: Matthew 5.1-3 — Jesus told His followers that those who recognized their need for God would find salvation. The secular world often judges Christians to be insane for traveling around the earth to serve the poor and needy. To the secular world, actions such as building a cement block church and putting in a water purification system to provide clean drinking water in an under-privileged area, carrying Bibles into China for underground churches, or even spending time with the elderly in a nursing home are ridiculous. They are not fun, entertaining, or personally profitable. But by God's standards, they are right on target!

Notice also that Christ teaches us that "God blesses" those who do what He calls them to. Another translation of this could be "happy are those who realize their need for Him." In other words, when we're fulfilling His purpose in our lives, He gives us tremendous joy. That means that building, digging, sharing and transporting can provide a happiness that only God can supply.

REFLECT: Christ has called His people to respond to the needy of this world like He did, with compassion and action. We can't all travel around the world, but we must do what we can, where we are, with the resources we have. Is there a place or project where you can minister in your community? Joy awaits you!

RESPOND: Pray for compassion and sensitivity to the poor in your neighbourhood. It's easy to pray for the poor around the world, but are you taking action to help those in your community?

Lord, grant me opportunities to be a missionary for you – whether it is in my community, through my church or in places I've only read about but never imagined that I'd visit.

TO KNOW MORE:
Psalm 1 and Ephesians 6 \\

Day 151 | *Extravagance*

PRAY: God connect with me here, as I seek you in your Word.

READ: 1 Kings 3.9-14 — Anna always treasured her Christmas memories of shopping with her granddad. Every year in mid-December, he would pick a night to take Anna and her sisters into the city. They loved this event for they knew that, once at the toy store, they would hear the words, "You may pick out anything you want." Granddad put no limit on their choices. After each girl had made a selection, he would purchase the toys. Anna could still remember the smile on his face and the joy in his eyes as he would hand out the gifts. She thought Granddad was the most generous person in the world.

In today's passage, God shows His great generosity by going one step further. He gives Solomon what he asks for and then gives him more. How surprised Solomon must have been to not only receive his one request, but to be given much more in addition. This passage shows God's heart for His children. Like Anna's grandfather, God delights in giving. He is at times even extravagant. Think about all He has created for us to enjoy: sunsets, rainbows, the myriad of colours and the variety of animals. He could have just made three colours, one kind of sunset and five or six animals. If you've ever doubted God's love then stop and think about the many amazing gifts He's given us – gifts we too often take for granted – that reveal how much He cherishes His children.

REFLECT: God promises us many gifts in the Bible. His most extravagant gift, of course, is His Son, Jesus. Yes, God is a generous God. But what delights God more than giving to His children is when He sees us imitating His extravagance toward others.

RESPOND: Thank God for his unlimited generosity. Then ask Him to show you how you can give extravagantly to a person in need or a worthy cause this week.

Lord, thank you for the many and abundant blessings you've given me – may I, in turn, bless others in your name.

TO KNOW MORE: Psalm 72 and Philippians 1 \\

Day 152 | *Shameless*

PRAY: God connect with me here, as I seek you in your Word.

READ: Joshua 5.2-9 — "Shame on you!" This phrase sends a chill down the spine of the guilty. It reminds the offender that he or she should feel bad about their offense and is guilty as charged. Certainly shame can serve a useful purpose, motivating a person to change his or her ways. But shame and guilt, like a heavy burden, can also weigh us down.

For centuries, the people of Israel carried this suffocating weight. But after four hundred years of slavery and forty years of wandering in the desert, God lifted the load from their back. In our reading today we find that circumcision was a sign of God's covenant relationship with Israel. And on that day – when Israel's men became circumcised – God sent a clear message to His people: I am removing the shame of your past and renewing my relationship with you.

Today, many people suffer from various forms of shame. Hebrews 12.2 tells us to keep "our eyes on Jesus" who was willing to die a brutal death for our sake. The Bible speaks of Jesus scorning the shame of the Cross. He essentially laughed in the face of guilt and shame, declaring that it would no longer have power over those who put their trust in Him.

REFLECT: God replaced the shame of the Israelites with the renewal of his magnificent plan to bring them into a land flowing with milk and honey. Today He replaces the shame of innocent victims as well as guilty sinners with love and forgiveness through Christ.

RESPOND: Pray that God will help you deal with any shame or guilt you have been carrying and that you will understand His unconditional love.

Lord, by the power of your death and resurrection remove the stains of guilt and shame that I bear for my sins and give me a new life in you.

TO KNOW MORE: Matthew 16 and Romans 4 \\

Day 153 | *Stewards*

PRAY: God connect with me here, as I seek you in your Word.

READ: Genesis 1.28 — What if you worked for a large corporation and the chief executive decided to take a month-long vacation and left you in charge? Imagine being the boss of everyone and everything in offices around the world. "Take care of things," are the only instructions you are given before he or she leaves. How well do you think you'd do? How hard would it be for you to make sure everyone and everything continued to perform well? What would things be like when the boss got back?

We are called stewards of God's creation. Stewards are people entrusted with caring for the wealth and property of their master. God has placed us in charge of the earth's resources. We are to use them properly so that everyone can share in its bountiful provision. How well would you say we have done in fulfilling our responsibility?

REFLECT: When we think about widespread pollution, hunger and the depletion of resources, such problems often result from being poor stewards. We all have a responsibility to do what we can to manage the earth's resources wisely. Several small efforts on a local level have the potential to yield large-scale benefits.

RESPOND: Ask the Lord for wisdom and inspiration as you seek to exercise your responsibility over the earth and its resources in ways that will honour Him.

Lord, help me to be a good steward of all you've entrusted me with.

TO KNOW MORE:
John 1 and Isaiah 45 \\

Day 154 | *Leadership*

PRAY: God connect with me here, as I seek you in your Word.

READ: Matthew 20.20-28 — In today's reading, Jesus challenges the expectations of those who would be part of His royal family and His Kingdom. The mother of James and John was convinced the Kingdom of Jesus would operate like every earthly kingdom with people scratching and clawing their way to the top. Her "power play" on behalf of her sons angered the other disciples because they shared her worldly view of success. They were probably irritated that she asked the question first. But Jesus shattered all their wrong expectations with his topsy-turvy explanation of spiritual leadership. To become important in my Kingdom, Jesus explained, you have to give up your attempts at self-promotion. You have to be willing to be unimportant. If you want to be seen as a leader, be willing to be unseen as a lowly servant who cares for others. You want glory? Okay, but only after you have served and even suffered. These statements must have shocked the disciples as much as they surprise us.

REFLECT: Jesus turned the idea of leadership upside down. Biblical leadership means giving up our lives for others, leading by serving and serving in obscurity.

RESPOND: Ask God to help you see that in His Kingdom, the way up is down. Thank Him that, as a believer in Christ, you are a member of the ultimate royal family.

Lord, I pray that I can become a true leader in your Kingdom – someone who puts the needs of others first.

TO KNOW MORE:
Psalm 110 and John 15 \\

Day 155 | *Christian Living*

PRAY: God connect with me here, as I seek you in your Word.

READ: Micah 6.8 — What does God want most from you? Your money in the offering plate? Your attendance at all church functions? Your listening only to Christian music? What is the bottom line? We find the answer in the ancient prophetic book of Micah.

Are you surprised by the list found in today's reading? It says nothing about wearing a cross around your neck or putting a Jesus bumper sticker on your car. There are no requirements about what books to read or stipulations about what kind of music is best. This verse seems to say that God is more concerned with internal matters than external issues; His emphasis is more on the heart. Why? Because a heart that is humble, a heart that has been stunned by the mercy of God, will produce a life filled with good things.

We are to "do what is right." That is, we are to act justly and be fair in our dealings with others. "To love mercy" is to show kindness to the unlovable, even though they may scorn us and mock our ways. Micah says God delights in showing mercy.

REFLECT: This week, instead of buying another Christian CD, consider giving that money to someone in need. Rather than merely putting on a cross necklace, remember that the most important adornment you must wear is love (Colossians 3.14). Love. Compassion. Humility. Faithfulness. That's what God wants!

RESPOND: Ask God to teach you more and more what He really wants from you.

Lord, give me the wisdom and maturity to do the things that are truly important as I seek to serve you.

TO KNOW MORE:
Jeremiah 22 and 2 Peter 1 \\

Day 156 | *Security*

PRAY: God connect with me here, as I seek you in your Word.

READ: Psalm 34.6-10 — In Mark Twain's classic novel The Prince and the Pauper, a poor young man named Tom is invited into a castle by a prince who befriends him. The prince convinces Tom to switch places with him. Tom agrees. Then, for the first time in his life, Tom has fashionable clothes, rich surroundings and all the food he can eat. His every need is met by the king.

The children of the heavenly King have even greater privileges, as the writer of today's reading declared. God hears and cares, and David appreciated that fact. He is never too busy to listen. The same verse goes on to say, "He set me free from all my fears." The world is filled with fear. But God promises to comfort us and to help us push through our fears. Verse 7 reminds us that God is our guard and rescuer. As our guard, He meets our need for security. As our rescuer, He meets our greatest need, the need to be rescued from sin. And if we trust and honor God, we will have all that we need.

REFLECT: What a wonderful King we have. And how fortunate that we who are Christians will enjoy the riches of the King – not just temporarily, but for the rest of our lives. David wrote in another psalm, "Once I was young, and now I am old. Yet I have never seen the godly forsaken" (Psalm 37.25). It's a promise that covers us like a warm coat on the coldest day. Praise the Lord for his unceasing care for our needs!

RESPOND: Thank God for giving you all you need to live an abundant life.

Lord, thank you for being both my loving Heavenly Father and my generous King.

TO KNOW MORE:
2 Samuel 22 and Matthew 18 \\

Day 157 | *Patience*

PRAY: God connect with me here, as I seek you in your Word.

READ: 2 Peter 1.5-7 — Can you believe how long it can take to connect to an Internet site? Must be several seconds! Do these people think we have all day or what? Regardless of our age, we're all part of the "instant generation" and we have finger drumming down to a science.

Often, people make the mistake of expecting the Christian life to be quick, easy and efficient. Compare today's reading with the world's attitudes and solutions: Trying to decide how to respond to an ethical dilemma? Need more Bible study? No problem — just sign up for a class at church and consider your void filled.

Peter, however, told us it would take a little bit longer. As a matter of fact, he presented a case for "spiritual bodybuilding". This is something that's not going to be accomplished in one day or one class. Instead, effort upon effort, day after day, consistent and decisive work builds a life of faith, moral excellence, knowledge, self-control, patience, godliness and love. There's nothing quick or easy about it.

REFLECT: Growing spiritually means patiently learning to do what is right according to God's Word and the leading of His Holy Spirit. Impatient finger drummers need not apply.

RESPOND: Reflect on the qualities listed in today's passage. Are you making progress in your spiritual growth? Pray for God's strength and the wisdom to grow.

Lord, I pray that you will give me the patience to grow spiritually and mature in my daily walk with you.

TO KNOW MORE:
Proverbs 4 and Hebrews 11 \\

Day 158 | *Loneliness*

PRAY: God connect with me here, as I seek you in your Word.

READ: Psalm 68.3-6 — Where do you turn when you're down and lonely? Maybe you call a friend who you know will listen and care and offer some good advice. Maybe you talk to you family and enjoy the easy interaction you find at home. But think about people who don't have families, friends or a church. What can they do to heal their hurting hearts? Today's Scripture gives us a glimpse of God's grace for the lonely.

God is "Father to the fatherless and the defender of widows." That's the kind of God He is – One who yearns to abundantly supply the love and security needed by those who have no one else. The root of much of our pain and need is loneliness. When we feel lonely, we sometimes try to soothe our pain in ways that not only fail to fill our loneliness, but remove us even further from others and from Him. God stands ready to fill up the emptiness in our hearts. He will build a support team – a "family" – for each of us, if only we'll take advantage of it. This group may take various forms but, whoever it is, God is pleased to provide for your need to "belong".

REFLECT: Make sure that those we rely on are truly ones God has provided for us. It's easy to fall into a group and discover that its purposes are counter to God's will. Trust God to fill your loneliness His way.

RESPOND: If you're feeling lonely or down, sometimes it's hard to pray. You just don't feel like it. Maybe you don't even have the words to say. Just think about God and His promises. Lift up your open hands and allow Him to fill you and your heart with joy and security.

Lord, I pray that you will bring people into my life who will strengthen me in my faith and I pray for those who are lonely and in need of a comforting word.

TO KNOW MORE:
Hosea 14 and Ephesians 4 \\

Day 159 | *Paying Back*

PRAY: God connect with me here, as I seek you in your Word.

READ: Leviticus 6.1-7 — Toward the end of the 20th century, Europe's poorest country, Albania, slid into chaos. Its people rebelled against a corrupt regime. Food soon became scarce as Albanians looted warehouses and stores. A missionary couple has since reported that they roamed the streets of their town looking for food. They were told that looting was the only way to ensure they could get something to eat. Reluctantly, they joined in. Unlike most people, though, they promised to find the store owner and pay him for the food they took.

Saying "sorry" does not make everything better in God's eyes. It's actually impossible to fully settle our account with God through our own efforts. Just one sin severs the relationship, and we can do nothing by ourselves to even the score. In Old Testament times, God provided animals to atone for sin. Today, by trusting in the perfect sacrifice of Jesus Christ, we can settle our account with God forever. But just as in the days of Moses, God requires us to be in good standing with others. True repentance results in taking action in the world in which we live.

REFLECT: The act of repayment, or giving back something that was taken, helps restore things to their original place. It's also a clear expression of a heart that is truly sorry, enabling the person wronged to more easily accept an apology and restore the relationship. Our gestures of repayment, even though they seem small, remind us that God will one day make everything right again.

RESPOND: Ask God to show you if you need to repay someone – perhaps even for something done a long time ago.

Lord, I pray that you will show me where I need to "repay" someone for something I've done in the past.

TO KNOW MORE:
Proverbs 24 and Colossians 3 \\

Day 160 | Endurance

PRAY: God connect with me here, as I seek you in your Word.

READ: Hebrews 6.9-12 — What is the most difficult job you can imagine? A police officer patrolling a gang-infested neighborhood in a major city? A window-washer balancing a hundred stories above the ground? A construction worker smoothing asphalt on a scorching summer day? A doctor in a refugee camp with few supplies and an endless stream of new patients? Some jobs require a daily dose of courage to complete the work at hand. These jobholders well deserve the compensation he or she gets for his or her efforts.

God recognizes that those who labor on His behalf merit their rewards too. The writer of the book of Hebrews reminds his audience that God will not forget how hard they have labored for Him. God is the perfect boss. He knows everything about His workers, including which jobs will best suit their abilities. He never gives his laborers a task that is too difficult for them, and He is always available to help them complete their work. In addition, He's extremely generous in His rewards for a job well done.

REFLECT: Work is extremely important to God. There is no room for laziness among His people. Fortunately for us, God recognizes how difficult it can be for us to carry out His work. That's why He's created such an incredible incentive program for us. Unlike our work on earth, which often goes unnoticed, God will reward everything we do for Him. God, the perfect boss, sees all and rewards all.

RESPOND: Ask the Lord to develop in you a spirit of endurance so that you will be equipped to carry out the work He has planned for you.

Lord, instill in me a desire to serve you with a proper attitude and a willing heart.

TO KNOW MORE:
James 2 and Titus 2 \\

Day 161 | *Trust*

PRAY: God connect with me here, as I seek you in your Word.

READ: Daniel 4.34,35 — It's a tricky subject—we admit it. The selfish, in self-satisfied indignation, puts it this way: "If God is in control, then this mess is His fault, and He has to take responsibility for it." Doesn't that feel good? Now we're off the hook. Or are we?

Just as we trust our eyesight to give us an accurate representation of reality, we tend to trust our perspective to define truth. God's present allowance of disobedience—and its inevitable suffering—is momentary. At His command, time and space will roll up like a scroll, and you will inherit the Kingdom Daniel describes. Then you will understand His purpose and His control. Trusting it now is the key to contentment.

REFLECT: Consider the breadth of God's revelation, from the cosmic to the microscopic. How comprehensive can your time-and-space-bound understanding be? We all yearn for something better than our current experience. You are created for heaven. And if you have decided to follow Jesus, you are already its citizen.

RESPOND: Focus on the character and magnitude of God, allowing yourself—his child—to rest in the security of his control.

Lord, I want to trust you completely. Thank you for the power of your word to help me gain your perspective.

TO KNOW MORE:
Psalm 145 and 1 Timothy 6 \\

Day 162 | *Values*

PRAY: God connect with me here, as I seek you in your Word.

READ: James 1.27 — A summary of our culture's messages would read as follows:

- Seek pleasure – it's the most important thing in life.

- Success comes when you have plenty of money and things.

- You have to control your destiny.

- You're nothing if you don't have power and prestige.

- Look out for yourself because nobody else will.

- Do what you want to do because you're the most important person in the world.

Few people actually say they believe these statements, but it's clearly the philosophy of our world's system which is based on money, power and pleasure. So where do believers fit in with all this? James made it clear. "Refuse to let the world corrupt us." Don't let it seep into your thinking. To keep away from the world's influence to corrupt us, we have to commit ourselves to the way of Jesus. Jesus' system is expressed in its essence by James: "Pure religion in the sight of God our Father means that we must care for orphans and widows in their troubles."

REFLECT: Being willing to serve others in need demonstrates you aren't putting yourself first. You're putting the needs of others before your own. You're serving and loving in Jesus' name. You have the needy on your heart, just like God has them on His heart. If that's your lifestyle, it proves that your faith is pure and lasting and the world can't touch you.

RESPOND: Ask God for a faith that's pure and lasting, for a heart that seeks to help others, for a life that shows you're walking closely with your Heavenly Father. Pray for the widows, orphans and needy people in your community and look for a way to help them.

Lord, I pray that you will show me ways I can be a blessing to others in your name and can share your love with them.

TO KNOW MORE: Isaiah 58 and Galatians 1 \\

Day 163 | *Greatness*

PRAY: God connect with me here, as I seek you in your Word.

READ: Mark 9.33-37 — Our society seems to have an obsession with lists and rankings. No matter what the category, we want to know what's the newest, what's the most popular, who's ranked number one and what's the greatest of all time.

Of course, as Christians, terms like "the greatest" and "number one" should have little or no meaning when they apply to who we are. Jesus' disciples found this out for themselves one day on the road to Capernaum. Note what happened in today's passage when Jesus asked the disciples what they'd been arguing about. No one answered Him. The disciples had been arguing about which one of them would be greatest in the coming kingdom. Jesus took this opportunity to teach His followers about true greatness. Jesus' strategy for finishing first is certainly unique. In God's arena, serving others becomes a path to greatness. Becoming a servant means making a deliberate decision to put others' needs before your own.

REFLECT: When we put others first, when we concentrate on helping others, we lose our inclination to seek the honor and fame the world clamours for. Remember, greatness in the Christian faith is not determined by status but by service.

RESPOND: Ask God to continue to develop in you a servant's heart and a desire to focus your attention on others rather than yourself.

Lord, instill in me a servant's heart and a desire to demonstrate your loving kindness toward others.

TO KNOW MORE:
Psalm 139 and Hebrews 4 \\

Day 164 | *Motivation*

PRAY: God connect with me here, as I seek you in your Word.

READ: Zechariah 7.4-10 — Think you're pretty smart? The following questions are guaranteed to test your insight. You have thirty seconds to answer each one. Did Adam have a belly button? If God is all-powerful, could He create a rock so large He couldn't lift it? If you do what is right for the wrong reasons, is it still right?

The first two questions are merely brainteasers. The answers aren't really important (assuming they're answerable at all). The answer to the third question, though, is extremely important. If the answer is no, it requires Christians to examine their motivations for being involved in God's work in the world. Do we minister to others out of our love for them and for the Lord? Do we gather for worship hoping to impress others with our musical abilities or our gifts for speaking? These are questions that must be tackled with brutal honesty and self-evaluation.

REFLECT: The best and most basic reason for worship and for ministering to others is obedience to God. God's instructions in Zechariah are pretty straightforward: Administer true justice; show mercy and compassion to one another; do not oppress the widow, the fatherless, the alien or the poor; do not think evil of one another. If we follow these instructions, we do what is pleasing to God; if we don't, we disobey Him. It's that simple.

RESPOND: Ask the Lord to assist you in evaluating your motives for ministry. Ask Him to bring to your mind any selfish ambitions that may be clouding your focus. Then ask Him to help you realign your desires toward His will.

Lord, help me to maintain my focus on you and your will for my life and to turn my back on my own selfish desires.

TO KNOW MORE:
Isaiah 10 and Matthew 6 \\

Day 165 | *Provision*

PRAY: God connect with me here, as I seek you in your Word.

READ: 1 Kings 17.4-6 — Imagine conversing with God as you read today's passage…

"Is that a true story – that one about the ravens bringing Elijah food?

"Well, why don't you do stuff like that anymore?

"You do? I haven't seen it.

"You're kidding. You do kid right? You're serious? It's easier to get birds to do that than to get people to do it? Wow! I never thought of it that way before."

REFLECT: How often have you been desperate for something before stumbling upon a better solution? You think you know what you need, but God really knows. It's that perspective issue; He is working from the big picture, and you are not. Can you trust Him to always provide exactly what you need?

RESPOND: Put God's work first and do what He wants. Then other things will be yours as well.

Lord I want you to be first in my life and I want my first thought to be how I can obey you fully.

TO KNOW MORE:
Psalm 147 and Hebrews 6 \\

Day 166 | *Unprepared*

PRAY: God connect with me here, as I seek you in your Word.

READ: Luke 12.35-47 — Have you ever been caught doing something you weren't supposed to be doing? Be honest now! Maybe when you were younger and your parents discovered some "harmless" mischief you'd gotten into. Of course, you've learned a lot since then and have never done anything like it again, right? Jesus told a story very similar but the consequences were much more devastating. They are eternal.

Jesus often told his disciples that He would leave this world only to return at some future time—a time only the Father knows. In the meantime, He wants His followers to be ready for His return. If we adopt the attitude that the unfaithful servant demonstrated, thinking, "My master won't be back for a while," and then waste time pursuing frivolous and ungodly activities then we may be in for an unwanted surprise. Jesus promises to reward those who live faithfully while they wait for His return. Our rewards in eternity will reflect our activities done in His name on earth.

REFLECT: God has given you a lot. And as Jesus explains, "Much is required from those to whom much is given, and much more is required from those to whom much is given." Wouldn't it be great to "get caught" doing something meaningful and wonderful for somebody who needs it?

RESPOND: Do you need to confess any activities and behaviours that have been keeping you from living a responsible, mature Christian life? Ask God to cleanse you, forgive you and fill you with His Spirit to help you be ready for Jesus' return.

Lord, I pray that you will forgive me of my sins and that I will remain faithful until you return for your followers.

TO KNOW MORE:
Philippians 1 and 1 Peter 1 \\

Day 167 | *Control*

PRAY: God connect with me here, as I seek you in your Word.

READ: Romans 8.26-28 — Many of us can quote Romans 8.28 from memory, taking comfort in God's work for our good. Few of us, however, are comfortable with the notion of our own weakness–an important part of verse 26. Weakness and devastating circumstances are the norm in a fallen world. God demonstrates His love in response to our weakness–and in spite of our unworthiness.

In so doing, He sets the standard for us–as members of His body–to demonstrate love for each other. Devastating circumstances become opportunities for ultimate good, both for those who respond in love and those who receive it.

REFLECT: Circumstances that seem devastating would not exist apart from the entrance of sin into the world. God's control does not prevent such circumstances, but it does prevent them thwarting His purpose. He uses them to discipline His children, develop their character and accomplish His plan. If you have ever lost your job for an extended period or suffered expensive medical bills due to illness or injury, you know how devastating it can seem. Living by faith is learning to trust God's control and care for you in the face of these circumstances.

RESPOND: Choose to believe that every circumstance brings you an opportunity to be victorious through Christ.

Lord, I yield to your control and thank you for your Spirit living in me and praying for me to accomplish your will.

TO KNOW MORE:
Zechariah 12 and Jude 1 \\

Day 168 | *Control*

PRAY: God connect with me here, as I seek you in your Word.

READ: 1 Samuel 2.5-8 — The swarms of reporters sent to cover the first game of the 1989 World Series in San Francisco had no idea they would spend little time talking about baseball that evening. The skies were clear, the temperature ideal. But during batting practice, while fans were filing into Candlestick Park, the earth began to tremble. Within seconds, the city was paralyzed by a powerful earthquake that cracked foundations, collapsed freeways and opened canyons in the earth. Although the stadium suffered little damage, the fans who left that evening surely thought for many days about their brush with the uncontrollable forces of nature.

In today's reading, Hannah affirms God's control over everything – not only the forces of nature, but the destiny of His chosen people. Verse 8 declares: "For the foundations of the earth are the Lord's and upon them He has set the world." The "foundations of the earth" are the base of His creation. God controls everything from the ground up.

REFLECT: Hannah praised God for surprising changes that revealed His control. She was no longer barren but "full" with "seven children" (v. 5). Seven is a number signifying completeness and God's richest blessings. Verse 7 says: "The Lord makes one poor and another rich; He brings one down and lifts another up." God does not endorse poverty or favor inequality. In verse 8; God gives the poor back their dignity: "He lifts the poor from the dust – yes, from a pile of ashes! He treats them like princes, placing them in seats of honor."

RESPOND: Thank the Creator God for being in control. Thank Him for blessing you on a daily basis.

Lord, I praise you for your many blessings and for being my sure and certain Saviour.

TO KNOW MORE:
Psalm 34 and Galatians 4 \\

Day 169 | *Honesty*

PRAY: God connect with me here, as I seek you in your Word.

READ: Romans 13.9,10 — Dishonesty always hurts someone. When people steal from an organization or cheat on their taxes, they may not think they are hurting anyone because a corporation or the government seems so impersonal. Shareholders and other citizens, however, suffer the consequences.

REFLECT: Have you thought about why God is so concerned about our honesty toward others? Because He loves them and requires us to love them, He forbids dishonest behaviours like stealing, lying, and cheating that hurt them.

RESPOND: Working to develop the habit of complete honesty in all your dealings will help you fulfill the law of love.

Lord, help me realize how any act of dishonesty reveals my lack of love for others and help me grow in my ability to love others as much as I love myself by dealing honestly in all situations.

TO KNOW MORE:
Ecclesiastes 19 and 1 Corinthians 13 \\

Day 170 | *Love*

READ: John 13.34 — Did you know that more songs have been written about love than any other topic? In fact, music has quite a bit to say on the topic. Let's see . . . Love can make you happy. Love changes everything. Love hurts. Love is a battlefield. Love is like oxygen. Love is alive. Love is all around. Love is forever. Love is in control. Love is in the air. And of course, love is like a rock. As informative as music may be, perhaps the most important thing we need to know about love is found in John 13.

This is really a two-part command that Jesus gives. The first part is a piece of cake: "Love one another". OK, no sweat. We Christians can show love to one another. We'll worship together in church. We'll pray for each other. We'll eat fellowship dinners together. The second part of the command, though, is more difficult—a lot more difficult: "As I have loved you, so you must love one another." Love each other as Jesus loved us? Now you're talking about sacrificial love, love that manifests itself not only through words but through actions. It's love that is unconditional. And we're supposed to have that kind of love for one another? How? Sacrifice, sacrifice, sacrifice.

REFLECT: If we are to love somebody the way that Christ loved us, we've got to be prepared to give up our time, our energy, our comfort and our material possessions for that person. That's a serious relationship, one that requires a tremendous commitment. That's the kind of relationship Jesus calls us to!

RESPOND: Take a few minutes to praise the Lord for His example of sacrificial love. Identify the aspects and demonstrations of His love that you most appreciate.

Lord, thank you for your limitless love for me and I pray that you will give me opportunities to share your redeeming love with others.

TO KNOW MORE:
Ephesians 5 and 2 John 1 \\

Day 171 | *Associations*

PRAY: God connect with me here, as I seek you in your Word.

READ: Proverbs 23.6-8 — A few years back, two friends went on a camping trip. They pitched their tents along the banks of a scenic river. For breakfast each morning, they would gather wild blackberries and make pancakes over an open fire. At night they would cook their dinner in the one pot they had brought along. At the end of the long weekend, they packed their car and headed home. Along the way they stopped for a snack. As they walked into the restaurant, people began to look at them a little strangely. They wondered what people were staring at and then it hit them: They both smelled like walking campfires. Everyone in the restaurant knew they had been around fire because the smell of smoke was in their hair and on their skin.

Today's passage reveals God's warning about hanging out with selfish and stingy people. Those close to selfish and stingy people stand in danger of picking up bad habits, attitudes and characteristics. God wants us to say what we mean and mean what we say. He is always direct with us, and he wants us to be direct with others. Another pitfall is an obsession with money. Some are always thinking about how much money everything costs rather than focusing on the people they could be helping. God wants us to be people centered, not money-centered.

REFLECT: Selfish and stingy people are always discontented and never satisfied with what they have. They always want more. God warns us to stay away from them. He knows that if we spend too much time with them we will surely be affected.

RESPOND: Think about your friends and acquaintances. Is there one person in particular who you are concerned about? Pray for that person and ask God to show you whether or not you should be spending time with him or her.

Lord, I pray that you will bring Godly people into my life so that we can support one another in our journeys of faith.

TO KNOW MORE:
Psalm 141 and Mark 7 \\

Day 172 | *Carefree Living*

PRAY: God connect with me here, as I seek you in your Word.

READ: 2 Corinthians 4.17-18 — When we put things in that perspective, looking at the big picture, "our present troubles are quite small and won't last very long" (v. 17). We can survive the troubles and toil and temptations now because they don't really amount to anything. And present troubles "produce for us an immeasurably great glory that will last forever" (v. 17). What did Paul mean by this? If we don't let our pains and troubles decrease our faith or disillusion us, we'll discover there's always a purpose for present suffering or something good that God can bring out of it.

Our human problems can give us opportunities to:

- Remember that Christ suffered for us.
- Stay humble and dependent on God.
- Look beyond life on earth and count on life in heaven.
- Grow in our faith as we trust God more.
- Identify with others and comfort them with God's comfort.
- See God's power at work in our lives.

REFLECT: Think of your problems as growth opportunities. Look beyond them to what waits for you, a child of God, in heaven forever.

RESPOND: Thank God for the gift of eternal life in heaven that He has already given you. And ask Him to give you some opportunities to grow through your hassles and heartaches.

Lord, I pray that you will help me to keep my mind on heaven as I live for you each day.

TO KNOW MORE:
Psalm 30 and Romans 8 \\

Day 173 | *Promises*

PRAY: God connect with me here, as I seek you in your Word.

READ: Deuteronomy 7.7-12 — Promises. We hear them all the time. People say, "I promise I won't tell anyone." "I promise I'll help you with that project." "I promise I'll meet you for lunch at 12:30." But sometimes promises are broken, and someone usually gets hurt in the process. Broken promises are unavoidable in a world of broken people. But there is one who will always deliver what He promises…. God.

In today's passage, God made a promise to His people. In these verses, He showed His care by delivering His people from their slavery in Egypt. How has God shown His care for you? By answering a prayer with a "yes?" By sending along a friend when you needed one? By providing extra money for you to be able to do something that you thought was impossible? God has many ways of providing for us. But if you think about it, the way that God provides for us most of the time is through other people. Perhaps God would like to use you to be an answer to someone else's prayer.

REFLECT: By helping others, you can reflect the faithful and caring nature of a loving God.

RESPOND: Recall incidents in the past week where God's faithfulness was evident to you. Then say a prayer of thanksgiving for His compassion.

Lord, I praise you for your faithfulness and ask that you will help me keep my promises to others and, especially, to you.

TO KNOW MORE:
Isaiah 51 and 1 John 3 \\

Day 174 | *Teamwork*

PRAY: God connect with me here, as I seek you in your Word.

READ: 1 Corinthians 3.1-9 — Each member of a sports team has a specific role. No player is more important than another because if anyone fails to do his or her job, the entire group suffers. The best teams function as a unit. Believe it or not, this same principle holds true for churches. The strongest churches are those whose members recognize their individual roles and perform them to the best of their ability, as the apostle Paul explains in his first letter to the Corinthians.

In order to emphasize the need for church members to work as a team, Paul used an example that hit close to home with the Corinthian believers. He pointed out that the various leaders whom the church singled out and looked up to were actually part of one team. Paul's role on the team was to plant the seed of faith and to spread the good news of Jesus Christ. Apollos' role was to water the seed Paul had planted. Neither task was more important than the other. After all, it was God alone who could make the seed grow. The same principle holds true for modem believers. Teamwork among Christians is every bit as important today as it was in Corinth two thousand years ago.

REFLECT: No matter what our ministry role is, we need to remember that it is no more or less important than the roles of other believers.

RESPOND: Ask God to give you the wisdom to understand your ministry role and the perseverance to perform it.

Lord, thank you that you have given me gifts that I can share with others and I pray that I will use me talents for your glory in a cooperative and loving way.

TO KNOW MORE:
Galatians 6 and 1 John 4 \\

Day 175 | *Good News*

PRAY: God connect with me here, as I seek you in your Word.

READ: Isaiah 61.1-3 — When was the last time you received some really good news? Do you remember how you reacted when you got the good news? Did your mouth drop open in amazement? Did you fall to your knees in thankfulness? Sometimes it's almost as fun to watch someone else receive good news as it is to get it. The fact is, nothing can brighten a person's day quicker than a happy, unexpected report. And God certainly understands this power. In fact, one of the most important aspects of the Christian life involves spreading the Good News.

God sent His only Son to mend the brokenhearted, to free those who are slaves to sin and to comfort those who mourn. Because of the salvation provided by Jesus, all who believe in Him can look forward to one day escaping the injustice, suffering and poverty of this present world. Working to meet the needs of hurting and broken people may lead to opportunities to talk to them about the fulfillment of their eternal needs. How wonderful it is to know that, with God's help, we too can turn ashes to beauty, mourning to joy and despair to praise.

REFLECT: Put yourself in the place of a homeless or needy person and answer this question: "What's the best news you could ever hope to get"? Probably the first answer that comes to mind involves food and lodging. And yet the news that the Lord gave to Israel in Isaiah 61 – the news that was later proclaimed by Jesus himself in Luke 4.18,19 – is much more exciting and meaningful.

RESPOND: Ask the Lord to make you aware of opportunities to share His Good News with non-Christian friends and acquaintances.

Lord, I pray that I can be a witness of your saving love to those I work with and those I meet throughout the day.

TO KNOW MORE:
Psalm 45 and Matthew 11 \\

Day 176 | *Not Forgotten*

PRAY: God connect with me here, as I seek you in your Word.

READ: Galatians 2.6-10 — Galatians 2 records a meeting between two of the most important figures in the early church—the apostles Peter and Paul. Interestingly enough, one of the main topics of their conversation was forgotten people. During the early days of the church, Jesus' disciples were looked to as the leaders of the Christian movement. Because Paul had not been one of the Twelve, it was important that he be accepted by James, Peter, and John. If these men recognized Paul's ministry as legitimate, so would other believers.

Fortunately, the three disciples were only too happy to welcome Paul into a position of leadership in the church. They had just one request of him. Now keep in mind, these were the early days of the church. Believers were facing a multitude of issues and problems including persecution, rapid growth, false teachers and squabbles among various factions, just to name a few. With all of these serious situations to consider, what did James, Peter and John want Paul to remember more than anything? The poor. Taking care of the needy is every bit as important today as it was in the early church. We must not fail to heed the advice that James, Peter and John gave to Paul.

REFLECT: Ask yourself three questions: (1) On a scale of one to ten, how well do you do at remembering the poor? (2) What are some things that tend to occupy your mind and cause you to forget about the poor? (3) What specific steps can you take to ensure that you will continue to remember the poor?

RESPOND: Ask God to help you focus your thoughts regularly on the poor and not forget the needy.

Lord, open my ears to the needs of others and give me a willing heart to answer their urgent pleas.

TO KNOW MORE:
Job 32 and 2 Corinthians 5 \\

Day 177 | *Faithfulness*

PRAY: God connect with me here, as I seek you in your Word.

READ: Luke 16.10 — Our responsibility as a steward or manager includes being faithful in all areas – in matters both large and small. Before we can be faithful, we must know what God wants us to do. The Bible gives instructions for living; some are direct commands, some are stories that provide examples, and some – like the Proverbs – are wise counsel for understanding principles of godly behavior.

REFLECT: Consider what it means to be faithful in matters both large and small by following these simply stated principles. They have their foundation in God's Word, as you will see in days to come.

- Seek counsel
- Practise honesty
- Work hard
- Give generously
- Save consistently
- Spend wisely
- Avoid debt
- Live for eternity

Can you see how faithfulness to these principles has a direct bearing on the quality of your life?

RESPOND: The more you realize God's loving power to care for you in every circumstance, the more eager you will be to honour Him with your faithfulness in every area of your life.

Lord, give me a hunger for your perspective on the practical areas of my life. I want to be faithful in everything, including the small things.

TO KNOW MORE:
John 13 and Ephesians 3 \\

Day 178 | *Hope*

PRAY: God connect with me here, as I seek you in your Word.

READ: Song of Songs 2.10-13 — The Song of Songs talks about the idea of "changing seasons." But, as you see in today's reading, weather is the farthest thing from the writer's mind. Life, like nature, has its seasons. Those who have endured bitter cold rejoice when spring arrives to warm the earth. In the same way, no one can appreciate security, stability and happiness as much as those who have experienced hardship and misery. Why are some people able to endure hardship in life? The secret is hope. For cold weather dwellers, the hope of spring helps them endure winter. For Christians, the hope of eternal life through Jesus helps them endure life's miseries. If we can recognize that our present "wintertime" suffering is temporary, we take a big step toward spiritual "springtime". Christians can also look forward to a more immediate hope – the assistance of fellow believers. God's people are called to look after each other, to support one another in times of suffering and hardship. In a sense, we are called to be spiritual "meteorologists", recognizing the seasons of life of those around us.

REFLECT: Many people in this world (and probably many people in your community) have endured, and are continuing to endure, long winters. For them, spring never seems to arrive. That's where we come in. Our job is to provide relief for these sufferers, to help them move from winter to spring. This help may involve personal contact, providing encouragement and emotional support to those who need it. It may also involve financial or material assistance, doing whatever we can to lessen the burden of the poor and the suffering in our community and around the world.

RESPOND: If you're in the midst of a winter in your life, remind yourself that God has prepared an eternal spring for those who trust in Him. Remind yourself that you have the ability (and the responsibility) to offer "springtime" relief to others who are facing their winter in life.

Lord, I pray that you will give me opportunities to bring hope, in your name, into the lives of others.

TO KNOW MORE: Jeremiah 31 and 2 Corinthians 11 \\

Day 179 | *Leadership*

PRAY: God connect with me here, as I seek you in your Word.

READ: Proverbs 29.2-12 — Today's verses shine a light on rulers, revealing the benefits of their honesty and the consequences of their dishonesty. God's concern for rulers is not limited to monarchs and presidents; the same principles apply to all leaders. Whether you lead a company, a church or a family, you are in a position of influence. Your decisions—even those that you think are private—have an impact on everyone around you. As a leader you set the pace. The greater your influence, the more you will be imitated—for good or for bad.

REFLECT: It seems so reasonable to think that no one will ever notice. Do you ever consider this line of reasoning in your decision making? Let it be a huge red flag in your mind. How would that ever justify anything?

RESPOND: Safeguard those who follow you—including your children—from following the path of least resistance. Your example is far more powerful than your preaching.

Lord, help me honor you in whatever role of leadership you have given me and help me stand against any hint of corruption without regard to whether it benefits me.

TO KNOW MORE:
Psalm 89 and Luke 15 \\

Day 180 | *Joy*

PRAY: God connect with me here, as I seek you in your Word.

READ: 2 Chronicles 7.1-10 — Joy. It's one of the finest feelings humans can experience. How long has it been since you really felt joyful? Maybe you haven't had much reason lately to experience the joy of the Lord. You're stuck in life's hassles, in the mundane matters of everyday existence or wallowing in some painful circumstances. Joy? That may seem like a huge cosmic joke. No matter how you're feeling right now, though, open your heart and mind to God's Word today and catch a glimpse of His joyful people from today's passage. Here we find that the Temple of God – ornate, gold-laden, and stunningly beautiful – took seven years and innumerable hours of labour to build. Now it was complete. And King Solomon and the people of Israel had dedicated it to the Lord God. God's glorious presence filled the building. It was so amazing that no one, not even the priests, could enter it. The people were overcome by praise and joy, falling on their faces and worshipping the Lord. They cried, "He is so good! His faithful love endures forever!" (v. 3).

You may never experience anything so dramatic. And yet the same God is at work in you and through you.

REFLECT: Lift up your eyes – away from your circumstances and onto the Lord. Recognize how good He has been to you, how faithful His love has been for you. Isn't He worthy of your joyful praise today?

RESPOND: Carve out some time in your schedule just to praise God for the many blessings and gifts He has given you. Make a list of the people, experiences, memories and possessions that have brought you joy. Think of as many as you can. Then thank God for them one by one.

Lord, I thank you for the many blessings you have given me and the great joy you bring into my life on a daily basis.

TO KNOW MORE:
Malachi 3 and Hebrews 7 \\

Day 181 | *Specialness*

PRAY: God connect with me here, as I seek you in your Word.

READ: 2 Timothy 2.20-21 — Does your family have a nice set of silverware or stainless steel utensils? It's the "good stuff" – the forks and spoons and knives you use for big dinners at Christmas, Easter, family birthdays and other special occasions. If so, you probably keep this silverware in a beautiful wooden box. Occasionally someone will lovingly polish every piece so it's shiny and beautiful and ready to use. Now compare that silverware with the plastic "sporks" you get at a fast-food restaurant, wrapped in plastic with a cheap napkin. They're used once and then tossed. Nothing special. If you were a utensil, which would you rather be: treasured silver or tossed-away plastic?

Paul uses picture language to get an important point across to Timothy. Followers of Jesus should aim to be the kind of people that God uses for special occasions: utensils that are clean and ready to use for joyful, loving purposes. That can happen only when they are pure, clean and ready to use.

REFLECT: Something clean and set apart for special use can easily become grungy and contaminated. When a spoon is gross with old food on it, it is set aside and left unused until it is cleaned up properly. Don't let that happen to you. Be careful with whom you associate and what you do in your spare time. Strive to keep yourself clean and ready for God to use. Be the kind of person Jesus can work through for His noblest purposes. Then God can use you as an instrument of His blessing in every good work.

RESPOND: Spend some time in prayer, confessing your sins and thanking God for cleansing and filling you. Ask God to give you an opportunity to be used for His glory today.

Lord, forgive me of my sins and make me clean so that I can serve you effectively and share your love with others.

TO KNOW MORE:
Lamentations 4 and Romans 9 \\

Day 182 | *Dishonesty*

PRAY: God connect with me here, as I seek you in your Word.

READ: Exodus 20.15,16 — Two of the Ten Commandments address honesty:

- Do not steal.

- Do not tell lies about others.

Today's verses link "living right" with respecting God (Proverbs 14.2), and doing what Jesus "commands" with loving him (John 14.15). When we examine what motivates us to be dishonest, we usually find fear as a root cause. Fearing that we will not get what we need, we take things into our own hands to get the outcome we want.

REFLECT: Linking honesty with loving God may be a connection you have not considered before. Reflect on how dishonesty simultaneously makes at least three subconscious statements to God:

- I don't trust you to provide what I need.

- I prefer my dishonesty to your character.

- I love my wants more than I love you.

RESPOND: Develop the habit of thinking through the implications of even the smallest acts of dishonesty.

Lord, help me realize how any act of dishonesty reveals my lack of respect and love for you. Help me remember that nothing is hidden from you and that you love me enough to provide the discipline I need.

TO KNOW MORE:
Psalm 15 and 1 Thessalonians 4 \\

Day 183 | *Greed*

PRAY: God connect with me here, as I seek you in your Word.

READ: Genesis 13.8-13 — The Bible provides a very accurate assessment of greed and its consequences. One of the earliest examples can be found in our reading today about Lot and his generous uncle Abraham. Lot saw that the plains of Jordan looked fertile and profitable, so he chose that land for himself. In his desire to prosper, Lot thought only of himself, leaving the less-desirable land to his uncle Abraham. In short, Lot made a greedy decision. And, as so often happens, he later paid dearly for his greed.

The land that Lot chose bordered on the wicked city of Sodom. When God decided to destroy Sodom, He had to evacuate Lot and his family. Even though they sensed a great danger, they were reluctant to leave their home. As Lot's wife was leaving the city, she looked back (despite God's clear warning) and died. Lot's greedy decision years earlier set in motion a chain of events that eventually tore his family apart.

REFLECT: Of course not every greedy decision results in death. And yet when we choose to satisfy our own desire for wealth and power and put others second, we can be assured that we will have to answer to God for it.

RESPOND: Ask God to remind you of any greedy decisions you've made lately. Ask Him to forgive you for those decisions and to give you wisdom and strength to make choices in the future that will honour Him.

Lord, help me to be generous with others and to not give in to selfish and greedy desires, no matter how personally satisfying those choices may seem at the moment.

TO KNOW MORE:
Psalm 133 and 1 Corinthians 6 \\

Day 184 | *True Worship*

PRAY: God connect with me here, as I seek you in your Word.

READ: Matthew 2.9-12 — The fact that giving and worship are closely related is not exactly a news flash. After all, most churches collect tithes and offerings during their worship services. But, unless we're careful, our giving may become a lifeless routine or a legalistic ritual. When we refuse to give beyond what's expected – be it a tithe or a standard we've set for ourselves – we may fall into the trap the Pharisees failed to see.

If we seek to honour the Lord, we'll do so by giving without thought for the cost. Whether we have much or little does not matter as much as our willingness to give what we have. If we maintain a joyful spirit and always consider the needs of others, God will look on our acts as a delightful offering of worship. We may feel like the Little Drummer Boy – that we have no gifts fit to give the King. But God asks us to give our best. We can take comfort, however, in the fact that the Lord accepts as precious gifts our efforts on His behalf.

REFLECT: Extraordinary needs may arise that require more time, energy or money than we're used to giving. Our reaction to such circumstances will tell us a lot about the state of our hearts. Do we worship God because we want to or because we're expected to?

RESPOND: Spend a few minutes in worshipful prayer, during which time you do nothing but praise God for who He is and what He has done. Offer to give Him all that you have.

Lord, I praise you for all that you've given me and for sending your Son to die for my sins so that I may live in your presence throughout eternity.

TO KNOW MORE:
Psalm 25 and Luke 2 \\

Day 185 | *Remembrance*

PRAY: God connect with me here, as I seek you in your Word.

READ: Nehemiah 9.7-16 — You've probably met people who can't seem to remember anything. How often do we as Christians act as if we have no memory of what God has done for us? We need reminders to strengthen our faith in times of weakness and turn us back to God when we rebel. At a time when Israel had once again turned from God, Ezra led his people in a beautiful prayer that recounted God's love and faithfulness to them from the time of Abraham.

God obviously thinks remembering is important (see verse 10). Ezra's prayer recalls the Israelites' repeated pattern of rebellion followed by God's mercy, grace and forgiveness. God showed remarkable patience with His people, refusing to abandon them despite their rejection of Him. They needed to remember that fact as they came before Him in repentance.

REFLECT: Just like Ezra, we need to remember and praise God for all that He has done for us. We must also honour His "regulations and laws that are just and right, and decrees and commands that are good" because each of these were given to us so that we can live holy and righteous lives that are pleasing to Him.

RESPOND: Keep a string tied loosely around your finger for one day. When you look at the string, say a prayer of thanks for one blessing God has given you recently.

Lord, thank you for blessing me with (_____) and may I never forget the mercy and love you show me each day.

TO KNOW MORE:
Genesis 15 and Hebrews 17 \\

Day 186 | *Generosity*

PRAY: God connect with me here, as I seek you in your Word.

READ: Mark 12.41-44 — He was a humble man, soft-spoken and preferring to talk about his God rather than himself. Living in a country ruled by a dictator, this man risked all to be an underground pastor. He was in prison for nearly nineteen years; while there, his entire family died. He had no citizenship. Denied even this by his government, he was literally a man with no country. He owned essentially nothing. Still, he gave abundantly to the churches he served. Poor? Oh, definitely, by the world's standards. But this man was like the woman whom Jesus observed in the temple. They both understood that generous giving goes far beyond monetary limits.

In fact, the woman in today's reading gave everything; all that she had. It boggles the mind, doesn't it, to think of that kind of faith and generosity? So our inner voice probably responds, I can't be like her! And I can't be like this pastor who puts his very life in danger for God. Actually you're right—none of us can serve with this kind of love. But, with God's help and the Spirit's guidance, we can all experience the blessing of giving generously to others.

REFLECT: Jesus didn't share His observations with His disciples to make them feel guilty. And He isn't asking us to empty our savings, sell our possessions and give away everything. But He is calling us to evaluate our giving. How generous are we? What is the spirit of our giving? Do we give first, trusting in God's provision? Do we follow a plan that allows us to give joyfully and with increasing generosity? And finally, does It cost us anything? It certainly cost the poor widow and the underground pastor.

RESPOND: Pray for the ability to trust God even more with your finances and consider the possibility of giving more than you currently do.

Lord, help me to have the same giving spirit as those who so generously live to see your Kingdom thrive and your people cared for.

TO KNOW MORE:
2 Kings 12 and Luke 21 \\

Day 187 | *Teammates*

PRAY: God connect with me here, as I seek you in your Word.

READ: 1 Corinthians 1.10-17 — Sometimes great athletes are referred to as a one-man or one-woman team. The truth is that even those blessed with extraordinary physical gifts need teammates. The apostle Paul recognized a Christian's need for "teammates", especially in the areas of support, encouragement and unity.

In the early days of the church, several Christian leaders traveled throughout the Roman Empire (and beyond), teaching people in various churches along the way. As you might expect, the people who listened to these evangelists began to develop favourites, preferring one leader's style over another. The church in Corinth, however, began to take this to an extreme. Little cliques, based on a preferred leader, were forming in the church. Some identified with Paul. Others preferred Apollos. Still others followed Peter. Some even believed that they were the only ones who truly followed Christ. Paul emphasized the need for unity among Christians.

REFLECT: One committed individual can have a tremendous impact when he or she determines to serve the Lord by ministering to others. When joined by two or three Christian "teammates" – people who support, pray for and accompany that ministry – the results can be incredible. When that group of teammates is working in conjunction with the church as a whole, the impact can rock a community to its core.

RESPOND: Confess any attitude that has kept you from being a team player. Ask God to provide an opportunity for you to begin or develop a relationship with at least a couple of other people from your church – people who are interested in the same type of ministry that you are interested in.

Lord, I pray that you will bring people into my life with whom I can become part of a team that serves you in joyful harmony.

TO KNOW MORE:
1 Thessalonians 5 and 2 Thessalonians 2 \\

Day 188 | *Strangers*

PRAY: God connect with me here, as I seek you in your Word.

READ: Deuteronomy 1.14-18 — For the most part, Canada has been a nation that has warmly and openly welcomed immigrants. For this reason, on June 25, 2009, Pier 21 – the Gateway to Canada – was designated a National Museum of Immigration. In today's reading we discover that God wanted Israel to have an unblemished record in its just treatment of foreigners. God weighed in on the topic when He urged Hebrew judges to rule fairly in cases involving those who lived among the Israelites but were not directly descended from Jacob. Of course Jesus' solution to the problem of xenophobia – or an unreasonable fear or hatred of foreigners – is as simple in its wording as it is difficult in its execution: "Love your enemies".

Some of the neediest and most oppressed people in our society today are foreigners. Squalid living conditions, extreme poverty, unsafe neighborhoods and limited language skills are just a few of the obstacles faced by strangers in our land. While these same obstacles may deter you from making an effort to show the love Jesus spoke of in Luke 6 to foreign families in your community, the simple truth is, they shouldn't!

REFLECT: There is a great deal of satisfaction and mutual benefit to be found in forming relationships with people of other cultures. Do not allow yourself to miss out on these opportunities.

RESPOND: If you struggle at all with xenophobia, ask God to create in you a spirit of love for the foreigners with whom you come into contact every day.

Lord, you are my refuge and my security – may I show the same welcoming attitudes to those who journey to our shores.

TO KNOW MORE:
1 Samuel 17 and 1 Timothy 5 \\

Day 189 | *Dignity*

PRAY: God connect with me here, as I seek you in your Word.

READ: Leviticus 19.9-16 — Picture the mad scramble and frenzy of children grabbing for candy spilled from a piñata at Christmas. That's a fairly accurate image of what adults are like. We want to get as much as we can before someone else beats us to it. In Leviticus 19, God presented Israel with a radically different model for behaviour. God told the Israelites to leave some of their harvest in the field for the poor and the foreigners to collect. The fact that He gave that command suggests that this practice didn't come naturally. People should reap what they sow, right. Yes, hard work should be rewarded, but God's command expresses two desires. One is that the prosperous should bless those who struggle. Corporate sin, individual sin and our fallen nature all contribute to poverty. It affects the just and the unjust. God has a heart of mercy for the poor, regardless of how they got that way. Passing out food is often necessary, especially in emergency situations, but it tends to lower the dignity of the recipient. Modern methods of "reaping the remains of the harvest" provide a way for the poor to work for what they receive.

REFLECT: In the book of Ruth, we find a well-known story about gleaning. Ruth, a poor widow, was noted for working in the field steadily from morning, collecting unharvested grain. Boaz, the owner of the field, went beyond the law's requirements to ensure that Ruth collected what she needed. He also took great effort to ensure that she wouldn't be embarrassed. Boaz reflected the heart of God for the poor: to bless them with dignity and grace.

RESPOND: Pray for ministries working among the poor that they will help provide for their needs in a way that builds self-esteem and dignity.

Lord, I pray for those whose compassion for the poor is coupled with their desire to give them outlets for developing skills along with self-respect.

TO KNOW MORE:
Deuteronomy 24 and Ruth 2 \\

Day 190 | Rulers

PRAY: God connect with me here, as I seek you in your Word.

READ: 1 Samuel 12.12-24 — In the last few decades, many Christians in North America have chosen to become part of the political process. Some argue that this is a healthy trend – that believers elected to positions of influence can be salt and light in a decaying, darkening culture. Others believe that spending so much money, time and effort to bring about political change is a waste. Both arguments have merit, but each side needs to remember the timeless truth taught by the ancient prophet Samuel in his farewell address to the nation of Israel found in today's reading. In essence, Samuel was warning Israel against forgetting that God was their true King. In order for their new system of government to work, the people had to maintain a primary trust in and fear of God. He is the ultimate Ruler. He is the only One who deserves full confidence and allegiance. Samuel was saying that when God is revered and remembered and when His laws are followed carefully, things would go well for the nation. We need this same warning today.

REFLECT: The temptation is for us to put our hope in whatever political party or candidate who claims to represent "traditional values". We get worked up over particular causes, as if a single legislative act can bring about godliness in our nation. We tend to rely heavily on economic forecasts and reports. Each of these is important, but the greater truth is that God is in control, and we need to trust Him and nothing else.

RESPOND: Pray that you and other believers would place the hope for justice in the hands of the Lord instead of in world leaders and governments.

Lord, I place my faith and trust in you for both my future and the future of all Canadians.

TO KNOW MORE:
Genesis 17 and Psalm 74 \\

Day 191 | *Proper Attire*

PRAY: God connect with me here, as I seek you in your Word.

READ: Job 29.11-18 — For several weeks you've been looking forward to a presentation you'll be making to what could be your company's biggest client. Because it's such an important meeting, you've invited key executive staff to join the gathering – which will be held in a private dining room at an expensive restaurant. You make it clear that this is a formal occasion and business casual attire isn't appropriate. As everyone arrives, however, you discover, to your horror, that while the potential clients are dressed in expensive, dark suits, the executives from your company show up in t-shirts, jeans and flip flops. As you stumble for words, your boss remarks loudly that "it's just a meeting" and who cares what anybody wears.

Yes, a special gathering, celebration or dinner meeting calls for appropriate clothing, doesn't it? And today's passage is about the splendid attire God provides for His people. Righteousness means having a special standing with the Father because of Christ's purity. God sees His Son's sinless life in place of our sinful one. God has covered our old sinful nature with the robe of Christ's righteousness.

REFLECT: You may feel awkward or overdressed if you wear a formal gown or business suit to a hockey game. There is no awkwardness in Christ's righteousness, however. Only awe at the splendour of the robe and crown. Thank the Righteous One, Jesus Christ, for "buying" your new wardrobe.

RESPOND: Thank the Lord for His righteousness that covers you. Ask Him to show you how you specifically can shine His righteousness where you are.

Lord, I am so grateful for the splendour of your righteousness and I pray that your holiness will be evident in my life for all to see.

TO KNOW MORE:
Proverbs 29 and Luke 11 \\

Day 192 | *Promises*

PRAY: God connect with me here, as I seek you in your Word.

READ: Isaiah 49.8-13 — The world is full of promises. You know, for things like sure-fire weight loss programs or get-rich-quick schemes. So how do you know whether a promise is believable or not? It all depends on the person making the promise. If it's a politician looking to get reelected or an advertiser trying to sell a product, you may want to take their guarantees with a grain of salt. If, however, the promise-maker is someone incapable of lying, someone who is perfectly trustworthy, then you'd better believe that the promise will be kept. We find one such promise in Isaiah 49.

God is speaking to Israel, reassuring the poor and needy that He will always be with them. He assures them that they will never hunger or thirst, that He will comfort them and that He will have compassion on the afflicted ones. The Israelites knew that the Lord was trustworthy, that He kept His promises. We should have the same confidence today because God never changes. He has promised to protect the weak and satisfy the needy. We must remain confident that the Lord will eventually fulfill His promises to the disadvantaged – in His time and in ways that we cannot imagine.

REFLECT: Where do you, as a believer, fit into God's promises? Recognize that you may be one of the ways God accomplishes His work of uplifting others.

RESPOND: Praise the Lord that His promises are rock-solid and that they can be depended upon when everything else in life seems untrustworthy.

Lord, thank you that your promises are certain and that you never waver in your commitments – may I demonstrate the same level of integrity to others as I serve the poor in your name.

TO KNOW MORE:
Psalm 2 and 2 Corinthians 6 \\

Day 193 | *Gifts*

PRAY: God connect with me here, as I seek you in your Word.

READ: Luke 19.12-26 — A friend calls you one day because she wants to borrow your most expensive necklace for a banquet she's attending. You're a little reluctant because she has a tendency to be careless with her belongings. Eventually, though, you agree to lend her the jewelry. Almost two months later, she finally returns it. Unfortunately the clasp is broken and some of the jewels are missing.

Some people are just as careless with the gifts God has given them, as Jesus shared in today's parable. Through this story the Lord wanted His followers to realize that He has given each of us certain resources to use for His glory. All of these come from Him and all should be used for Him. He also wanted the world to know that He is coming back one day and we should live with an ever-present awareness of His imminent return.

REFLECT: We will one day be judged for how well we have served God with the resources He has given us. Our future rewards will be determined by how faithfully we are serving Him in the present.

RESPOND: Pray for faithfulness in managing all God has entrusted to you. Pray for opportunities to multiply your "allowances". Trust God for opportunities to share the gift of the Gospel with those who have yet to receive it.

Lord, thank you for the many gifts and talents you have given me and I pray that your Holy Spirit will guide me as I strive to use them to further your Kingdom.

TO KNOW MORE:
Philippians 2 and Hebrews 9 \\

Day 194 | *Judgment*

PRAY: God connect with me here, as I seek you in your Word.

READ: Revelation 7.1-17 — Non-believers can ask a lot of tough questions. In fact, you may have just recently heard someone say, "Where is God when a child is hurt or a widow is mistreated?" or, more commonly, "How can a loving God judge and punish people?". We can't really give an adequate answer to these questions until we shake off any flawed ideas we have about God's love, mercy and justice.

Revelation 7 gives us a clear portrait of God as both a loving heavenly Father and a stern, frightening Judge. More important, it allows us to see how these two sides of His nature fit together. In the minds of most people, love and judgment are contradictory actions. Yet, God judges sin because He is holy and perfect. Sin, on the other hand, is destructive. Therefore, because God is a loving God, sin must be judged.

REFLECT: God demonstrates His love by protecting the people who have chosen to follow Him. He marks them with a seal that sets them apart from those who will be judged. As followers of Jesus Christ we will escape the wrath of His judgment. What a motivation – and responsibility – to tell others about the Good News of Jesus Christ!

RESPOND: Ask the Lord to give you the wisdom and courage to tell an unbelieving friend or family member about Him and the salvation He offers.

Lord, I pray that you will give me the resolve to share my faith with others so that they will have an opportunity to escape your coming judgment.

TO KNOW MORE:
Malachi 4 and Ephesians 4 \\

Day 195 | *Deluge*

PRAY: God connect with me here, as I seek you in your Word.

READ: Amos 5.18-27 — Anyone who has ever witnessed a raging, flooded river knows the frightening and devastating effect this powerful force of nature can wreak. And yet there is a kind of flood that is NOT disastrous. In fact, it's desirable! Consider the words of the prophet Amos in today's reading.

What does God mean by "a flood of justice"? Well, we know that floods wash over everything in their path. The waters seep into every crack and crevice. Even when the "wet stuff" recedes, the residue of the flood remains. So God desires fairness and rightness to cover the world — washing over and in and through the lives of His people. But what is meant by "a river of righteous living"? If you've ever seen a fast-flowing river, you know that it doesn't let anything stand in its way; it chisels at everything it encounters. Fast or slow, every river flows relentlessly to its destination, bringing life to the land in the process. God wants us to be like that — faithfully working with other believers to provide refreshment, even as we slowly but surely erode the sin in our culture.

REFLECT: Practically speaking, we become human floods of justice and rivers of righteousness by helping the victims of injustice. As we allow God's Spirit to change our attitudes, values, and priorities, we begin to recognize every person as important and special.

RESPOND: Ask God to flood your life with a passion for Him and compassion for those hurt by injustice. Pray that you and your believing friends and family can join together to be a river of righteousness.

Lord, help me to be a "river" of loving care for those who need your love and who desperately seek your justice.

TO KNOW MORE:
Joel 1 and 2 Peter 3 \\

Day 196 | *Good News*

PRAY: God connect with me here, as I seek you in your Word.

READ: Psalm 37.12-18 — A farmer who was on vacation called his farmhand to see how things were going. "Oh, just fine," the farmhand replied. "The good news is the dog's leg should be all healed by the time you get home. The bad news is the truck rolled over it." "The truck rolled over it?" the farmer asked. "Yep, the bad news is that someone forgot to set the brake. But the good news is that when the truck rolled over the dog's leg, it slowed the truck down a bit before it hit the barn." "Hit the barn!" shouted the farmer. "Yep," replied the farmhand. "That's the bad news. But here's the good news. The truck didn't do much damage to the barn because most of it had burned down the day before."

Today's passage shares the ups and downs of a good news / bad news message. You can be sure, however, that David, the author of this Psalm, didn't find anything funny about the content. For the wicked – those who would oppress the poor and needy – the news is bad. They will be pierced by their sharpened swords and their bows will be broken (vv. 14-15). But for believers, the news is good because the Lord takes care of the godly (v. 17) and they will receive an everlasting reward (v. 18).

REFLECT: The information age allows us to witness and read about the evil things that plague our world. But we have a source of hope that surpasses the world's despair. By reading the Bible – God's Good News – we can be reminded daily that God has overcome whatever trial wc facc. Now that is good news indeed!

RESPOND: Ask God to make His Word the lens through which you view the world. Ask Him to help you study Scripture in a thoughtful, life-changing way.

Lord, I pray that you will open the truths of your Scriptures to me so that I can be filled with the assurance that you are ultimately in charge and that soon the world will be transformed by the return of your Son.

TO KNOW MORE:
Esther 3 and Galatians 5 \\

Day 197 | *Vows*

PRAY: God connect with me here, as I seek you in your Word.

READ: Judges 21.19-25 — In Disney's Mary Poppins, the Banks children are introduced by their new nanny to the "pie-crust promise": easily made, easily broken. While she may have helped the medicine go down, the lady with the magic umbrella didn't keep promises very well. The Israelites knew that keeping promises was important, though they often failed to keep their end of the agreements they made with God. During the shameful war between the tribes of Israel and Benjamin, which began with the brutal murder of a concubine, the Israelites swore they would never give their women in marriage to the Benjamites. When the fighting was over, Benjamin lay in ruins, and only a few warriors survived. Victorious Israelites decided they didn't want to annihilate Benjamin completely, so they came up with a roundabout way to repopulate the tribe while still keeping their vow. They permitted the surviving Benjamites to nab festival dancers. Since fathers of these dancers had not given their daughters voluntarily, they had kept their pledge (Judges 21.22), while the Israelites technically avoided breaking their vow. Jesus provided a superior alternative—use plain words and avoid hasty declarations or inflammatory oaths (Matthew 5.33-37).

REFLECT: We learn from the Israelites the importance of keeping our word. To do rightly in the Lord's eyes means to keep promises to Him and to others. There should be no "pie-crust promises" made by Christians.

RESPOND: The last verse of Judges says the people often did what was right in their own eyes and that they had no king. Christ is your King. Ask Him to help you keep promises to Him and to the people He has placed around you.

Lord, I pray you forgive me for any promises I have made that I have yet to fulfill, and help me to guard my tongue whenever I am tempted to quickly and foolishly make a vow to you or to others.

TO KNOW MORE:
Psalm 81 and Matthew 10 \\

Day 198 | *Justice*

PRAY: God connect with me here, as I seek you in your Word.

READ: Exodus 22.3-8 — If a group of thieves broke into your house and took your laptop and jewelry, you'd want to make sure they were punished, right? If a stranger stole your car, you'd want to see the person arrested and jailed. If somebody carelessly spilled grape juice on your new white shirt or blouse, you'd probably want that person to pay for a replacement. This is because most people want restitution. Restitution is the act of making good for loss, damage or injury. In other words, restitution is making wrongs right.

Fairness is essential to justice. And clearly, justice is important to God's heart. Now, you may never have an ox stolen, but chances are you've been treated unjustly a time or two in your life. Naturally, you'd want the wrongs to be made right. But consider the other side of the coin. What about when you hurt somebody else, whether intentionally or unintentionally? How strongly are you in favour of justice then? As a child of God, you're called to a higher standard. So consider going beyond what is merely just and fair. Go beyond what's expected. As Jesus said, go the second mile.

REFLECT: A caring person wants not only to replace what was lost but to ease the pain caused by the loss. By going beyond the "letter of the law", you'll do more than the mere basics for someone you've hurt. It's an attitude that will make you more "other-focused" rather than "self-focused". Best of all, you could make a huge impact in the lives of people who have been hurt by lovingly paying them back, in Jesus' name, more than what's expected.

RESPOND: Praise God for His justice and His mercy. Ask Him to make you sensitive to the ways in which you may hurt or rob others and to give you guidance for offering a generous payback. Ask Him to give you a heart for justice.

Lord, help me to be just in all my actions and that I will demonstrate fairness whenever I am the cause of someone's misfortune.

TO KNOW MORE: Proverbs 6 and Hosea 7 \\

Day 199 | *Investments*

PRAY: God connect with me here, as I seek you in your Word.

READ: Matthew 6.19-24 — Where do you keep your riches? In a world that seems consumed by money and possessions, Jesus' words are kind of shocking, aren't they? He simply says, "Don't store up treasures here on earth". What's the use? It'll just rust, be eaten by moths or stolen by thieves. And you certainly can't take it with you.

So, Jesus says, spend your time creating heavenly, not earthly, wealth. Nothing can hurt those treasures, and you can enjoy them forever. Giving money regularly to God's Kingdom is one way. Set aside a portion of every paycheque to give back to God, recognizing that it's all His anyway and He's just letting you use it. But that's not the only way to store up treasures in heaven. Every good deed you do, every act of obedience, every gift of your time and energy in service to others who need it is an eternal investment.

REFLECT: Jesus says you can't serve two masters. In this world, you'll be continually tempted to pursue money and possessions. To some people, that's all there is to life. They spend their time collecting things only to leave them all behind when they die. Which master do you follow? Jesus calls us to make a decision to live contentedly with whatever we have. It's a decision we'll benefit from forever and ever.

RESPOND: Ask God to give you a heart that pursues Him rather than money or possessions. In prayer, acknowledge that He is your master and that you desire to follow and serve Him as long as you're on this earth. Thank Him for the Heavenly treasures that await you because of your obedience.

Lord, I am thankful for the abundance you have given me and pray that you will show me ways I can use your blessings to further your Kingdom so that the riches I gain will be eternal and not fleeting.

TO KNOW MORE:
Ecclesiastes 2 and James 5 \\

Day 200 | *Favouritism*

PRAY: God connect with me here, as I seek you in your Word.

READ: James 2.1-9 — It's natural to show favouritism toward someone who's rich. Why? First, most of us don't feel entirely comfortable around poverty – partly because we know we're responsible to help the poor as best we can. Second, deep down, most of us want to be rich ourselves. And we think that if we hang around someone who's rich, maybe it will rub off on us.

Of course, these motives are selfish. They indicate that we think we're better than poor people. We're not. In fact, James says, "Hasn't God chosen the poor in this world to be rich in faith? Aren't they the ones who will inherit the kingdom God promised to those who love him?" (v. 5). If we really believe in Jesus and want to follow Him, then we need to show favouritism . . . to no one!

REFLECT: We should love everyone regardless of whether they are rich or poor. God looks at all people as equals. We are commanded to follow His example.

RESPOND: If you realize you've been playing favourites, especially with people who are rich, confess your sin to God. Ask Him to give you a heart that sees all people as equals – regardless of their economic status, race, colour, neighbourhood, clothes or hairstyle. And ask Him to help you love them all equally, just as His Son does.

Lord, forgive me for times when I've been less than kind to someone who is poor and help me to view everyone as equal and deserving of mercy.

TO KNOW MORE:
Jude 1 and Revelation 14 \\

Day 201 | *Treasures*

PRAY: God connect with me here, as I seek you in your Word.

READ: Luke 12.33-34 — Look around your home at the little treasures you have on shelves, desks or tables. As you look at each object, take note of why you kept it, why it's special to you, what it means to you. We treasure things because of the memories associated with them and because of the people they bring to mind. Think about these feelings in the context of today's reading.

Heavenly treasure is far more valuable than earthly wealth. To get that across, Jesus goes so far as to suggest that we sell everything we have and give to those in need. He challenges us to decide to put God and eternity first. Then He explains, "Wherever your treasure is, there your heart" (v. 34). Whatever we value will become the centre of our lives. If we choose God above all else, our thoughts will dwell constantly on Him. Remember, too, that God-given treasure cannot be taken from us. Money, on the other hand, is a relentless master. When it becomes our reason for living, it consumes our thoughts, our plans, our interests, our time and our energy; but it does not satisfy. An obsession with money also keeps us from using God's gifts as He intended.

REFLECT: Jesus doesn't say there's something wrong with having possessions that are meaningful and precious to us. But He is challenging us to think about what our hearts and minds routinely dwell on. Is it money and earthly possessions or heavenly treasures earned by obedient, sacrificial acts of service? Let those meaningful objects around your home prompt your prayer time today.

RESPOND: Pray for your family members and friends who are connected to cherished objects. Then ask God to give you treasures in heaven that are far more important than these perishable things.

Lord, I pray for my family and friends and I ask that you will give me both the opportunities and the desire to share my abundance with others.

TO KNOW MORE:
John 12 and Daniel 6 \\

Day 202 | *Limits*

PRAY: God connect with me here, as I seek you in your Word.

READ: 1 Chronicles 17.7-15 — Some people who really don't understand Christianity downplay it as "pie in the sky when you die"—in other words, they think it's just vague, empty promises of sweetness and light in heaven. They assume that the Christian life on earth is tough, hard and grim—a bunch of do's and don'ts without much joy or excitement. Take note of the ways God rewarded David both in the present and in the future, because that's just what He'll do for you too. David had been a fabulously successful leader of his nation. Israel was prosperous, peaceful and promising. In fact, God had given David so many blessings in this life that he was beginning to feel a little guilty. David felt bad that, while he lived in an incredibly beautiful palace, God was still worshiped in a tent. He wanted to build God a proper temple.

But God spoke to Nathan, David's trusted advisor. Through Nathan, God assured David that he had been chosen to lead His people Israel. He promised He would raise up David's son after him and make him a great king. And that son would be the one to build the temple. When he heard this message, David was overwhelmed with gratitude. It was almost too good to be true. Yet that's just the kind of God He is. He wants to lavish on us every blessing in this life including fellowship, joy, peace and much more.

REFLECT: Sure, life can be tough. And yes, there are limits to our behaviours here on earth. But these are limits that God gave us for our own protection. And there's much more than just the "sweet by and by". There are the blessings here and now.

RESPOND: David prayed, "What more can I say about the way you have honoured me? You know what I am really like" (1 Chronicles 17.18). Recognize that God does know what you are really like, inside and out, and He still loves and treasures you. And He looks forward to spending eternity with you. Take some time to enjoy that truth with God in prayer.

Lord, thank you for loving me despite my flaws. Help me to show similar patience and kindness toward others.

TO KNOW MORE: Psalm 78 and Amos 7 \\

Day 203 | Excuses

PRAY: God connect with me here, as I seek you in your Word.

READ: Deuteronomy 15.7-11 — There are a lot of excuses for not helping poor people. How many have you yourself made?

- Somebody else will help them.

- I have to take care of my own needs first.

- It's their own fault that they're poor.

- I really don't have enough money to help anyway.

The Israelites were preparing to enter the land they had been forced to wait forty years for because of their disobedience. Would they dare disobey God now? He tells them that if they found any poor people living in the towns of their new land—the land God was giving them—that they were to generously lend to these people whatever they needed. They were not to be "hardhearted" or "mean-spirited". If they refused to lend a needy person what he or she needed, they would "be considered guilty of sin". This principle stands out clearly: "Give freely . . . and the Lord your God will bless you in everything you do".

REFLECT: God first speaks of loans, then of gifts. The people of God were to be free with lending money and materials to help the poor get on their feet. Loans, by definition, are intended to be repaid. And that was the goal of helping the poor—to help them get established so they could repay their loans and prosper. But then God moves to gifts. Gifts are free, with no strings attached. Be free with your giving. Don't expect repayment. God will repay you with blessings beyond what money can buy.

RESPOND: Ask God to wipe the excuses away from your heart. Ask Him to prepare you so that the next time you have an opportunity to help a poor person, your initial reaction will be to give freely as you are able rather than to find a hard-hearted, tight-fisted excuse.

Lord, I pray that you will forgive me for the excuses I've made in the past to not help the poor, and instill in me a generous heart for those in need.

TO KNOW MORE: Proverbs 21 and 1 John 3 \\

Day 204 | *Pretense*

PRAY: God connect with me here, as I seek you in your Word.

READ: Proverbs 13.7-8 — We've all "enhanced" the truth about ourselves at least once or twice in our lives. Whether we'd care to admit it or not, most of us have at some point pretended to be someone we're not. The book of Proverbs has some interesting things to say about pretending, as we read in today's passage. According to God's accounting method, money does not necessarily make a person rich. If a person has a wealth of material possessions but is lacking spiritually and socially, he or she has nothing. He or she is only "pretending" to be rich. Likewise, a person who possesses very little materially may have great wealth spiritually and socially. Thus, he or she is only "pretending" to be poor.

The writer of Proverbs also makes another interesting distinction between the rich and the poor. People who own much material wealth may need to use that money to buy their way out of trouble or to pay off criminals and enemies. A poor person (one with no material wealth), on the other hand, doesn't have to worry about such threats.

REFLECT: When was the last time you heard of a homeless person being held hostage while their kidnappers demanded a shopping cart full of old blankets and rags? The folk singer Bob Dylan said it best: "When you ain't got nothin', you got nothin' to lose". The book of Proverbs affirms that it's important to decide what kind of wealth we decide to pursue.

RESPOND: Ask the Lord to help you shift your focus from material wealth to social and spiritual riches.

Lord, I pray that you will reprioritize my desires so that my heart is focused on you and eternity rather than the passing pleasures of this world.

TO KNOW MORE:
Zephaniah 3 and 2 Peter 2 \\

Day 205 | *Motivations*

PRAY: God connect with me here, as I seek you in your Word.

READ: Matthew 6.16-18 — People sometimes do good deeds for the wrong reasons. Only God knows our deepest motivations. Like the attention we really want when doing something virtuous. Or the applause we were really after for a job well done. And even the thank-you we were seeking for a supposedly unselfish act. Going without food for one whole day calls for self-denial – something that we might be pretty eager to let others know about. But Jesus makes it quite clear that if we're doing this publicly, if we're intent on others knowing we're fasting, then we've missed the point and missed out. That praise will be the only reward we receive. The blessing comes from keeping it secret.

Likewise, anything we do for others should not be a reason for publicity and applause. That should not be our motivation. It kind of comes down to showmanship, doesn't it? Are we doing religious things for applause from others? Are we merely performing? Essentially, we've circled back to where we started, for once again we're called to evaluate: Why am I doing this? If we do any religious or unselfish act, including fasting, for selfish reasons, we need to be changed from within.

REFLECT: What are your motivations? Why do you do religious things? Why do you do any unselfish act? If it's for praise, ask God to change your heart.

RESPOND: Ask for God's help to always do right for the right reasons. If your self-esteem is such that you need to be acknowledged for good deeds, ask God to change your heart.

Lord, help me to treat all people with kindness and mercy without consideration for the praise I may receive from others.

TO KNOW MORE:
Psalm 69 and Acts 13 \\

Day 206 | *Entitled*

PRAY: God connect with me here, as I seek you in your Word.

READ: Proverbs 28.19-27 — You need some cash – and you need it now. What do you do? Ask for your Christmas bonus early from your boss? Contact a close relative? Give up and bear the consequences? How about taking on a second job in the evening? God's Word seems to keep hitting us over the head about our attitude toward money, doesn't it? Notice the distinction that's made between hard work and playing around, being a trustworthy worker and wanting to get rich quick, being greedy as opposed to being a giver. If you have the attitude that the world owes you, that you are entitled to get whatever you want by whatever means you can, then the Bible says you will end up poorer than when you started – not only financially, but emotionally and spiritually as well.

If you have the attitude that the hard work of a wise and trustworthy person will bring great rewards from the hand of God, then you will surely prosper in all areas of your life. Remember the promise in verse 27: "Whoever gives to the poor will lack nothing. But a curse will come upon those who close their eyes to poverty."

REFLECT: In the world's eyes, today's reading doesn't make sense; it seems you'd be richer if you kept all your money rather than giving some of it away. But that's just how God's economy works. He promises abundant riches – not necessarily in the wallet but certainly in the heart – to those who live and work according to His will.

RESPOND: Ask God to show you how you can give generously of your time and resources. Pray that He will keep you heart from being greedy.

Lord, open my eyes to the needs of others around me and help me be generous to them in your name.

TO KNOW MORE:
Micah 7 and 1 Timothy 6 \\

Day 207 | *Power*

PRAY: God connect with me here, as I seek you in your Word.

READ: 1 Samuel 8.10-18 — Prophet Samuel had warned God's people of the dangers that would come with giving wide-reaching power to an earthly ruler. Samuel had foreseen the corruption of future kings. The prophet's words were, well, prophetic! This is precisely what happened. To build kingdoms, kings need money and servants—lots and lots of both. Kings, Samuel warned, are very greedy. Look at all the possessive verbs: "take," "take away," "want," "demand". Before long, the people of Israel were complaining about high taxes (1 Kings 12.4). With such power to demand money and command subjects comes kingly pride. Almost all of Israel's leaders yielded to the alluring trappings of power. Even the godly King David occasionally forgot that he was under God's authority. Such failures from power-intoxicated leaders always produce unhappiness among the populace.

You can learn a lot from this chapter of Israel's history. Remember that while humans are corrupted by power, God is not. His ability to do anything and everything is rooted in His inherent goodness. He will never act selfishly or ruthlessly. He rules the world with absolute fairness and kindness. Thus, we can have full confidence that He will govern our lives in ways that are good.

REFLECT: Be extremely careful that you don't get tripped up by pride if you are in a position of prominence or power. Depend on His wisdom. Rely on His guidance. "When you bow down before the Lord and admit your dependence on Him, He will lift you up and give you honour" (James 4.10).

RESPOND: Pray for wisdom to avoid an ego trip of pride, no matter how great your success.

Lord, help me be humble in all circumstances so that I will never forget that you are the true source of power and authority.

TO KNOW MORE:
1 Kings 12 and 1 Chronicles 27 \\

Day 208 | *Strangers*

PRAY: God connect with me here, as I seek you in your Word.

READ: Exodus 22.21-27 — Imagine that you wake up one morning in an unfamiliar room, in a strange house, on an unknown street, in an alien land. You must get up, get dressed and go about your day. There are no familiar faces. In fact, you can barely understand a word anyone says. It wouldn't be much fun, would it? Foreigners who wandered into Israel's camp must have been grateful for the kindness they met. God made it a point to tell His people to treat strangers who lived with them fairly because, after all, the Israelites knew what it was like to suffer in a strange land.

God shows us many times in Scripture that He takes the needs of foreigners, widows and orphans very seriously. When you move to a new town, it's not easy to develop new friends, or learn which plumber or electrician is the best, or find a new church where you feel at home. It's easy to feel alone, frustrated and out of place. North America draws hundreds of thousands of refugees and immigrants from other countries. And every year, families move into your community. So you can have the opportunity to reach out to these "strangers in a strange land" with God's love and acceptance.

REFLECT: God calls His people to be kind to "foreigners" – whether they be from another land or not – to make them feel welcome; to make them feel at home in their new land. Open yourself up to those who are new to your community. Be sensitive to the struggles they face. Show them God's kind and generous heart through your own words and actions.

RESPOND: Thank God for the many blessings He has given you, your family, your friends and members of your church community. Ask Him to open your eyes and your heart to the excluded. Ask for His blessings on them. And ask Him to make you a blessing in the lives of each one.

Lord, I pray that our church can be a blessing, in your name, to those who are new to our community – whether they be from a foreign land or another province.

TO KNOW MORE: Isaiah 10 and James 1 \\

Day 209 | *Darkness*

PRAY: God connect with me here, as I seek you in your Word.

READ: Jonah 4.11 — God said that the Ninevites didn't know their right hand from their left. Most likely, He was declaring that the Assyrian people had lost all sense of good and bad, right and wrong. They were hopelessly lost, cut off from the truth of their Creator. He wanted the people of Nineveh to have a standard by which to measure their lives and actions in the light of God's holiness and righteousness. If the people turned from their sins and asked for God's mercy, they would be spared destruction.

For darkened hearts, life itself has little or no meaning or purpose. Existence is a short time in a shadow world where right and wrong disappear. For these people, satisfying immediate desires becomes an all-consuming goal. The more they pursue worldly desires, the farther away from God they move. And since He is the Light of the World, running from Him only takes them further into the darkness.

What the book of Jonah teaches us is that God loves those in the darkness. He sees their plight and cares enough to send a reluctant prophet to invite them to turn back to the light. It's an amazing testimony to the compassion and mercy of God.

REFLECT: If you have a hard time believing that God would care so much about people living in spiritual darkness, fast-forward back in time some 750 years and witness a strange star twinkling above a ramshackle stable in Bethlehem. On a dark night comes an infant in a manger who would grow up to be the Light of the World. In this One lies hope for everyone who stumbles in the dark.

RESPOND: Ask God to help you shine for Him "in a dark world of crooked and perverse people" (Philippians 2.15). Pray for friends and family who still haven't come out of the darkness in the light of Christ.

Lord, I pray that I can be a messenger of your Light and a witness to those who live in darkness.

TO KNOW MORE: Psalm 36 and Isaiah 1 \\

Day 210 | *Abundance*

PRAY: God connect with me here, as I seek you in your Word.

READ: John 6.10-13 — Have you ever gone to a restaurant and noticed the amount of food that's left on plates and, eventually, is thrown away? Do you regularly go through your refrigerator and clean out the produce that has gone bad? Do you ever wonder what people in impoverished countries would think if they saw the wasted food that we thoughtlessly toss away and that ends up in landfills? It would (or should) shame us all into managing our abundance more carefully.

The Gospel of John provides a thoughtful example of dealing with leftover food. We need to be careful not to overlook the example Jesus sets for believers at the end of the story. "Let nothing be wasted," he instructed, as His disciples collected every piece of bread that was left over after the five thousand had been fed. What would happen if our society adopted the motto "Let nothing be wasted"? We live in a land of abundance. Unfortunately, one of the things that seems to go along with abundance is waste. Perhaps with some careful planning, we can begin to take small steps toward correcting this situation.

REFLECT: What if we reduced our grocery bills – and thus, the amount of food we bring home – by 15 percent a month and donated the extra money to a local homeless shelter? What if, rather than spending money to eat out, we eat the food we have at home and use the extra money to support a needy child overseas? These are just two suggestions to get you thinking. If you put your mind to it, you'll probably be able to come up with a much better plan for reducing the amount of food you waste and then wisely distributing your extra resources.

RESPOND: Ask the Lord to give you wisdom as you think of ways to keep from wasting food.

Lord, I pray that you will give me both a willingness and the opportunities to share my abundance with others.

TO KNOW MORE: Matthew 15 and Luke 9 \\

Day 211 | *Hunger*

PRAY: God connect with me here, as I seek you in your Word.

READ: Lamentations 4.2-10 — You see images of hungry children in Sub-Saharan Africa. Their bellies are painfully distended. Their eyes are bottomless pools of pain. They haven't the energy to swat the flies swarming around their noses and mouths. You see news reports about children in Mumbai who live and work on giant mountains of garbage. They are neglected by parents and forgotten by the public.

The Bible offers another description of the ravages of hunger. We find an example in today's reading. The world's hungry suffer for many reasons – drought, political turmoil, wars. For the most part, they are innocent victims. But that was not the case with the Israelites. Their hunger resulted directly from their own sin. After many years of warnings, God was allowing the enemy to lay siege to Jerusalem.

As you read these descriptions of mistreated, crying children and people searching bits of rotting food, you get a glimpse of how devastating sin can be. It destroys life. Ask God to help you reach those who are devastated by sin so that they can turn away from it. Do not let it destroy your own life.

REFLECT: Christ has called His people to respond to the spiritually and physically hungry with compassion and loving-kindness. We can't all travel to places where there is great need but we can share the resources we have through Christian organizations that are dedicated to caring for the world's poor in the name of Jesus.

RESPOND: If your harbouring sins, confess them now so that they won't ravage your life.

Lord, I pray that you will forgive me of my sins – the things I do that are an offense to your holiness – and I ask that you will give me opportunities to help those who struggle because of the sins of others.

TO KNOW MORE: Psalm 22 and 2 Corinthians 4 \\

Day 212 | *Tasks*

PRAY: God connect with me here, as I seek you in your Word.

READ: 1 Chronicles 28.11-20 — You have a big job ahead of you. Maybe it's a major presentation to a key client. Maybe it's preparing a banquet for a large wedding party. Maybe it's finalizing the specs and budget for an enormous construction project in a foreign country. How do you feel when you face a monumental task? Overwhelmed? Inadequate? Scared? Weak? You may even feel like giving up.

King David was preparing his people – and his son Solomon – for a huge job. Today's passage reveals his very helpful advice. David had dearly wanted to be the one to build the great and awesome Temple of God in the land of Israel. But God had other plans. So David gave to his son Solomon, who would be the next king, all the plans God had given him for the Temple and the surrounding areas.

Now, how would you feel if you were young Solomon? Talk about pressure! But David passed along some encouraging words full of God's power. And Solomon undoubtedly took them to heart. You see, when you face a task given to you by God – no matter what size it is – He stands ready to give you all the strength, wisdom and help you need to finish it.

REFLECT: When you consider the work that must be done for the Kingdom of God, the job can seem overwhelming. But the key is simply to live closely in the power and wisdom of God. Rely on Him to guide you and to give you the strength and wisdom for what he has called you to do.

RESPOND: Turn 1 Chronicles 28.20 into a prayer asking God to give you the strength and courage to enable you to do His work.

Lord, in the words of King David, I pray that I will be strong and courageous to do the work you have called me to and that I will not forget that you will never fail nor forsake me.

TO KNOW MORE: Joshua 6 and Ezra 2 \\

Day 213 | *Retribution*

PRAY: God connect with me here, as I seek you in your Word.

READ: Proverbs 25.21-22 — A co-worker keeps putting you down in front of your friends. A neighbour spreads a false and totally embarrassing rumour about you. When somebody intentionally does something to hurt or embarrass you, how do you feel? Not good! You really want to get them back for it. Verse 21 doesn't give much room for excuses, does it? It doesn't say you have every right to seek revenge. Instead, it clearly states you are to go out of your way to be kind to your enemies – to help meet the needs of those who oppose you.

In other words, don't hold back doing good. Rather, two interesting and surprising things according to verse 22: First, your enemies will feel guilty for what they've done because you've shown them compassion. The point is, by returning good for evil and showing kindness to those who have hurt you, you could actually win them over and cause them to change. This doesn't mean that it's alright to manipulate someone. God wants his children to serve others with a pure, honest, giving heart – no matter who they are. The second thing that happens is that God will reward you because you're trusting Him to take care of the situation. You're letting him be the ultimate Judge who will make things right in the end.

REFLECT: The next time you face a situation in which someone has hurt you, remember today's verses. It won't be easy, but it will provide a positive and God-approved outcome.

RESPOND: Think of one or more people who have hurt you lately and lift them up to the Lord in prayer. Ask God to bless them abundantly. Ask Him to give you the power and grace you need to be kind to these "enemies".

Lord, I pray for those who have hurt or mistreated me and ask that you will give me the strength to forgive them and to allow you to handle the situation in your timing and according to your will.

TO KNOW MORE:
Matthew 5 and Romans 12 \\

Day 214 | *Stewards*

PRAY: God connect with me here, as I seek you in your Word.

READ: 1 Samuel 30.23-25 — Imagine you're a companion of David, the man who would become king of Israel. You and six hundred other Israelites are in hot pursuit of the Amalekites, who have taken your wife and children captive. Two hundred men in your group give up the chase. You and the other four hundred continue on until you finally catch the Amalekites, defeat them in battle and head for home with the spoils of victory.

As you approach home, some of the guys around you start grumbling, saying that the plunder should not be split with those who did not fight. Do you agree with them? Like David, we often hear from people who have ideas about what we should or shouldn't do with our material possessions. We would do well to learn what David understood: Every blessing we receive – material or otherwise – comes from the Lord. It's not ours; it's His. We are merely stewards or caretakers of God's riches. When we start trying to determine who "deserves" to share our blessings, we are ignoring the fact that we ourselves are undeserving of those blessings.

REFLECT: Think about it: What did we do to earn the privilege of being born in one of the wealthiest and most advanced countries in the world? What makes us so special that we don't have to worry about dying of starvation or finding a safe place to spend the night? We have been blessed by the Lord. Who will you allow to share your blessings?

RESPOND: Spend some time thanking God for blessings that you have taken for granted or believed you deserved in the past. Ask Him to help you be a wise steward of those blessings.

Lord, I pray that I will never forget the source of my blessings and that I will be as generous with others as you have been with me.

TO KNOW MORE:
Psalm 121 and Acts 7 \\

Day 215 | *Forgiveness*

PRAY: God connect with me here, as I seek you in your Word.

READ: Matthew 5.38-48 — You're standing in line, waiting for tickets for the game of the year. You've been at the stadium since 5 a.m., hoping for some choice seats. Then you see a group walk past you and start up a conversation with some friends ahead of you in line. They gradually work themselves into the line, as if they had been there all along. Now you're angry. What should you do? You start scanning the faces of the line ahead of you, seeing if you can find a new "friend" to talk to. After all, we have to stand up for ourselves, don't we? And those cheaters shouldn't be allowed to get away with it! Or so the rationalizing goes.

But Jesus has something else in mind, as we discover in today's reading. So much of what our Lord said comes down to the issue of control. Which will you decide to do: allow your anger to control you? Or will you take control of your anger by demonstrating strength of character as you decide to forgive?

REFLECT: If we allow our anger to take charge, then we're also giving that person – the one we're so intent on seeing punished for what he or she has done – control over us, too. Essentially, we're giving them permission to make us miserable! That's why it's so important to forgive. Forgiving is for our sake, for our contentment and for our ability to grow spiritually.

RESPOND: Ask God to help you deal with the feelings of anger you may be holding toward someone. Then seek reconciliation with that person.

Lord, I pray that you will help me forgive others just as you have forgiven me of my transgressions.

TO KNOW MORE:
Leviticus 24 and 1 Corinthians 6 \\

Day 216 | *Gifts*

PRAY: God connect with me here, as I seek you in your Word.

READ: Romans 12.3-8 — Someone you love is having a birthday. You thought long and hard about what gift to give. You shopped carefully, being sure to get just the right colour and style. You can't wait to see your friend enjoy it. At the party, your eyes dance with joy as your friend rips the paper open. "Oh! Isn't that nice," your friend says and then puts the gift aside. Last time you checked, it was still stuck in your friend's closet. Never used. How do you feel? God gives His children gifts in order to build up His church. When everyone exercises their gifts—of service, administration, giving, teaching—then a church operates smoothly, meets needs regularly and grows continually.

To use your gift effectively, you have to:

- Realize that all gifts and talents come from God.

- Recognize that people have been given different gifts.

- Know what gift or gifts you've been given.

- Commit yourself to use your gifts to serve God, not to promote yourself.

- Determine to use your gift wholeheartedly, whenever you can.

REFLECT: God doesn't expect any one person to do all the work himself or herself. He wants the body of Christ to work together—just as the parts of a human body must work together for His glory. Don't let your gift gather dust, stuffed away somewhere. Use it. Enjoy it. The Giver will be very happy when you do. And He will give you all the faith and power you'll need to succeed.

RESPOND: Ask God to help you see things as He does. When you gave your heart to Him you also gave Him your trust that He knows best and that our assumptions, when not backed up by Scripture and fervent prayer, are misguided.

Lord, I pray that you will show me ways that I can serve you effectively and help me embrace the important role you have given me in our church family.

TO KNOW MORE: Colossians 2 and 1 Peter 4 \\

Day 217 | *Empathy*

PRAY: God connect with me here, as I seek you in your Word.

READ: 1 Peter 2.21-24 — One of the most common accusations people hurl at each other is "You don't know what it's like". Jesus has no trouble empathizing with suffering people. He was subject to so much suffering during His short time on earth that he is called "man of sorrows". Jesus displayed this endurance throughout His life – especially during the events leading up to His crucifixion. Facing vicious taunts, insults, physical abuse and other forms of persecution, Jesus refused to retaliate. Instead He placed himself in God's hands, recognizing that the Father is the ultimate source of justice. When we face persecution or suffering today, we too should have the confidence that He will eventually make things right. No matter how much we suffer in life, we will encounter people who suffer even more. Some do bear hardships that the rest of us can't imagine. But we must stay focused on the great truth that no matter our situation, God understands fully how much we hurt. He remains the One who will put an end to all grief and injustice. He gave us His own Son, who suffered an agonizing death beyond the experience of any human. He remains our comfort when all else is empty and cold.

REFLECT: God charges us with a responsibility to follow Christ's example in assisting others in their times of suffering. We may not be able to prevent sorrows from happening, but we can be the agents of healing made possible through the incredible work of Christ.

RESPOND: Praise God not only for the fact that He suffered and gave His life for us but also that He understands our suffering, having experienced it Himself.

Lord, thank you for sending your Son to die for my sins and I pray that you will continue to meet my physical and emotional needs as well as the same concerns of those around me.

TO KNOW MORE:
2 Timothy 3 and Hebrews 2 \\

Day 218 | *Trust*

PRAY: God connect with me here, as I seek you in your Word.

READ: Exodus 16.1-3 — If only life were simple and you could go back to the way things were before life started getting complicated. For more than 400 years, the Israelites had lived a horrible life in Egypt as slaves who worked hard under awful conditions but received very little for their labour. With Moses as their leader, God had miraculously rescued them and was leading them back to their own land. Just one month after leaving Egypt, the Israelites found themselves in the middle of the Desert of Sinai—a huge, barren, unforgiving land. They had jumped out of the frying pan of Egypt but they had then jumped right into the fire of the wilderness. They were surrounded by danger, uncertainty and fear. And they were hungry. And they yearned for the past. Had they taken the time to listen, the people would have heard God urging them to depend solely on Him. They had to realize that the only certainty of their lives was His provision. Instead, they complained and attacked their leaders, Moses and Aaron. Sure, they were under tremendous stress; and complaining is a natural reaction to tough circumstances. Unfortunately, their untrusting attitude steered them into even worse problems.

REFLECT: Like the Israelites, you know how it feels to be stressed out sometimes. How will you respond the next time you feel overwhelmed by all your responsibilities? If you need to vent, talk to your spouse, best friend or pastor, as well as to God. But don't just complain. Learn to trust your Provider every step of the way.

RESPOND: God ultimately provided everything the Israelites needed. He can do the same for you and for anyone else who asks in faith. Talk to Him about the pressure points of your life, and ask Him to make you sensitive to the many ways He guides and provides for you.

Lord, I pray that you will give me the faith to trust in you each day of my life.

TO KNOW MORE:
Numbers 33 and Psalm 106 \\

Day 219 | *Comfort Zones*

PRAY: God connect with me here, as I seek you in your Word.

READ: Deuteronomy 10.17-19 — Some of us have a very limited idea of what the world is like. We have been living inside our comfort zones for too long. In today's verses, God challenges us to step into the bigger world that needs His love. Verse 18 says, "He [God] shows love to the foreigners . . . and gives them food and clothing." But you might ask, "Who are the foreigners?" Foreigners can be people who live in other countries or people who live next door to you. They are people who look, think, talk, act and have beliefs different from you. But Christians are called to imitate God's nature by showing love to everyone.

Sometimes we are afraid to reach out to those who are different from us because we don't understand their customs, language or beliefs. But underneath the differences, we have many similarities. And who knows, you may be a foreigner some day in need of a helping hand as well.

REFLECT: Stepping out of your comfort zone could mean having dinner with a family that has few friends in your community. It may involve volunteering your time to help someone with language skills. Or it could mean simply being a friend at work. Every act of kindness matters to someone who stands outside looking in.

RESPOND: Pray that God will help you step out of your comfort zone by giving you a greater awareness of people who are different from you.

Lord, help me to identify those who need a friend or helping hand and give me the courage to go beyond what I'm comfortable with to show them kindness in your name.

TO KNOW MORE:
Daniel 2 and Acts 10 \\

Day 220 | *Appearances*

PRAY: God connect with me here, as I seek you in your Word.

READ: Isaiah 53.3-9 — How do you picture Jesus during His time on earth? How did He act? How did He carry himself? What impression did His physical appearance make on other people? His teachings were so unique that they completely altered the way people thought about God. He confounded even the most respected religious leaders of His time. Yet people did not necessarily respond well to Jesus. The Son of God, in the book of Isaiah, is said to come to earth as a servant—a despised, rejected, oppressed and afflicted servant. He endured the world's hatred and gave His life for the human race He loved. How does that description compare with the mental image of Jesus you had earlier? If He had taken the form of a wealthy and powerful leader, it would have contradicted God's emphasis throughout the Old Testament. God constantly identified himself with the poor and needy of the world, saying that those who oppress the poor show contempt for their Maker (Proverbs 14.31). It makes perfect sense that our Lord would assume the 'personhood' of a lowly servant.

REFLECT: The Lord understands what it's like to be looked down upon by society. He knows what it means to be poor. He experienced the suffering of the downtrodden. And as a result of this personal experience, He knows exactly how to help those in need.

RESPOND: Thank the Lord for the fact that He is able to empathize with us when we face rejection, oppression and suffering because He Himself faced the same type of experiences.

Lord, thank you for dying for my sins and the sins of the world—and I praise you for entering the world as a suffering servant who has empathy for the needs that I and others face.

TO KNOW MORE:
Psalm 22 and Mark 9 \\

Day 221 | *Possessions*

PRAY: God connect with me here, as I seek you in your Word.

READ: Luke 12.13-21 — If you only drove a certain car, you'd be cool. If you only lived in a certain neighbourhood, you'd be truly admired. Advertisers spend billions every year trying to make you think you need their product in order to be happier and fulfilled, more accepted and satisfied. Can pieces of metal and plastic, threads woven together or brick and mortar really have that much power over our lives? Silly, isn't it? But think about it. Do you have an unconscious list of things you really "need" to own in order to be truly happy? And what does Jesus have to say about all this? Our Saviour uses the opportunity of a family squabble that a man brings to his attention in order to make a broader point to His listeners: "Don't be greedy for what you don't have. Real life is not measured by how much we own" (v. 15). You see, the "good life"–the life that is fulfilling, exciting, satisfying and real–has nothing to do with how much money we have or what possessions we own. Our society wants us to believe differently, but Jesus is speaking the truth.

REFLECT: Remember the words of Jesus when you're tempted to place high importance on possessions: "Yes, a person is a fool to store up earthly wealth but not have a rich relationship with God" (v. 21).

RESPOND: Ask God to make your relationship with Him richer and deeper. This may involve rethinking your finances–and your giving to Him. Talk to Him about how you can be more generous on earth . . . and more "worthy" in heaven.

Lord, I pray that you will help me to always remember that you are the only real treasure in my life and that all that I have is from your generous hands.

TO KNOW MORE:
Psalm 17 and 1 Timothy 6 \\

Day 222 | *Communion*

PRAY: God connect with me here, as I seek you in your Word.

READ: 1 Corinthians 11.33-34 — Nothing beats a good party! Laughing with friends, meeting new people—generally having a good time. Unfortunately, parties often have a way of getting out of hand. All it takes is for a disagreement to erupt over an old dispute for the party to be ruined for everyone. Often these unpleasant situations are fueled by alcohol and simmering resentment.

The first-century Corinthians were world-class party people. Apostle Paul had a few things to say about these out-of-control celebrations. Before their communion service, the Corinthians would hold an agape (love) feast. The wealthy people ate and drank heavily at these dinners. In fact, they were such drunken gluttons that the poor people often went home hungry. You can imagine what this type of celebration did to the fellowship in the Church—especially right before the Lord's Supper. Paul offered a rather simple solution to the problem: If the Corinthians had such a hard time controlling their appetites at the agape feast, perhaps they should eat at home. The Lord's Supper is a time for Christians to remember the sacrifice of Jesus on the cross and to celebrate the fact that we are all part of His body.

REFLECT: We can learn from the experience of the Corinthian church. First, we see the importance of unity among believers. As members of the body of Christ, believers are called to support each other. Second, and perhaps most important, we can learn that the church should be a place where we look out for others first. We should not go primarily to have our needs met but to meet the needs of others.

RESPOND: Ask God to help you prepare for your church's next communion service and to look for ways to help those who are going through hard times in your congregation.

Lord, I pray your blessing on our next communion service and ask that it will be a time of deep fellowship and spiritual connection within our congregation.

TO KNOW MORE: 1 Corinthians 16 and Titus 1 \\

Day 223 | *Paradise*

PRAY: God connect with me here, as I seek you in your Word.

READ: Revelation 21.1-4 — Travel agencies and airlines make a business of selling paradise on earth. They lure you with images of tropical islands with white sand beaches, deep blue water and gentle breezes. Or maybe you're tempted by the scene of perfectly powdered Alpine slopes with virgin snow swooshing beneath your skis while a brisk wind reddens your cheeks. In the book of Revelation, John gives believers a very brief taste of what their eternal home will be like. Here there is no more pain, death, sorrow or crying. And heaven will be a place of incomparable beauty because it is filled with God's presence. God will dwell among His people. He will not be separated from us—He will be present at all times! Imagine what it will be like to live in the presence of pure goodness, joy and happiness.

Think about what our world would be like today if we found a way to end hunger and drought, everyone on earth learning to live together peacefully—no more wars, no more skirmishes, no more armies and the medical community discovering a cure for every sickness people suffer. It would still be a long way from what eternity will be like for those who trust in Christ.

REFLECT: It's important for believers—especially those who are struggling—to remind one another of our eternal future. Christians who suffer hardship now in this dark world can find strength in the bright, glorious hope of heaven. Let this thought fill your mind with joy as you commit your life to serving God.

RESPOND: Pray for the resolve to bring "heaven to earth" by doing everything you can to relieve those who suffer in the name of Christ.

Lord, I pray that I will always keep my eyes on eternity and that the cares of this world will not distract me from my mission of serving you each day.

TO KNOW MORE:
Isaiah 66 and 2 Peter 3 \\

Day 224 | Tithes

PRAY: God connect with me here, as I seek you in your Word.

READ: Deuteronomy 14.22-29 — Today's passage is about a main concern God has for us. These verses teach us about tithing in the ancient Israelite community. First we learn that there were two types of tithing. One tithe went to God (v. 23) and a second went to help everyone, especially the Levites – the priests and religious officials of Israel (vv. 28-29). How seriously should we take tithing today? Do the laws given to a people three thousand years ago have anything to say to us today?

In the New Testament, we don't see any specific commands about tithing. That does not mean, however, that we are left with no guidelines for giving. Rather, we are encouraged to give freely and generously to help other people and the work of the church. Keep in mind Paul's advice to the Corinthians: "Don't give reluctantly or in response to pressure. For God loves the person who gives cheerfully" (2 Corinthians 9.7).

REFLECT: If you really want to know how much of a priority God is in your life, take a look at your giving. How you distribute your time, talents, money and material goods is a clear indicator of what your priorities really are. You might say that God is first in your life, but do your actions show it?

RESPOND: Ask God to help you put Him first by using your money and abilities wisely.

Lord, show me where my tithes can do the most good and help me to be generous with the gifts you have given me.

TO KNOW MORE:
Ecclesiastes 9 and John 2 \\

Day 225 | *Treasure*

PRAY: God connect with me here, as I seek you in your Word.

READ: Psalm 49.16-20 — Born in 1797, Mytton inherited a sizable fortune as a young man. He drank heavily and spent his days conducting foolish experiments, such as seeing if a horse and carriage could jump a toll gate. He hunted even in the worst weather, sometimes wearing no clothing! He often threw bundles of money to servants and friends without concern for the future. Soon he had bankrupted his estate. He died in a debtors' prison at the age of 37. Mytton's life may be an extreme example, but it does show us that wealth can be a great trap. It can insulate us from God's truth and encourage us to indulge ourselves, sometimes to death. David recognized this truth when he wrote today's reading.

When people die, they take nothing with them into the afterlife. All that wealth will ultimately gain them nothing. Believers, on the other hand, are promised the "riches" of God forever: eternal life with Him. And that's worth far, far more than any earthly riches.

REFLECT: One day every person – whether rich or poor – will stand naked and empty-handed before God in heaven. The only rewards we can claim at that time are those we have stored up by our actions while on earth (read Matthew 6.19-21). How are these rewards built? By serving God with our time and talents; by ministering to others in His name, even if it costs us something we value; by setting our priorities in life according to His will, not according to the world's standards of success. To build treasure in heaven, our faith must be in God, not in money or possessions or power. The more we use our gifts and resources for His glory on earth, the greater our treasure in heaven will be.

RESPOND: Search your heart before God and evaluate your desire for money, wealth and possessions. Ask Him to keep you free from the love of money.

Lord, I pray that you will help me never forget that true wealth is stored in heaven, not here on earth, and that I need to always place my values on the things eternal.

TO KNOW MORE: Proverbs 28 and Luke 12 \\

Day 226 | *Money*

PRAY: God connect with me here, as I seek you in your Word.

READ: Ecclesiastes 10.16-20 — Solomon has some interesting and rather startling things to say about cash and currency. Look at the last line of verse 19: "Money gives everything". Is Solomon being sarcastic or serious? From a spiritual standpoint, he's awakening. It's no coincidence that the wealthiest people in the world are often the most miserable. Anyone who attempts to fill his or her life with riches and material possessions will ultimately discover they are empty inside. Only God can provide ultimate, eternal happiness and fulfillment.

From a social standpoint, however, Ecclesiastes 10.19b is a pretty accurate statement. Money is the answer for most problems in society today, particularly the problems that face the poor and needy. This is why we are called to share the money we have with those who have very little.

REFLECT: It's important to keep in mind that money itself is useless. It's what you do with it that counts. The best way to look at money is as a tool—nothing more, nothing less. It's an instrument that can be used for good or for evil. Used appropriately, it can bring great blessing to others.

RESPOND: Ask God to help you become a "craftsperson" with your money, putting it to use in wise ways to help the poor and needy in your community.

Lord, help me to creatively think of ways to help others with the abundance you have given me.

TO KNOW MORE:
Jeremiah 21 and Philippians 4 \\

Day 227 | *Hunger*

READ: Mark 16.15 — Don't you just hate it when you're hungry and you can't figure out what you want? You probably end up shuffling through the cupboards, rejecting the two stale slices of bread or a piece of candy from last Christmas. Next stop: the pantry. Soup? Ravioli? Cereal? The last resort is the refrigerator, where you might stare at its depressing contents: leftovers, wilted lettuce and lunch meat . . . So you dial the number for Chinese take-out!

Just like we may crave something and not know what it is we want, the unsaved people of this world have a need too. They know the deepest void possible within their hearts, yet they have no answers for their emptiness and pain. They desire a saviour they haven't met. They long for forgiveness and cleansing that knows no substitute. They thirst for Living Water when their spiritual lives are dry. They hunger for the Bread of Life because they have no fulfillment in their lives. And, sadly, they won't find what they need . . . unless we tell them.

REFLECT: Around the world, people are literally dying from spiritual hunger. They cover up their symptoms with materialism, political solutions, new ideologies and twisted ideas, but their hunger remains. "Go into all the world," Jesus said. He didn't suggest. He didn't ask. He commanded. As a follower of Jesus, the responsibility rests squarely on our shoulders. But we are not alone – God has promised His Spirit to help us every step of the way. It's a big world out there. But we have an even bigger God!

RESPOND: Ask God to give you a passion for those who are physically and spiritually hungry.

Lord, may I be a witness to your life-giving salvation to those who hunger for spiritual nourishment.

TO KNOW MORE:
Psalm 98 and Acts 1 \\

Day 228 | Widows

PRAY: God connect with me here, as I seek you in your Word.

READ: 1 Timothy 5.3-8 — She sits alone in her small, tidy house watching game shows. Occasionally she glances at the phone sitting beside her on a white doily, wondering why it never rings. Is it broken? Has the phone company cut off her service? Sometimes she even picks up the receiver to listen for the dial tone. Then she notices the mail truck out front, depositing her mail. She works hard to get up out of her easy chair and walk to the mailbox, her arthritic hips nagging at her all the way. Perhaps there'd be a letter or a card from a friend. But there are only a couple of bills. Slowly, even more painfully, she returns to her house. Perhaps she will take a nap and try to escape her sadness for a time.

Paul sets forth some guidelines about caring for widows and the elderly to his son in the faith, Timothy, a young pastor. First and foremost, a widow's family is to take responsibility to care for her. But if a widow has no family, it is the church's responsibility. The principle is clear: The church is designed by God to support those who have no families.

REFLECT: Often, families who must care for their ill or elderly members are placed under a heavy financial burden. They may need extra money, encouraging support, a helping hand. And believers should be there for them. Something very interesting usually happens as the church acts as a truly caring community. Those who receive the blessing of support often become a blessing to others. And that's the way it's supposed to work.

RESPOND: Ask God for a heart that's sensitive to the needs of the elderly, especially the widows in your church.

Lord, I pray that you will give me opportunities to be a blessing and a friend to the lonely in my church and community.

TO KNOW MORE:
Psalm 94 and 1 Thessalonians 2 \\

Day 229 | *Lending*

PRAY: God connect with me here, as I seek you in your Word.

READ: Leviticus 25.35-40 — St. Leo the Great, the fifth century pope who stood at the gates of Rome and persuaded Attila the Hun to turn back, once gave a sermon on lending. "Be steadfast, Christian giver," he wrote. "Give what you may receive, sow what you may reap, scatter what you may gather. Fear not to spend, sigh not over the doubtfulness of the gain. Your substance grows when it is wisely dispensed. Set your heart on the profits due to mercy, and traffic in eternal gains . . . He that loves money, and wishes to multiply his wealth by immoderate profits, catches men hampered with difficulties, and by treacherous assistance entangles them in debts which they can never repay."

Today's passage is about lending and repaying. Do not demand an advance or charge interest on the money you lend. God teaches that He upholds us and provides for us. The duties and possessions we owe each other should be seen from the perspective of the source of all generosity, God himself. We owe God our lives. Jesus said we can't serve both God and money (Matthew 6.24).

REFLECT: In ancient times as well as today, God chooses people to do special work. But His choosing is not based on wealth or talent. Jesus ministered to corrupt tax collectors and blind beggars. He gave His life for people from all classes. Now Christ "lends" us His love and purity through His Holy Spirit. Our response should always be to reflect that generosity to others – without regard to their ability to repay any small or great kindness.

RESPOND: Ask God to help you look beyond earthly success to see people with the same way God does. Pray that you will give more of yourself to others, even if no one notices your generosity or returns the favour.

> *Lord, help me to be a cheerful giver without any thought for repayment so I can use the gifts you have given me in service to others.*

TO KNOW MORE: Psalm 112 and James 2 \\

Day 230 | *Giving*

PRAY: God connect with me here, as I seek you in your Word.

READ: Exodus 35.20-24 — Why does a rich God ask us to give to Him? First of all, giving begins with God. It is an essential part of His character. The Lord placed the desire to give in the hearts of the Israelites. Nobody's arm was twisted. "If their hearts were stirred and they desired to do so, they brought to the Lord their offerings" (v. 21). Second, God is honoured by our giving. By willingly and joyfully sacrificing the best that they had, the Israelites showed their devotion to God. It's one thing to say "I love you" and another to demonstrate it. Words and actions are both important, but by giving up something which is precious to us, we show God that we mean business. In this way, we teach ourselves to submit our entire being to the will of God. Third, God is very practical: He has a job to do and He wants to use us! We have the privilege of participating in the building of His Kingdom. When we give to the Lord, according to His guidance, we contribute to His work in the world: to clothe and feed the naked and hungry and proclaim salvation through Jesus Christ.

REFLECT: There is no greater joy than living in harmony with how God created us. To be a giver is to allow God's rich blessings to flow through us and transform the lives of others.

RESPOND: If you find the thought of giving difficult, ask God to show you if there is anything you value more than Him. God wants to stir your heart and give you the joy of dispensing His blessings.

Lord, show me ways that I can be effectively generous with the bounty you have given me and the abundance you have blessed me with.

TO KNOW MORE:
Psalm 110 and 2 Corinthians 9 \\

Day 231 | *Fasting*

PRAY: God connect with me here, as I seek you in your Word.

READ: 2 Samuel 3.31-37 — Think of all the things that could possibly cause you to miss a meal. Sickness could do it. People on crash diets often skip meals, although it isn't recommended. Surgery and other medical procedures require abstinence from food for a certain period of time. A more extreme circumstance, of course, is not having access to food, whether as a result of poverty or famine. What about prayer and meditation? Could they be added to the list? Is it likely or even possible that you would give up one or more meals in order to focus your thoughts on the Lord or a special request that you were bringing to Him? In today's reading we find an example from the life of King David.

Though fasting today is not as prevalent as it was during biblical times, it is still an important spiritual discipline. Fasts can last for a few hours or longer. Fasting allows believers to shift their focus from their physical to their spiritual needs.

REFLECT: Fasting is an intensely private issue; it's between you and the Lord. However, if you have a personal issue or a societal concern (such as homelessness in your area or famine in another land) that you would like to bring to the Lord in a special way, you might consider embarking on a fast.

RESPOND: If you're not sure about fasting ask the Lord to give you some direction. Talk to some mature Christians and read Bible passages that concern fasting. Then ask the Lord whether denying yourself food as a spiritual discipline is something you should add to your devotional life.

Lord, I have several needs and concerns I would like to bring to your throne. Please guide and direct me as I dedicate myself to a fast that will focus my mind entirely on you.

TO KNOW MORE:
Joshua 7 and Ecclesiastes 2 \\

Day 232 | *Down and Out*

PRAY: God connect with me here, as I seek you in your Word.

READ: Psalm 10.9-14 — Did you play on your high school or college sports team? What would you have felt like if you had an open shot at the net to win a championship but missed and your team lost. You would have felt pretty low. How about getting anonymous calls from people who cursed you for losing the game. God frowns on this kind of behaviour, especially when those being "kicked" are the poor and needy of the world. Of course, these verses don't really apply to us. After all, we're not the type of people who would lash out at the poor and needy when they're down, are we? We would never laugh and jeer at a homeless person asking for handouts on the street.

Truth be told, most of us have been guilty at one time or another of being less than kind to those who are filled with despair and deep needs. Or, we've simply ignored their pain. Anytime we speak or act insensitively toward those less fortunate than us, we hurt the person and we hurt God.

REFLECT: Like it or not, we have a responsibility to the poor and needy of this world. God calls us to show them love, compassion and concern for their well-being. To do this, we must hold our thoughts in check when we're tempted to be dismissive or unkind; otherwise, we may end up "kicking" ourselves later.

RESPOND: Ask God to remind you of situations and circumstances in your life in which you purposefully or inadvertently ignored a person when he or she was down. Pray that you will show more compassion in the future.

Lord, open my ears to the needs of others and give me a willing heart to answer their urgent pleas.

TO KNOW MORE:
Habakkuk 3 and Hebrews 4 \\

Day 233 | *Dividends*

PRAY: God connect with me here, as I seek you in your Word.

READ: Matthew 19.29-30 — Peter was a bottom-line kind of guy. He and his fellow disciples had given up their careers, and almost everything else in their lives, in order to follow Jesus. Now Peter was starting to wonder what kind of dividends he could expect to see from his "investment". So, in typical fashion, he put the question to Jesus in the most blunt manner possible: "We have left everything to follow you! What then will there be for us?" How do you suppose Jesus responded to Peter's interesting (but rather tacky) question? If you had been one of Jesus' disciples, how would you have reacted to His words in Matthew 19? Would you have been disappointed to learn that you wouldn't be receiving much in this world; that you would have to wait until you got to heaven to be repaid for your efforts? Would you have asked Jesus for more details about what exactly you would be receiving in heaven? Think about your answer carefully because the same situation applies to us today. The first in this world will be the last in God's Kingdom; the last in this world will be first throughout eternity. The Lord offers His followers abundant life. God offers us peace, joy, security and a passion for living – things that have long-lasting value. We will also be given eternal life with our heavenly Father. What a combination!

REFLECT: Abundant life follows from an obedient life. God demands our very lives, but He also promises to restore them in ways we cannot imagine. We must invest ourselves in the work of his Kingdom, but we can look forward to the rich return that will never stop providing dividends.

RESPOND: Ask the Lord to help you recognize the non-material wealth He has blessed you with. Thank Him for the fact that He has eternal rewards waiting for you in heaven.

Lord, help me to keep a proper perspective on the rewards you have promised your followers and to remember that, while life can be difficult, the rewards for believers in heaven are endless.

TO KNOW MORE: Mark 10 and 3 John 1 \\

Day 234 | Promises

PRAY: God connect with me here, as I seek you in your Word.

READ: Deuteronomy 23.21-23 — He stood at the altar. The hymn had challenged him to go out into the world and take the love of Christ to those who desperately needed it. Together, they vowed to obey God's command to "go". He felt excited. It was good to stand with his friends and make this commitment before God. Of course, he felt a little guilty too; this was the third time this year he'd gone forward to make the same promise to God. This time, he hoped, he'd have the strength and desire to follow through with it. This time would be different.

When it comes to making promises, what does God think of an attitude like this? God's Word doesn't beat around the bush when it comes to making vows or promises to Him. Not only are we to follow through, but we're to do so promptly. Vows are serious business. Making a vow or promise is a way of recognizing God's truth and obeying His will. It involves mind, heart and desire. It involves standing before the God of the universe. That's why vows aren't to be made lightly.

REFLECT: What vows have you made? Have you promised to follow Christ? Have you promised to be sensitive to the needs of the poor? Have you promised to be open to God's leading? Have you promised to be a witness for Him? God's calling on your life is precious. Handle it with care and commitment.

RESPOND: Search your heart before God to see if there are any unkept promises or unfulfilled vows that you've made to Him. If necessary ask God to forgive you for a lazy attitude or forgetfulness. If you feel led to do so, promise God right now to be sensitive to His calling and obedient to His will for your life, no matter where He may lead you.

Lord, I pray that you will forgive me for any promises to you that I have left unfulfilled. Please bring them to mind and help me to keep my word to you, both now and in the future.

TO KNOW MORE: Nahum 1 and Jonah 2 \\

Day 235 | *Trampled*

PRAY: God connect with me here, as I seek you in your Word.

READ: Habakkuk 2.9-11 — Can you imagine what it must be like to have hundreds of people stepping all over you and not being able to do anything about it? The prophet Habakkuk recognized that the poor were being stepped on by the wealthy people of Israel – specifically the rulers and other leaders. Habakkuk lived thousands of years ago. How has the situation changed since then? Are the poor, needy and weak still being pressed down today? Our society places a great deal of importance on getting ahead. In every area of life, we're told there are winners and losers. Those who have the power, money and glory are the winners; those who don't are the losers. It's a dog-eat-dog world. To get to the top of the company ladder, you have to step on a lot of people on the way. Only the strong survive. Many have unfortunately taken these messages to heart.

The problem for Christians is that the people we have to step over and on to get ahead (according to the world's philosophy) are the very people God instructs us to protect and care for. Does this mean that Christians who work in the corporate world are doomed to fail? Absolutely not. It simply means that we choose to play by a different set of rules.

REFLECT: Thousands of Christian businesspeople have become successful without grinding down those who are weaker or less fortunate than they are. They operate ethical companies that show compassion for employees and a burden for the well-being of others. Such blessings await anyone who chooses to play by God's rules and refuses to press down others.

RESPOND: Ask God to point out any areas of your life where you may be stepping on others in order to get ahead. Ask Him to help you see people as He does.

Lord, I pray that you will give me a heart of compassion for others and that I will not be tempted to hurt others in a quest to get ahead.

TO KNOW MORE: Obadiah 1 and Jude 1 \\

Day 236 | *Priorities*

PRAY: God connect with me here, as I seek you in your Word.

READ: Haggai 1.3-6 — The prophet Haggai knew that living for one's own pleasure led only to unhappiness. Observe what he tells the people of Judah. These words were directed specifically at the Israelites who had built fancy houses for themselves but had neglected to rebuild the Temple of the Lord. God urged the people to rethink their priorities, abandon their self-centredness and make Him first in their lives again.

Even though God's words in Haggai were intended for Israel, they might also apply to any Christian today whose priorities are skewed. The Lord's main concerns should be our priorities. Because the Lord places a special emphasis on the poor and needy, we should make ministry to the disadvantaged one of our principal desires.

REFLECT: God requires a radical shift in thinking, from self-focus to a heart for others. We need to honestly assess what we have (including our time, money and energy), what we would like to have and what we can give to those in need. Rather than taking for granted the blessings we have been given, we can now share those blessings with others.

RESPOND: Ask the Lord to make you aware of things in your life that you take for granted. As He brings these things to your mind, thank Him for them and ask His forgiveness for any selfish attitudes you may have.

Lord, I pray you will forgive me for times when I have taken your blessings for granted and ask that you will give me many opportunities in the future to share what you have given me with others.

TO KNOW MORE:
Ezra 5 and Lamentations 2 \\

Day 237 | *Hospitality*

PRAY: God connect with me here, as I seek you in your Word.

READ: Matthew 10.5-10 — Hospitality means making somebody feel at home, comfortable, enjoyed, wanted and welcomed. The disciples were continually doing good things: praying, healing, declaring the coming Kingdom, ministering in Jesus' name, and they received good things in return. But what was the standard for them to follow? "Give as freely as you have received!" (v. 8b).

We can learn a lot from the example of the disciples.

- We are called to reach out to the world in Jesus' name.

- We should freely accept any hospitality offered to us as we minister. Not only is that a blessing to us, but it is to the giver as well.

- Anytime a guest preacher, singer, missionary or other minister comes to our church, we should do all we can to make sure that person's needs are provided for and that he or she feels at home.

REFLECT: As Jesus' best friends, the disciples had certainly received incredible blessings. Now they were given the opportunity from their Master to go out into a hurting, sick, scared world and pass their blessings along. Of course, Jesus also encouraged the disciples to be discerning (vv. 11-15). If someone was antagonistic to them, they were to move on. But if someone received them and their message, they were to give that home a blessing.

RESPOND: Take some time today to pray for those who travel from church to church and town to town to proclaim Jesus. Think of all those who have blessed your own church with their presence in recent years. Ask God to meet their every need through the hospitality of fellow believers.

Lord, I pray that both me and my church will show hospitality to everyone, especially to those who selflessly travel on your behalf while serving the needs of others in your name.

TO KNOW MORE: Jeremiah 50 and Acts 1 \\

Day 238 | *Impartiality*

PRAY: God connect with me here, as I seek you in your Word.

READ: Exodus 23.1-6 — Honesty check: Have you ever fibbed just a little to make yourself look better in the eyes of someone else? Maybe you just wanted to be accepted by a person you thought was a little better than you, more popular, richer, better looking. You wanted to get on their good side. Did it work? And was it really worth it? How about people who are not as well off as you? Maybe they live in a poorer part of town, they don't wear the best clothes, they drive a broken down car. Ever tried to make yourself look good to impress them? Probably not. Why bother, right? But God's Word is clear: We are supposed to "bother" to do right.

God wants His people to be authentic, real, transparent. He doesn't want us to put on an act to impress anybody – rich or poor. In today's reading, God makes a strong case for justice by coming at it from both sides: "Do not slant your testimony in favour of a person just because that person is poor." And, conversely, "Do not twist justice against people simply because they are poor" (vv. 3; 6). In other words, be true and do right, no matter what.

REFLECT: Justice, by definition, is impartial. And impartial is what we should be. So when it comes to the way you treat a person, be fair. That may mean standing up against the pressure of the crowd. After all, you want to be treated fairly and accepted for who you are. God calls you to do the same for others, regardless of whether they are rich or poor.

RESPOND: Is an acquaintance of yours being unfairly treated? Accused of something he or she didn't do? Not accepted by others because of something superficial? Pray for that person right now. Ask God to provide them with an abundance of grace and acceptance. And ask Him to make you an instrument of His peace in that person's life.

Lord, I pray for (name) who is being unfairly treated. I pray that you will protect and comfort them and that I will be a source of encouragement to them.

TO KNOW MORE: Psalm 101 and Romans 3 \\

Day 239 | *Plans*

PRAY: God connect with me here, as I seek you in your Word.

READ: Genesis 41.33-36 — Have you ever had a looming deadline for a project that will have an impact on not only your future but the lives of your co-workers as well? Whether you have or not, you can imagine the weight of responsibility you would feel. God, through Pharaoh, had given Joseph the task of preparing a nation for an upcoming famine. Because God had seen the many times that Joseph had acted responsibly in his daily life, He knew that Joseph was the man for the tough job ahead. And Pharaoh obviously sensed that Joseph was someone who could be trusted. By acting responsibly in the areas where God had placed him, Joseph was also reflecting a part of God's nature to those around him.

God has wonderful plans for your life. And it's important to remember that even the smallest tasks for Him are part of His training. Take advantage of the numerous opportunities you have to grow in being responsible.

REFLECT: Henry Wadsworth Longfellow wrote, "We judge ourselves by what we feel capable of doing, while others judge us by what we have already done." Would people consider you a responsible person?

RESPOND: Pray that God would entrust you with greater responsibility by being faithful with the tasks you do for other this week.

Lord, I pray that you will give me more and greater opportunities to serve you today, tomorrow and throughout my life.

TO KNOW MORE:
Deuteronomy 1 and Acts 6 \\

Day 240 | *Vigilant*

PRAY: God connect with me here, as I seek you in your Word.

READ: Psalm 35.9-10 — Even in the darkest circumstances, God gives us hope. And His ceaseless care for His people shines through the words of today's Psalm. Like a lighthouse keeper who remains vigilant during a storm, God is always scanning the horizon for those who need His help. His attentive and eternal watch locates victims who are lost or adrift, unseen to everyone else. He also rescues them from their plight. We should be filled with wonder knowing that God cares for us so intimately.

But God's care goes beyond us. It extends to orphans, widows, shut-ins, the homeless, the jobless, those who are ill, the disabled, the starving – the list could go on and on. God loves those whom the world mistreats and sometimes even forgets.

REFLECT: Don't forget, that you can be God's eyes to see and help the poor, the weak, the needy. Scan the horizon for those who need rescue and ask God to give you greater vigilance to find the ones whom no one else notices.

RESPOND: Ask God to give you the eyes to see those in need and the courage and compassion to respond.

Lord, help me to be ever watchful for ways I can help others in your name.

TO KNOW MORE:
Isaiah 61 and Galatians 5 \\

Day 241 | *Compassion*

PRAY: God connect with me here, as I seek you in your Word.

READ: Psalm 109.26-30 — David, speaking of an unidentified enemy, writes what may not seem like a very godly prayer – to call down curses on someone. But David was deeply disturbed and angry. It bothered him that this individual had been so harsh to the poor and needy. And so David prayed that the wicked would be judged and the innocent vindicated. David wanted God to be honoured and obeyed. He understood that as long as the powerful mistreated the powerless, this was not fully possible.

What about you? Does it bother you when you see injustice? How do you feel when you see refugees or immigrants being treated unfairly? Are you moved to pray in such situations? When evil governments starve their own people, do you pray for God to bring down those in power? We cannot right every wrong or rectify every unjust situation. But we can pray for God to work on behalf of the oppressed.

REFLECT: One thing we can certainly do for the down-trodden is show them kindness and mercy through our prayers and our giving. What we never want to do is become callous to those in need for then we are no better than the one David condemned in Psalm 109.

RESPOND: Ask God to work through you on behalf of the oppressed.

Lord, help me to be compassionate to those who are suffering at the hands of others and I pray that your love and mercy will be revealed to them.

TO KNOW MORE:
Job 37 and Hebrews 5 \\

Day 242 | *Relaxation*

PRAY: God connect with me here, as I seek you in your Word.

READ: Leviticus 23.15-21 — Do you enjoy summer celebrations? Picnics in the park, annual family reunions, swimming parties at a nearby lake. Today we read about a summer celebration enjoyed by the Hebrew nation called the Festival of Harvest.

The Festival of Harvest happened in May or June. It was a day of thanksgiving at the start of the wheat harvest. Families brought sacrifices to thank God for their crops. Notice that verse 21 says, "That same day, you must stop all your regular work and gather for a sacred assembly." While priests sacrificed to obtain forgiveness for sins and to show thanks to God, Israel stopped working and rested. God wasn't talking only about physical rest, like sleeping late. God wanted to give His people spiritual rest. And He wants to do the same for us today.

REFLECT: God values rest. And He wants you to value rest as well, both physical and spiritual. Learn to take the time for physical rest. And learn how to rest in Him.

RESPOND: Pray for God's rest in your life whether through emotional peace or physical strengthening. Pray also for God's rest in the lives of your family, friends and church leaders.

Lord, thank you for opportunities to rest and enjoy time with my family. May these also be occasions when I grow closer to you and can listen more fully for your voice and your guidance.

TO KNOW MORE:
Numbers 28 and Romans 8 \\

Day 243 | *Selfishness*

PRAY: God connect with me here, as I seek you in your Word.

READ: Proverbs 28.2-11 — Today's verses from Proverbs indicate that there are two kinds of people in the world: the evil and the Godly. You see the distinction in society among men and women of all ages and classes. What causes evil people to do what they do? Think about it: their ultimate objective is to promote themselves and their interests. In essence, they are behaving selfishly.

Selfish people have one thing on their minds: themselves. Any way they can get more attention, more power, more money, more pleasure, they will do it. Sadly, the souls of such people can resemble a bottomless pit. Nothing can ever fill it up. Self-centred people are never truly satisfied.

REFLECT: Selfless people are those whom God honours. People who follow the Lord are honest and kind to the poor. It's vital that we consider eternity when our thoughts turn to selfish desires.

RESPOND: Ask God to help you become more "selfless".

Lord, I pray that you will give me a heart that is loving, self-sacrificing and thoughtful toward others and their needs.

TO KNOW MORE:
Hosea 13 and Ephesians 5 \\

Day 244 | *Greed*

PRAY: God connect with me here, as I seek you in your Word.

READ: 1 Kings 21.5-10 — Living near a river's edge can be wonderful in summer and beautiful in fall. But in the spring, one needs to keep a close eye on a river because of the spring melt. If left unmonitored, the lazy water can become a raging torrent of destruction and death. In today's verses, we find something else that can destroy lives if left unmonitored. Ahab was a king who had everything he wanted. So why did he desire a poor man's vineyard enough to kill for it? It was because he had become a slave to his greed. While possessions and wealth in and of themselves are not evil, love of possessions can lead to horrible crimes and injustices, such as the one Ahab encouraged.

Greed is the same today as it was in Bible times. Left unchecked, it can push people to do all kinds of senseless, wicked things. On the nightly news we see nations and corporations alike attack each other for very little gain. And not a month goes by that we don't hear of someone being killed or hurt badly during a carjacking or robbery. Greed is indeed an attitude to take seriously.

REFLECT: Do you have a problem with greed? Do you long for money, possessions or acclaim? Ask God to help you surrender your greedy tendencies to Him.

RESPOND: Pray that God will help you be content with what He has blessed you with.

Lord, forgive me for any greedy attitudes I may have and help me to have a generous and loving heart.

TO KNOW MORE:
Proverbs 14 and Micah 2 \\

Day 245 | *Revolution*

PRAY: God connect with me here, as I seek you in your Word.

READ: Genesis 47.23-25 — The Egyptians living more than 3,000 years ago confronted a more faceless kind of oppression. Famine ravaged their land, and they were powerless to stop its misery. The courage of one man, Joseph, was needed to blunt the impact of the disaster.

Because of his power and position, Joseph could have demanded much more from the Egyptians. But he chose instead to treat them with kindness. Oppressed people live among us today. They deserve our kindness now as much as they did then. Who are the oppressed? The oppressed are those who have suffered abuse by someone in authority or those who are "weighed down." Can you identify these people in your community? What about people struggling with drug or alcohol addiction? The homeless? Or families who have fled their homelands to avoid starvation or war?

You may not feel very powerful when it comes to making a difference in the lives of so many hurting people. But small steps can lead to giant strides.

REFLECT: Throughout history, courageous people have taken a stand to make the world a better place for everyone. What can you do to start a kindness revolution in your neighborhood, church, or workplace?

RESPOND: Pray for the courage to act on behalf of the oppressed

Lord, I pray that you will give me a heart for the needs of others and that I can find ways to help those who are suffering in my community.

TO KNOW MORE:
Isaiah 55 and 2 Corinthians 9 \\

Day 246 | Service

PRAY: God connect with me here, as I seek you in your Word.

READ: Matthew 23.11-12 — Jesus was condemning the Pharisees for the prideful way they wanted to be noticed by others (vv. 6-7). Everything they did was selfish and "for show" (v. 5). We've seen in previous devotions that the most important (and the most rewarded) members of God's Kingdom do not seek earthly (or even heavenly) notice. That's because they understand that Jesus is the one who should be our focus. He alone deserves all glory and honour and praise.

Do the things no one else is willing to do. Do the things no one else will ever see. According to Jesus, that's the real test of greatness: the willingness to do things in secret, without ever getting earthly recognition (Matthew 6.1-18). In so many words, Jesus challenges us to be a secret servant. How's that for a job description or for a career objective?

REFLECT: Imagine the impact if every follower of Christ would say, "I'm going to quietly and faithfully serve God, with no fanfare, with no expectations, with no strings attached. And I'll do this because He is the great King of the universe and of my life and because He has loved and blessed me so much." Will you make that your goal? There's not a greater ambition to be found.

RESPOND: Confess any areas of pride or selfishness in which your most important goal has been promoting yourself rather than proclaiming Christ. Pray for a humble heart that is willing to serve – even in the shadows.

Lord, I pray you will forgive me for times when I have thought only of myself and not the needs of others – and forgive me when I've not placed you first in my life.

TO KNOW MORE:
Galatians 5 and Philippians 2 \\

Day 247 | *Tithes*

PRAY: God connect with me here, as I seek you in your Word.

READ: Leviticus 27.30-33 — Verse 30 requires that "a tenth" of the produce of the land belongs to the Lord and must be set apart to Him as holy. The word tithe, which we use today to mean a gift to God, is another way to say tenth. In the Old Testament, the amount of "a tenth" was often given to a king – whether to the Lord and His priests and Levites or to an Israelite king. In Genesis 14.20 Abram gave the priest Melchizedek, and to God, a tenth of what he captured after rescuing Lot. In Genesis 28.22 after Jacob's vision of an angel-crowded staircase, he promised God a tenth of everything he had. Still later in Israel's history, Samuel the prophet warned that future kings would "take a tenth of your grain and of your wine."

We should not rob God of what is rightfully His. By giving our money or time to God, we acknowledge Him as our King.

REFLECT: Since the Creator God owns everything, we are not actually doing Him a favor by offering our gifts. Instead, we are praising Him for His favor to us.

RESPOND: Proclaim Christ as your King by giving Him what is rightly His – not only your time and money but your entire self.

Lord, I pray that you will accept my tithes as an offering of my thankfulness and my life as an offering of my praise.

TO KNOW MORE:
Malachi 3 and Matthew 23 \\

Day 248 | *Value*

PRAY: God connect with me here, as I seek you in your Word.

READ: Luke 12.4-7 — Jesus was speaking to his followers. Already they were attracting the attention of the people in charge, who didn't like the waves Jesus was making in their very comfortable system. Jesus knew that whoever followed Him ran the risk of upsetting the authorities. Even today, in various places around the world, being a Christian can cause you to lose your life.

Jesus set his listeners' minds at ease. He said, God knows every single sparrow–and they only cost a couple cents for five at the Temple. If a simple bird is known by God, certainly we are, too. In fact, Jesus said God knows exactly how many hairs are growing out of our heads. That may sound kind of ridiculous. But the point is that God knows every single detail of our lives. "So don't be afraid," Jesus says, "you are more valuable to him than a whole flock of sparrows" (v. 7).

REFLECT: God values you. You are important to him. He knows everything about you–every imperfection, every sin and doubt, everything. And still He loves you. Amazing! A God like that is absolutely worth praising and serving.

RESPOND: Spend some time in prayer thanking God for His infinite love and care for you. He is worthy of your praise. Turn to a psalm of thanksgiving (like Psalm 145; 146; 147 or 148) and pray or sing it aloud in His honor.

Lord, I praise you and thank you for your unlimited love for me.

TO KNOW MORE:
Jeremiah 1 and 1 Peter 3 \\

Day 249 | *Neighbours*

PRAY: God connect with me here, as I seek you in your Word.

READ: Deuteronomy 24.10-15 — In this passage, God again encourages us to treat our poor neighbors fairly and compassionately. We are to give and lend freely – and if they're poor, we're not to press for repayment or inconvenience them by taking something they need as security for a loan. We're supposed to trust God to repay us. God demands justice for all, especially the poor who receive justice so rarely. Poor people are often taken advantage of. Many are considered lazy or stupid when they are actually victims of oppression. For instance, usually a poor person can only get credit or loans from dishonest firms that extract huge amounts of interest. As a result, they end up in an even worse financial condition.

God calls us to a higher standard. He challenges us to do all we can to help the truly needy. We are not to demand a profit from them or insist they repay loans quickly. God's laws encourage the poor to improve their place in life. And if they're unable to do so, we are to treat them compassionately.

REFLECT: The poor are closer to you than you may think. Perhaps even some of your neighbors are struggling to keep their heads above the financial waters. Be open and ready to help in any way you can.

RESPOND: Pray for your neighbors in need today – those who live near you and those who live around the world. Ask God to provide for their needs and to use you in whatever way He can do so.

Lord, I pray you will show me how I can be of service and help to my neighbors in your name.

TO KNOW MORE:
Job 24 and James 1 \\

Day 250 | *Feelings*

PRAY: God connect with me here, as I seek you in your Word.

READ: Romans 13.8-14 — "Love your neighbor as yourself." Such a simple statement! And one we're so familiar with that it really doesn't even register. But Paul, like Jesus before him, summarizes the whole law of God with these simple words.

No matter who offends us, the right thing to do is to respond in love and to let God work His love through us. A lot of people have the idea that loving yourself is wrong. But if it were, then the idea of loving your neighbor as yourself wouldn't make any sense. How do you love yourself? Think about it: You feed yourself, clothe yourself, take care of your body. You protect yourself from pain and hurt and need. That's exactly what we need to be doing for our neighbors. We need to do what we can to see they are fed, clothed and housed as well as possible. We need to be concerned with issues of social justice. That's what loving your neighbor as yourself is all about.

REFLECT: But how do we do this when people have hurt our feelings or accused us of something? Let the Lord take control of you, and don't think of ways to get back at them(v. 14). The truth is, we can't continually live a life of loving our neighbors through our own power. But Jesus can, and He lives inside you. So let Him work through you today.

RESPOND: Ask God to help you forgive those who offend and hurt you. Ask Him to love others through you as only He can.

Lord, I pray you will give me a forgiving heart, even toward those who have done things that have been hurtful and caused heartache.

TO KNOW MORE:
Proverbs 3 and 1 Timothy 1 \\

Day 251 | *Mercy*

PRAY: God connect with me here, as I seek you in your Word.

READ: 2 Samuel 19.18-23 — Mercy might be defined most simply as kind and compassionate treatment. Yet mercy also involves choice. Being merciful means choosing not to repay others for how they have hurt you. A good example of mercy can be found in the Old Testament account of David's return to Jerusalem after his son Absalom's rebellion.

We don't know for sure what David was thinking when Shimei made his requests, but it's quite likely that he put himself in the other man's position. Shimei, who had earlier cursed the king and hurled dirt and rocks at him, had realized the horrible mistake he had made. The key to showing mercy to another person is to ask, "What would I like that person to do for me if our situations were reversed"? Hard as it may be to do, we can gain a great deal of perspective by putting ourselves in the place of those who may have wronged us.

REFLECT: When we are able to empathize with others, we are much more likely to respond to them in a merciful and God-honouring way.

RESPOND: Thank the Lord for the mercy He has shown you. Then ask Him to help you learn to show mercy to others.

Lord, I pray for mercy for the things I have done that have been displeasing in your sight and I ask that you will, in turn, give me a merciful heart toward those around me.

TO KNOW MORE:
Psalm 66 and 2 Corinthians 5 \\

Day 252 | *Worth*

PRAY: God connect with me here, as I seek you in your Word.

READ: Philemon 10-12 — In the shortest book of the New Testament, the apostle Paul told the story of a man named Philemon who was betrayed by one of his slaves, Onesimus. Take a look at Paul's surprising request of Philemon on behalf of Onesimus. This is why Paul wrote a letter on Onesimus' behalf. The apostle urged Philemon to receive Onesimus not as a slave but as a Christian brother. He wanted Philemon to forgive Onesimus the way he would forgive any other member of his church. He wanted Philemon to welcome Onesimus with the same respect and affection that he would give Paul himself.

The book of Philemon is not just a lesson in forgiveness, however. It also shows the importance of recognizing people's true worth. In the world's eyes, Onesimus was just a slave – an unimportant, "disposable" servant. In Paul's eyes, however, Onesimus was a valuable Christian brother.

REFLECT: How do you regard your brothers and sisters in Christ? Do you spend more time remembering their liabilities, their faults and their past slip-ups? Or do you love them as Christ would, encouraging them in their faith and helping them do good?

RESPOND: Ask the Lord to provide some opportunities for you to help those who have done things in the past that were wrong but are now hoping to turn their lives around. These are people who God wants to restore – and you can play a vital role in His purposes.

Lord, I pray that I will see value in all people, just as you do, and that I can be an encourager to someone who is trying to turn his or her life in a new and positive direction.

TO KNOW MORE:
Colossians 4 and Titus 1 \\

Day 253 | *Sacrifice*

PRAY: God connect with me here, as I seek you in your Word.

READ: Psalm 50.7-15 — Why do you go to church? Why do you read your Bible? Why do you give money to charitable causes and ministries? Why do you volunteer for mission activities? In short, when it comes to being a Christian, why do you do what you do? Is it because that's what you're used to doing? Or is it because you genuinely want to love, serve and know God as best as you can?

God is concerned foremost about the motives that drive us, as we see in today's passage. As believers, we're called to serve God out of a heart of thanks. We're called to sacrifice our time and energy for His glory. We're called to know Him intimately because we're going to spend eternity with Him. We do these things not in order to gain God's favour, but to reflect the changes He has already made in our lives.

REFLECT: God is pleased with sacrifices that come from true love and obedience. From where are your sacrifices coming?

RESPOND: Examine your motives before the Lord. Search your heart with the guidance of His Spirit to determine the true reasons why you do what you do as a believer.

Lord, I pray that I will be a person of pure intentions and humble thoughts as I seek to serve and worship you daily.

TO KNOW MORE:
Isaiah 1 and Hosea 6 \\

Day 254 | *Foolishness*

PRAY: God connect with me here, as I seek you in your Word.

READ: Isaiah 32.5-8 — According to the Bible, God is all-knowing. He not only sees everything people do, He is fully aware of motives and attitudes. He sees right into the heart and soul of each person. The Scriptures also declare that God is a just judge. Every person will one day stand before God and be required to give an account for the life he or she has lived.

But that day seems like a mere fantasy. Here and now, sinful behaviour is "no big deal." And so most people live selfishly and thoughtlessly. They take advantage of others and then try to justify their actions. They rationalize their deeds. They make excuses. They blame others. They thumb their noses at rules and decency. They live to shock. And though they may be treated as heroes in the current culture, they will one day be exposed in God's Kingdom. This is a lesson everyone needs to grasp: Because God is an all-knowing, perfect judge, nobody will get away with anything.

REFLECT: How can you live the kind of life that will be celebrated and blessed by God?

RESPOND: Tell God that you don't want to be like all the foolish people in our culture who gleefully do wrong things.

Lord, I pray that I will live a life of meaning and substance; a life that is pleasing to you as I strive to do what is right regardless of the way others conduct themselves.

TO KNOW MORE:
Psalm 15 and James 1 \\

Day 255 | *Caring*

PRAY: God connect with me here, as I seek you in your Word.

READ: Exodus 23.10-11 — God built into the Israelites' life the concept of caring for the poor. In today's verses, for instance, God made it clear that He expects His people to care for others by helping them to meet their need for food in various ways. God established a system of farming in which the people would work the land and harvest crops for six years, and then take the seventh year off. During this "Sabbath year", no work would be done and no crops would be harvested. This enabled the land to recoup its nutrients and become rich and fertile again.

If the people would obey his commands, God promised that the sixth year's crop would provide enough food not only for that year, but for the seventh year and all the way to the time when the eighth year's crop was harvested. The only thing the people had to do was trust Him to provide, and He would.

While they let their land rest during the seventh year, some crops would come up on their own. God's people were not to harvest these "voluntary crops". They were to leave them in the fields and allow the poor and hungry to come and harvest whatever they needed. What they didn't take was left for animals to eat. In this way, God would provide for everyone's needs.

REFLECT: Unfortunately, there's no record that Israel ever fully obeyed this command. But you can certainly obey the spirit of it by making sure the needs of the poor are regularly on your mind, in your prayers and in your plans to help.

RESPOND: Pray for the many ministries designed to provide food and other necessities to poor people in your city, throughout Canada and around the world.

Lord, I pray that you will bless the many churches and outreach organizations that are caring for the needs of the poor – along with the men and women who serve in these ministries.

TO KNOW MORE: Leviticus 25 and Isaiah 58 \\

Day 256 | *Selflessness*

PRAY: God connect with me here, as I seek you in your Word.

READ: John 3.13-17 — Coaches often talk about sacrifice. They want their players to think only about the good of the team and do whatever it takes to help their teammates win. In today's reading, Jesus talks about the personal sacrifice He will make for the good of the world.

The idea of sacrificing means letting go of personal goals and working selflessly for larger purposes. Christ is the ultimate example of this. As the Creator (Colossians 1.16), all of life is under His control. But by offering Himself as the ultimate sacrifice, Jesus put the needs of His creatures above His own desires. He surrendered His chance for quick fame and glory (Matthew 4.8-11 and John 6.15). He humbly and willingly complied with the wishes of His Father (Philippians 2.5-8). All of His energies were focused on "advancing us" to heaven. What else can explain the cruel agony He endured at the cross on our behalf? He laid down His life that we might find eternal life with God in heaven.

REFLECT: To sacrifice is to "lay down your life." It means letting go of your own ambitions, exchanging your agenda for God's plan. And so the question is, in view of the great sacrifice that Christ has made on our behalf, how much do we sacrifice for Him? For others?

RESPOND: Take a moment to thank God for His sacrificial love. Pray for the selflessness and strength to follow Christ as a "living sacrifice" (Romans 12.1), loving others no matter how different they may seem.

Lord, I pray that your love will shine through me and be a blessing to others and a witness to the sacrifice your Son made for the world upon the cross.

TO KNOW MORE:
Romans 10 and Acts 20 \\

Day 257 | *Actions*

PRAY: God connect with me here, as I seek you in your Word.

READ: Proverbs 14.31 — People typically don't like or trust those who brag about their accomplishments. Their outsized egos apparently don't allow them to consider that their words cause people to hold them to higher standards. And, if their skills don't match their words, they'll be ridiculed and never get the respect they crave.

The author of Proverbs may not use the same phrasing, but he has a lot to say about matching words with actions. We can talk and talk about how much we love the Lord and want to follow His will, but unless we back up our talk with actions, our words are hollow.

One of the best and most obvious ways to show our love for the Lord is to treat everyone according to His instructions. God identifies Himself so closely with the poor and needy that anything we do to (or for) them, we do to (or for) Him. If we oppress or mock the poor, we show contempt for God; if we are kind to the needy, we honour the Lord and will be rewarded for our actions.

REFLECT: God gives us opportunities to tangibly show the world how we feel about Him. He also gives us a chance to show our thankfulness for all that He has done for us. So helping the poor is not just a matter of being kind and generous to other people; it's a matter of honouring the Lord.

RESPOND: Ask the Lord to make you aware of opportunities to help the poor and needy in your community.

Lord, I pray that I will live a life that is above reproach, that is welcoming to those in need and that consistently honours you.

TO KNOW MORE:
Psalm 12 and 1 John 4 \\

Day 258 | *Prosperity*

PRAY: God connect with me here, as I seek you in your Word.

READ: Deuteronomy 6.10-12 — Born around 600 B.C., Aesop loved to tell clever stories. These stories are known today as Aesop's fables. The fable titled The Dog and His Reflection has a good lesson to teach about prosperity. It seems that a dog was given a bone. While on his way home, he had to cross a bridge. On crossing, he looked down in the water and noticed what he thought was another dog with a bigger bone. This made him unhappy. It wasn't enough to just have a bone. He wanted a bigger bone. So he opened his mouth to get the bigger bone and lost the one he had. His greed was his undoing.

Isn't it interesting that human nature is such that the more we have the more we want? And the more we get from God the more we forget Him? When do you pray the most? When things are going well or when you are in a difficult situation? The answer is probably when you are struggling. Most people act this way. That may be one reason that God allows hard things to come into our lives. He knows they will draw us closer to Him.

REFLECT: Proverbs 30.8-9 asks for neither poverty nor riches because with poverty comes great need but with riches we tend to turn from the One who is the source of all blessings. It's important to never forget the Lord, in difficult time or in times of bounty.

RESPOND: Ask the Lord to keep His blessings before you so that you will constantly be reminded of His boundless grace.

Lord, I thank you for your many blessings and I pray that, as you continue to supply my needs, I will never forget that everything I have comes from you.

TO KNOW MORE:
Nehemiah 9 and Psalm 78 \\

Day 259 | *Passions*

PRAY: God connect with me here, as I seek you in your Word.

READ: 2 Kings 19.29-31 — Have you ever heard something like this on television: Jeff and Ginger take passion to new limits in an all-new episode tonight. Don't miss a single minute! Sad to say, the word "passion" is one of the most abused words in our language today. It is often used to define any strong feeling. And having that "feeling" justifies all kinds of selfish behaviour. Television and movie advertisers, for example, use this word to put a positive spin on a destructive extramarital affair or an angry confrontation. Politicians like the word too, because it expresses deep concern without any accompanying commitment. "I have a passion for the poor" is a common but too often hollow political phrase.

But passion has a much larger and richer meaning than the examples just cited. Passion can be defined as a powerful emotion such as love or anger, but it can also mean the energetic and unflagging pursuit of an aim or devotion to a cause. God has a ceaseless devotion toward His people. And we should share His passion through our dedicated concern for others.

REFLECT: What are your passions? Art, music, sports, helping people? Ask God to help you discover your passions and use them to further His Kingdom.

RESPOND: Ask God to help you discover your spiritual passions.

Lord, I pray that you will make me passionate for causes that help others and that share the good news of salvation through your Son.

TO KNOW MORE:
Isaiah 37 and Psalm 80 \\

Day 260 | *Pride*

PRAY: God connect with me here, as I seek you in your Word.

READ: 2 Corinthians 10.12-18 — In our world of information overload, it takes a particularly vivid image or character to stick in our minds.

As a result, people looking to stand out are forced to go to more and more extreme lengths to promote themselves. This climate has produced a culture in which boasting thrives. This isn't to say that boasting is a new phenomenon, of course. The Bible, for one, certainly contains its share of boasters. In New Testament times, the apostle Paul faced off against some especially troublesome boasters in the Corinthian church.

Apparently false teachers had invaded the church in Corinth. Even worse, they were a rather cocky group, boasting of their ministry and behaving as though there was no higher standard than themselves. Paul, in contrast, recognized that if any boasting was to be done concerning his work, it would have to be boasting in the Lord. Paul understood that it is the Lord who deserves credit for any good that results from our labor.

REFLECT: The other principle that Paul makes crystal clear is that when people boast about themselves, it doesn't count for much. What does count? The Lord's commendation. So don't seek the spotlight. And trust God to commend your work as you serve him in your life.

RESPOND: Ask God to help you walk humbly each day, trusting Him to commend you for your efforts.

Lord, I pray you will give me a humble heart that seeks only your approval and a tongue that speaks encouraging, not boastful, words.

TO KNOW MORE:
Proverbs 26 and Romans 15 \\

Day 261 | *Standards*

PRAY: God connect with me here, as I seek you in your Word.

READ: James 5.1-6 — Life is serious business. The way we live here and now on earth will determine the way we'll live forever. Every attitude, every action, every word, every deed matters. Too often our faith is something we do on Sundays. The rest of the time, we're really looking out for ourselves. Doing what we want to do. Treating others indifferently or worse. Pursuing money, people, things, or other dreams of happiness. Let James shake you up a bit today. Let his words grab you and rattle your thinking. Let him help you get back on track.

Of course, money isn't the problem. We need money to live. Churches and ministries use money to serve effectively. Missionaries must have money to spread the Good News. It's the love of money that brings about all kinds of evil (see 1 Timothy 6.10). It's the love of money that causes some people to mistreat others in order to get more. So James warns all believers not to follow the world's standards of success but rather God's standards of service.

REFLECT: What you believe, and how you put those beliefs into action, matters. Only then can we find true happiness and satisfaction.

RESPOND: Let James' stern words lead you in a prayer of confession over any wrong attitudes you hold about money, about poor people, about possessions. Open up to God about your life. About your need for more boldness and direction, your desire to walk closer with Him and your opportunities to serve Him by reaching out to others.

Lord, forgive me for any sinful attitudes I have and help me to walk closer to you so that I can serve you more effectively.

TO KNOW MORE:
Micah 6 and Luke 23 \\

Day 262 | *Running*

PRAY: God connect with me here, as I seek you in your Word.

READ: Psalm 49.8-13 — On New Year's Day in 1929, a packed Rose Bowl Stadium watched the University of California battle Georgia Tech. After a scoreless first quarter, Georgia Tech began to move the ball down the field. The quarterback passed the ball to a running back, but the back fumbled as he was hit. The ball squirted into the hands of a California defensive back, who latched on to the ball and chugged toward the goal line. Everyone began to yell. The California player imagined that the spectators were celebrating his moment of glory. But ten yards from the end zone, he was tackled by one of his own teammates. He realized, to his horror, that he had been running the wrong way. This blunder allowed Georgia Tech to score a safety (two points) moments later when they tackled a California player in the end zone. And the crowning blow was the final score of the game: Georgia Tech 8; California 7. The infamous player became known in sports history as "Wrong Way" Riegels.

When we make wealth the goal and our reason for living, we begin running the wrong way. That course ends in exhaustion and despair. Instead, we should be running after true riches: life with God and a life of service to others.

REFLECT: When we pursue God's path, we are strengthened and encouraged with every step we take. As you choose to run after true riches, the crowd may try to convince you that you are running the wrong way. Just remember that God is the one who designed the game and the field. Run His way. Listen for His cheers.

RESPOND: Ask God to keep you turned in the right direction as you pursue your goals. Seek His strength as you look for endurance to finish the race.

Lord, I pray that you will keep me focused on the right goals – the things that bring glory to you and that help those around me discover your love and mercy.

TO KNOW MORE:
Ecclesiastes 8 and Matthew 16 \\

Day 263 | *Ambition*

PRAY: God connect with me here, as I seek you in your Word.

READ: Numbers 16.1-7 — The book of Numbers gives us an example of fierce greed and ambition. Korah was what you might call an ambitious self-starter. Not content with his duties at the tabernacle, he wanted to become a full-fledged priest. He was so intent on achieving his goal that he challenged Moses, God's chosen leader for the Israelites. And that's where Korah's ambition and greed got him into trouble. He and his followers were killed when the earth split open and swallowed them.

So is it wrong to be ambitious? Should those of us who have goals we're trying to achieve keep one eye on the ground to watch for cracks that might open up? No, but we should constantly assess our ambitions to make sure they're not motivated by greed. If we're willing to use, exploit or damage others in our quest to "get ahead", it's time to reexamine our goals and motivations.

REFLECT: God has instilled in each of us a desire to pursue excellence in everything we do. Some people ignore their particular calling and prefer to drift aimlessly through life. Their laziness is an affront to God. On the other hand, however, some desire greatness at all costs and will do anything to achieve their goals. God wants us to succeed but He wants us to achieve great things according to His laws. Only then will we find true satisfaction and peace.

RESPOND: Pray for the awareness and insight to recognize when your ambitions are motivated by greed.

Lord, I pray that my ambitions will be tempered by my desire to serve you in harmony with your Word.

TO KNOW MORE:
Ezekiel 16 and Jude 1 \\

Day 264 | *Unlovable*

PRAY: God connect with me here, as I seek you in your Word.

READ: Luke 6.27-36 — Rush hour traffic can bring out the worst in people. Traveling at a snail's pace (even bumper-to-bumper), blaring horns, aggressive and impatient, many drivers tend to be incredibly irritating, annoying and often just plain obnoxious. The result: We too often respond with the same bullying spirit. We become just as pushy. Just as intolerant. Generally out for me and me alone. But what if we determine to stay courteous, looking out for the other person and giving him or her a break? What if we try to operate even our cars by Jesus' charge to love the unlovable?

Doing good to those who do good things for us doesn't take a lot of effort on our part. But it takes someone special to love the unlovable. To do good things for people who have been cruel to us. To lend money to someone who we know can't repay the loan. To love an enemy. These efforts aren't easy or effortless; they take sacrifice and determination and power from the Holy Spirit. At this point, you might also be asking why you should even attempt this challenge. Well the answer's simple: Jesus loved us when we were unlovable so, as His followers, we should go and do likewise.

REFLECT: Will you accept the challenge? How about determining to love and allowing that driver to pull out ahead of you during the peak of rush hour traffic? Quite honestly, the look of shock on his face will be worth it!

RESPOND: Think of an "unlovable" person in your life. Pray for his or her needs and the grace to love that person unconditionally.

Lord, today I pray for (Name) and ask that you will give me patience with him / her regardless of how they respond to me.

TO KNOW MORE:
Proverbs 24 and 3 John 1 \\

Day 265 | *Freshness*

PRAY: God connect with me here, as I seek you in your Word.

READ: Colossians 3.1-10 — Nothing can bring about a more radical shift than when a person gives his or her life to Christ. In today's reading the apostle Paul describes the changes that occur when a person becomes a Christian. The way Paul describes it, turning away from the old self and embracing the new person – going from sinfulness to righteousness – is almost like changing clothes. Christians should be recognizable by the "clothing" of the new self: compassion, kindness, humility, gentleness, patience, forgiveness and love. Of course we all know what it means to be compassionate, kind, humble and so on. The key is making a conscious decision to demonstrate these qualities to others every day.

If you're at a loss as to how and to whom you can demonstrate these qualities, start with simple gestures. Befriend the lonely coworker. Show kindness to family members. Be a visible light of compassion in a world of darkness. It's a style that never goes out of fashion.

REFLECT: Are you all cleaned up and ready for God to use you for every good work? If not, spend some time in prayer confessing your sins and thanking Him for cleansing you and filling you. Ask God to give you an opportunity to be used for His glory today.

RESPOND: Ask God to help you take off the old and put on the new nature and to show your changed heart in a meaningful way to others.

Lord, I pray that I can be a source of encouragement to someone today, in your Name.

TO KNOW MORE:
Psalm 16 and Romans 8 \\

Day 266 | *Strength*

PRAY: God connect with me here, as I seek you in your Word.

READ: Judges 16.15-17 — Samson would be quite a celebrity if he lived in our culture. Agents would beat a path to his door, clamoring for book and movie rights to his life story. He would make the talk show circuit, discussing again and again his superhuman feats – ripping apart a lion with his bare hands, lifting the city gates of Gaza and carrying them to the top of a nearby hill.

Samson's life, as judge over Israel for 20 years, highlights several important facts about God's dispensing of gifts. One is that He often gives them to flawed people. Another is that character does matter. God chose Samson before he was born. Samson had nothing to do with his calling – it was at God's initiation. The angel of the Lord shocked Samson's barren mother with an appearance, promising that she would bear a son who would rescue Israel from the Philistines. To fulfill that purpose, God gave Samson supernatural strength. One has to wonder how much greater Samson could have been and how much more good he could have done if only he had lived a righteous life.

REFLECT: God longs for people who will subject their desires to His will. Samson's last heroic feat, great as it was, pales in comparison to the humble deeds of service carried out by obedient, willing believers.

RESPOND: Ask God to increase your ability to appreciate all that He has given you and to strengthen your love for Him so that it is more powerful than your desire to do wrong.

Lord, I pray that you will strengthen me spiritually so that I can consistently serve you and your Kingdom.

TO KNOW MORE:
Proverbs 5 and John 14 \\

Day 267 | *Anticipation*

PRAY: God connect with me here, as I seek you in your Word.

READ: Leviticus 19.23-25 — Do you remember the excitement of sitting next to your family's Christmas tree when you were a child? Surrounded by presents and beautifully decorated, it seemed to invite you to open every gift under its branches. Yet you knew it was better to wait patiently until Christmas morning. In verses 23-25 of Leviticus 19, God commanded His people to wait five years before eating any fruit from trees they planted in the Promised Land. Why the wait? Because the yield would be increased (v. 25). God knew branches have to grow before fruit appears. By the fourth year, enough fruit had grown for the people to give it all back to God as an expression of praise (v. 24). Finally, in the fifth year, there was plenty to eat.

Notice God's commands in these verses. After waiting three years, Israel spent another whole year giving thanks to Him. Like the trees in Leviticus 19, you may be going through a time of waiting and growing. This is a time to learn God's Word and talk to Him in prayer. God has work for you to do. He promises this. But while you're waiting, don't be lazy. Think of all the praising you've got to do! It may be as simple as thanking Him for being alive or for all the things He's given you. If you spend time getting to know God and praising Him, He promises to increase your yield for Him.

REFLECT: Waiting for fruit to grow takes patience. God wanted the waiting to be a time to praise Him for His generosity. And God wants you to wait as well. When it seems like He is not hearing your prayers, wait patiently. The bounty of His blessing will be worth the wait!

RESPOND: Pray that as you follow God today, He will increase your patience and trust in Him.

Lord, I pray that you will give me a patient heart and I thank you for the many blessings you have given me in the past and will faithfully supply me in the future.

TO KNOW MORE:
Jeremiah 9 and Acts 7 \\

Day 268 | *Control*

PRAY: God connect with me here, as I seek you in your Word.

READ: Exodus 10.13-17 — Today's passage is about an ecological disaster that happened in Egypt. Looking at these verses, we see that God can cause natural disasters to accomplish His will. Pharaoh had received numerous and clear warnings, but he chose to defy them. God thus showed the Egyptian ruler His great power to soften his hard heart.

But disasters can result from natural causes as well. For example, some countries experience starvation because humans have harmed the environment. By encouraging soil erosion and crop failure, they have created disasters that have harmed millions. Because the world is fallen and sinful, people will suffer, even the innocent.

People caught up in blaming God for random disasters often fail to see God at work in the middle of the suffering. He works through His children, showing mercy and healing to the helpless.

REFLECT: Rather than questioning God when natural disasters strike, we should reflect on our own actions and responses. We should be willing to help, in ways both large and small.

RESPOND: Pray for Christian organizations involved in disaster relief that they might have the funds, staff and volunteers to make a difference in the lives of those impacted.

Lord, I pray for ministries that are reaching out to those suffering due to a disaster that has befallen them, especially (Organization).

TO KNOW MORE:
Psalm 148 and Matthew 8 \\

Day 269 | *Trusting*

PRAY: God connect with me here, as I seek you in your Word.

READ: Matthew 6.25-34 — Are you a worrier? Everyone is, to one degree or another. Unfortunately, life gives us plenty to worry about. Job assignments. Challenges at home. Saving money to fix a leaky roof. And what about an impending physical exam? A new boss? A strange clicking from your car's engine?

It's easy to find something to worry about every waking moment, isn't it? Is that good? We discover what Jesus had to say in today's reading. The people Jesus was talking to had to worry about the basics of life – food, clothing and shelter. Life was pretty rough then. But Jesus knew that worry didn't help. Why waste time and energy worrying about the needs God has already promised He'd meet? Besides, it's unhealthy and unproductive and it keeps us from trusting God. In short, absolutely nothing good comes from worry.

REFLECT: So how do we break the bonds of worry in our lives? It boils down to faith. Those who don't believe in God have every reason to worry. They haven't put their trust in the God who cares for them. But Jesus challenges us to live differently. He says, "Your heavenly Father already knows your needs and He will faithfully meet them." All we have to do is trust and obey.

RESPOND: Pray that your faith will increase in the God who provides everything you need forever.

Lord, I pray you will give me a spirit of confidence as I trust in you to meet my daily needs.

TO KNOW MORE:
Mark 4 and Hebrews 13 \\

Day 270 | *Money*

PRAY: God connect with me here, as I seek you in your Word.

READ: Luke 16.1-9 — Imagine you've just become the manager of a new health food store. Business is sluggish so you decide on an aggressive sales campaign: You discount every product to the bone for one weekend only. You're anxious to get customers and are willing to take the risk. And it works! People come from miles around and buy out your inventory. The owner is so encouraged he gives you a big raise.

We can use money in three basic ways: (1) We can spend it to fulfill our basic needs, such as food, shelter and clothing; (2) we can use it to satisfy needs – some of them important, some trivial; or (3) we can give it away to help others. With that in mind, carefully examine in the days ahead the way you spend your money.

REFLECT: Here are a couple of questions to ask yourself about money: First, do you demonstrate with your resources that you can be trusted with greater responsibilities? Second, what changes can you make in your spending in order to invest more in God's Kingdom?

RESPOND: Ask God to help you become a wise steward of the money and material possessions He has blessed you with.

Lord, thank you for your many blessings – may I use them wisely and for the benefit of your Kingdom.

TO KNOW MORE:
Romans 14 and 1 Peter 4 \\

Day 271 | *Impactful*

PRAY: God connect with me here, as I seek you in your Word.

READ: John 17.9-19 — Aside from Jesus, name five people whose actions, accomplishments or lives have changed the world. Can you think of five off the top of your head? How about Alexander the Great, Copernicus, Galileo, Albert Einstein and Dr. Martin Luther King Jr.? It would be interesting to compare lists with other people. Of course, it's quite possible that we're not even aware of the five people who have changed the world most profoundly. After all, who's to say what actions are actually responsible for a change?

Jesus calls each of His followers to impact the world. In John 17, He offered a fairly detailed prayer for His disciples and their future work. In praying for them, Jesus clarified the Christian's relationship with and responsibility to the world. Even though believers live in this fallen place, we are not of it. Such a contrast may seem confusing but our eternal home is in heaven while our work is right here on earth.

REFLECT: Jesus spoke the prayer in John 17 as He anticipated his arrest and crucifixion. Jesus gave Himself entirely so that we might belong to the Father. Such faithfulness has had a bigger impact than the most exciting worldly achievements ever made.

RESPOND: Ask God to help you recognize the great sacrifice Jesus made on your behalf. Then seek His help as you try to impact the world for the sake of His Kingdom.

Lord, I praise you for all you have done for me and I ask that you will guide me as I seek to serve you and fulfill your purposes on earth.

TO KNOW MORE:
Luke 22 and Revelation 20 \\

Day 272 | *Choices*

PRAY: God connect with me here, as I seek you in your Word.

READ: Esther 4.15-17 — If you've ever read the book of Esther, you know the end of the story. God put Esther in a position of influence. He then used her uncle, Mordecai, to speak words of truth and conviction. Finally, Esther's courage saved the Jewish people. It's a great story with a happy ending. But before all the smiles and hugs and pats on the back, there were some tense and scary moments.

Chances are you will never face the awesome responsibility of trying to save an entire nation. But you do face tough choices all the time: Will you look out only for yourself, or also for others? Will you use your gifts and abilities to serve God and others, even when it's risky? Always listen to the still small voice of God rather than the suggestions of friends and family or your own pounding heart.

REFLECT: Like Esther, you can have a positive impact on those around you. But to do this you will need to make seeking and following God your top priority. You will need others praying for you (as Esther had "all the Jews of Susa" remembering her before God). And you will need someone in your life like Mordecai—someone who can challenge you to do right when you're scared and leaning the other way. Who knows? By living in such a fashion, God may use you to make a huge difference in the lives of those who are right on the edge.

RESPOND: Ask God to show you situations—large or small—where you have the ability and the opportunity to bring about change. Trust Him for the courage to do what's right regardless of the circumstances.

Lord, I pray you will give me the courage to do what is right and just at all times, regardless of how it will affect me.

TO KNOW MORE:
Luke 22 and Revelation 20 \\

Day 273 | *Hungry*

PRAY: God connect with me here, as I seek you in your Word.

READ: Deuteronomy 8.1-3 — So often when a person who has been successful at something for a long time and is asked how they maintain their drive, they'll answer, "I simply stay hungry." The dictionary defines hunger as "a strong desire or craving." So, in essence, many people define hunger as being eager for new challenges in their work and in their lives.

Today's passage is also about being hungry. But the hunger God speaks of is a craving that everyone should have. These verses tell how God allowed His people to go hungry in the wilderness and then how He met their need for food. But more important, the passage shows how He used their hunger to teach them an essential lesson – a lesson that is just as vital to us today. You see, they had a hunger even greater than the hunger for food. They had a hunger for God. And this hunger is present in every person and can only be satisfied by a relationship with Jesus Christ.

REFLECT: Sometimes being well fed and having plenty can cause people to ignore their spiritual hunger. Reading God's Word, fellowshipping with other Christians and sharing God's love are all ways to keep your spirit growing and healthy.

RESPOND: Seek to take God's Word into your soul today through careful study and prayerful thought. Pray that His words will nourish you and cause you to grow.

Lord, I pray you will nourish me with your Word and fill me with your Holy Spirit so I will have the spiritual strength to accomplish all you have set before me.

TO KNOW MORE:
Psalm 119 and 1 Thessalonians 4 \\

Day 274 | *Perspective*

PRAY: God connect with me here, as I seek you in your Word.

READ: Philippians 4.10-14 — Malcolm Muggeridge, the famous British journalist who became a Christian late in life, spent several years in India. His keen eye noticed a quality among the people in India that contrasted sharply with those who live in the West. He wrote: "They were all so poor; they all had so very little. Anyone from the West was a sort of millionaire by comparison . . . When floods came and they had to leave their homes, they could comfortably carry all they possessed on their heads: a tin box, a mat, some cooking vessels, no more. They had no sales potential; the siren voices recommending eating this, wearing that, urging them to consume. Their poverty immunized them against the chief sickness of the age. Perhaps it is in this that the blessedness of the poor – the least appreciated of the Beatitudes today – resides."

The apostle Paul knew the blessedness of having little. Obviously, he discovered and practiced the secret of contentment. And you know what that is? The power to decide to be positive in all circumstances. That's it. Such a little thing but such a major impact.

REFLECT: It's all a matter of perspective, isn't it? We can whine and complain that we don't have enough, or we can decide to be content – as Paul told us in v.13 – through Christ who gives us the strength we need. He lives within you and He's able, willing and waiting.

RESPOND: Prayerfully evaluate what areas of your life make you feel unsatisfied. Confess these and ask God to help you decide to be content.

Lord, you have given me so much – may I be happy in all circumstances and content in every situation.

TO KNOW MORE:
Hosea 14 and Galatians 6 \\

Day 275 | *Attributes*

PRAY: God connect with me here, as I seek you in your Word.

READ: 1 Corinthians 1.26 — Fame ... power ... wealth. These are the human attributes and distinctions that our culture admires and glorifies. Those who possess any of these characteristics are accepted anywhere and are always treated with special care. They are also considered ideal neighbours, friends and church members because their prestige and glory reflect on those around them.

God cherishes qualities in a person that have absolutely nothing to do with superficial, human values. Yet so often we critically judge others because he or she isn't successful or attractive or popular. Look with God's perspective. Is he kind? Is she generous? Does he share the love of Christ with others? These are the qualities that make a person truly great.

REFLECT: It's easy to be drawn to those who have an abundance of qualities and gifts the world admires – just as it's not difficult to ignore those who have few advantages and are generally shunned by others. Is this an attitude that is pleasing to God? Did Jesus turn His back on "the least" among us or did He comfort them, help them and enjoy their fellowship?

RESPOND: Compliment someone you know who isn't often praised or affirmed – point out the positive attributes you admire most about his or her character.

Lord, I pray you will help me not to judge others according to the world's temporary and ultimately meaningless standards.

TO KNOW MORE:
Zephaniah 3 and James 3 \\

Day 276 | *Sharing*

PRAY: God connect with me here, as I seek you in your Word.

READ: Exodus 12.1-5 — Have you ever had to carry something heavy by yourself? And just as you were ready to drop it, someone came along to help? Or perhaps you had a project to do at your job and you were stuck. Then a coworker offered to help you. How did it feel? Like a heavy load was lifted off of you? Well, that's the way it is with sharing. God commands us to share so that we can help each other with the heavy loads we all bear.

In today's passage we discover the types of things God wants us to share. These few verses tell us a great deal about God's nature. Notice that God is the one who told the people to share. He required such sharing because he knew it would be difficult for smaller families to afford a lamb. God is in the business of lightening loads, not adding to them. These verses should encourage us to share our resources as well: money, time, talents and material possessions.

REFLECT: God commands believers to share each other's burdens. People all over the world need encouragement and help. God commands us to share. So it is not a question of "Do you share?" but rather "What do you share and with whom?"

RESPOND: Pray that God will give you eyes to see people in need and a heart to share with them.

Lord, I pray you will show me how to help those who need someone to join them in sharing their burdens.

TO KNOW MORE:
2 Chronicles 35 and John 12 \\

Day 277 | *Plan*

PRAY: God connect with me here, as I seek you in your Word.

READ: Galatians 1.4 — "God has a plan for your life." There are many popular books, Sunday school resources and church conferences that focus on this theme. Generally these revolve around subjects like career paths, relationships and Christian outreach activities. Today's verse, though, deals with the ultimate "plan" – salvation.

God's plan was always to offer humanity a perfect source of deliverance from our sins through the death and resurrection of His Son, Jesus Christ. As a result, we have been rescued from the power of this evil world – a world ruled by Satan and filled with cruelty, tragedy, temptation and despair. Being saved from the powers of darkness doesn't mean that we are taken out of all the messes caused by sin, however, but that it no longer has any real power over us. We have been saved to live holy lives for God and compassionate lives for others. And, thankfully, our salvation includes a promise of eternity with our Saviour.

REFLECT: Helping others meet their physical needs is vitally important and should be part of every Christian's personal ministry. But it's God's plan that we share the good news of salvation with them as well. After all, eternity is a long time and sharing our faith is the most loving gesture of all.

RESPOND: Dedicate your life to the Lord and seek His wisdom each day so that your steps will be guided toward righteousness and compassion.

Lord, thank you for sending your Son, Jesus Christ, to die for my sins and the sins of the world – may I be a witness to others of your mercy.

TO KNOW MORE:
Psalm 72 and Romans 12 \\

Day 278 | Refugees

PRAY: God connect with me here, as I seek you in your Word.

READ: Luke 6.20-26 — Refugees from a ravaged, war-torn land are camped in a dense area, seeking one thing: survival. The smell of hopelessness and meaninglessness and victimization hang in the air like a fog. The lack of dignity hovers there, too, along with a complete loss of identity, significance and hope. The desperation is almost palpable.

This scenario plays out too often around the world. We can nearly be overwhelmed by the global despair of the countless innocent people who suffer daily. Fortunately, however, Christ brings hope to the refugees of this world, as promised in today's reading. You can see it if you've ever visited a refugee camp. Sorrow and pain still exist, but those who have placed their trust in the One who truly saves have a sense of peace and determination that doesn't exist otherwise. They may have nothing but the clothes they are wearing and their only food source is through relief agencies. But in their eyes exists a glimmer of hope because Christ has promised them that one day soon their tears will be turned into laughter and their uncertainty will be replaced with joy.

REFLECT: God does indeed provide blessings for the poor and hungry. Many of His promises will come true only in His future heavenly Kingdom. But even today, on this often cruel planet, His inner riches can make an intolerable situation bearable. Among poverty and pain, God can still provide satisfaction and joy. The refugees and poor of this world only need to be told of the One who freely provides these gifts. And this can only be done through those who care enough to tell them.

RESPOND: Hopelessness is a terrible thing. But the glimmer of hope brings joy. Only Christ can provide that glimmer,.

Lord, I pray for the refugees of this world and I ask that you will give me opportunities to share what I have with them through the Christian relief agencies and missionary societies serving their needs.

TO KNOW MORE: Isaiah 29 and James 1 \\

Day 279 | *Babylon*

PRAY: God connect with me here, as I seek you in your Word.

READ: Revelation 18.7 — Babylon. The very name stirs images of decadence and carnality and corruption. In today's verse we read that Babylon boasted, "I am queen upon my throne . . . I will not experience sorrow." The powerful, wealthy people of this world are susceptible to this same attitude. A person who is financially comfortable often feels invulnerable, secure and in control. They have no need of God or anyone else.

This type of attitude defies God, and God's judgment against it is often harsh. If you are financially secure, don't become complacent or deluded by the myth of self-sufficiency. Instead, use your resources to help others and advance God's Kingdom.

REFLECT: In Isaiah 47.10-11a we read, "You hid behind evil like a shield and said, 'No one can see me!' You were fooled by your wisdom and your knowledge; you felt sure that you alone were in full control. But without warning, disaster will strike" (CEV). The truth is that while the world may be unaware of our actions, God knows all that we do, think and say. Purify your heart by daily turning to God's Word and prayerfully responding to the calling of His Holy Spirit.

RESPOND: While pride, godlessness and self-glorification characterized the citizens of Babylon, be known for your kindness, generosity and faithfulness — virtues that gain treasures in heaven that will never fade or die away.

Lord, thank you for the resources you have given me and I pray that you will help me avoid the temptation to become blindly self-assured and self-centered.

TO KNOW MORE:
Psalm 45 and 2 Thessalonians 2 \\

Day 280 | *Fairness*

PRAY: God connect with me here, as I seek you in your Word.

READ: Leviticus 14.21-22 — That's not fair! How many times have you heard someone say this? Better yet, how many times have you thought or said it? Most of us have a good sense of what's fair and what's not. Sometimes, however, we fail to understand what God considers just and reasonable. Take, for instance, God's instructions for the Israelites who had been cured of a contagious skin disease. The payment varied according to a person's financial status, as we see in today's reading.

In ancient Israel, diseases made a person ceremonially unclean. God required all of His people, regardless of status, to make an offering before they could rejoin their community. However, He made special provisions for the poor: If you can't afford two lambs then bring one. This was the essence of God's instructions.

God doesn't issue commands without considering who we are and the circumstances we face. His wisdom produces a fair judgment. He knows us intimately—even down to the number of hairs on our heads (Matthew 10.30). He knows everything about our past and present situation and has prepared a glorious hope for our future. When we trust His divine wisdom and obey His commands, we gain His blessing.

REFLECT: Fairness is a relative concept. Our assessment of what's fair is based on what happens to others in similar circumstances. But when you trust in God's divine wisdom, you won't worry about what He requires of or gives to other people.

RESPOND: Make an effort to pray more specifically for people you see every day. Learn about their particular needs and concerns and pray they will receive all that God desires for them.

Lord, help me not to look jealously at what others have but to consider their needs and to be grateful for the many blessings you have given me.

TO KNOW MORE:
Proverbs 17 and Luke 6 \\

Day 281 | *Distortions*

PRAY: God connect with me here, as I seek you in your Word.

READ: Luke 15.1-7 — Imagine that every wall you faced was lined with funhouse mirrors–the kind that distort your features. Every time you looked up the image you saw was twisted and distended in an unnatural way. If you saw this every day you might begin to believe this is what you looked like. If nobody ever told you the truth, you'd live your entire life thinking you were different from other people, simply because you had a distorted self-image.

In today's reading we see that tax collectors in Jesus' day had a reputation for being corrupt. That's why the Pharisees and the teachers of the law complained when Jesus shared a meal with such "sinners." The Pharisees wondered why Jesus associated with such people when He could have been spending time with religious leaders and teachers of the Law. Today's parable shows how deeply God cares for those who are lost. No matter how far a person strays into sin, the Lord will look for him or her. If and when that person is found, all heaven rejoices. That's why it's important for us to join the "search party" for those who don't yet know Jesus as their Saviour.

REFLECT: Like the Pharisees, some Christians today have a tendency to isolate themselves from undesirable and obvious sinners–despite the fact that these are the people who need to hear of Jesus' love the most. Jesus set the example. He didn't spend His time on earth preaching to the Pharisees and other religious leaders. He met "sinners" where they lived. In order to follow Christ's example, we need to break out of our comfort zones and learn to approach people–all people–with God's message of hope.

RESPOND: Ask God to help expand your circle of acquaintances to include people you might normally not associate with while at the same time maintaining a strong Christian witness.

Lord, help me to be a witness to those who need you most and not to allow my preconceived judgments keep me from sharing your love.

TO KNOW MORE:
Ezekiel 18 and Romans 5 \\

Day 282 | *Roots*

PRAY: God connect with me here, as I seek you in your Word.

READ: Colossians 2.6-7 — Are you a gardener? Or do you just like to eat the bounty that comes from gardens? In either case, you know the dining pleasure that can only be found in a plate full of colourful vegetables. In today's passage, Paul describes the survival and growth of plants to illustrate the relationship Christians should have with their Saviour. Just as a flower draws nourishment from the soil through its roots, so we receive our life-giving strength from the Lord. The more we draw life from Him, the less we will be fooled by those who wrongly claim to have all the answers.

Throughout your life you have no doubt received advice and counsel from many different people—each with unique life experiences and points of view. Be sure to always use Scripture and the guidance of the Holy Spirit to judge what they say. While godly people can be used in a wonderful way to advise and encourage others, your first source of spiritual nourishment must be from the One who died on the cross for your sins.

REFLECT: Each of us have many opportunities throughout our lives to be the one who provides "counsel and encouragement" to others. Just as you should judge all advice you receive according to the Word of God, be sure you are offering solutions to others that are grounded in the pages of Scripture.

RESPOND: Ask God to guide you daily in your words and deeds so you can be a true spiritual blessing to those around you.

Lord, help me to grow stronger each day in my faith and commitment to you so that I can share your message of love and hope with others.

TO KNOW MORE:
Micah 4 and Colossians 3 \\

Day 283 | Responses

PRAY: God connect with me here, as I seek you in your Word.

READ: Job 16.1-16 — Perhaps you've worked for a boss with a one-size-fits-all approach. In every situation he or she has the same reaction. Criticism. Complaints. Disdainful looks. No matter what you do or how hard you try, you always know what's coming. On the other hand, you probably know bosses who are master motivators. They can tailor their comments to the needs of the moment. Today a person needs a word of encouragement. Tomorrow that same person may need to be pushed a bit to meet a deadline. To bring out the best in people takes wisdom to know how to respond to moods and situations.

The story of Job and his "comforters" is a good lesson on how to relate to those who are grieving. We need to be extremely sensitive in such situations. We need to guard against speaking an endless flow of words—especially foolish words that are not prayerfully and Scripturally grounded.

REFLECT: It's important to listen and share the pain of those facing trials. Eventually we may have to speak hard words, but we should never be eager to chastise with the "truth." Don't criticize someone until you have first cried with and for that person.

RESPOND: If you are suffering, pray for some truly wise people in your life. If you see suffering in others, pray for the opportunity to bring comfort and support to them.

Lord, I pray you will give me the opportunity to share the peace that can only come from you with someone who needs encouragement.

TO KNOW MORE:
Psalm 69 and Philippians 1 \\

Day 284 | *Jubilee*

PRAY: God connect with me here, as I seek you in your Word.

READ: Leviticus 25.1-7; 20-22 — In today's passage God told the Israelites to rest and enjoy His blessings and share these gifts with others. The Sabbath of complete rest for the land came every seven years. "Don't plant your crops or prune your vineyards during that entire year," God said. The Year of Jubilee marked the passing of seven Sabbath years – 49 in total. The Jubilee year followed the seventh Sabbath year. That meant there were two consecutive rest years. How could the people eat during this time? Because God promised enough for everyone – even for those considered to be the least in that culture: the slaves, servants and foreigners. Verse 21 highlights this promise.

So what does all this have to do with us today? First, we should thank God for His provision. Living in one of the world's richest countries, God has given us so much more than we need. Second, like the Israelites in Leviticus, we should rest in the promise that He will keep providing for us. Third, share with others. That includes loving and feeding the "least" among us.

REFLECT: When we love people who don't fit in our group or are hard to get along with, we are doing exactly what Jesus did for us. The first Christians came into a faith that started in the Jewish religion. They didn't fit. Today, people of many races and backgrounds believe in Christ. Paul says in the New Testament that we are "no longer strangers and foreigners" but now we rest in Christ and His forgiveness..

RESPOND: Thank God for all He has given you. Ask Him to open your heart to others to help meet their needs.

Lord, thank you for your many blessings – may I be a blessing to others out of the abundance you've given me.

TO KNOW MORE:
Exodus 19 and Galatians 4 \\

Day 285 | *Compromise*

PRAY: God connect with me here, as I seek you in your Word.

READ: Galatians 2.11 — The Judaizers accused Paul of watering down the Gospel to make it easier for Gentiles to accept. At the same time Paul accused the Judaizers of nullifying the truth of the Gospel by adding conditions to it. The argument came to a head when Peter, Paul, the Judaizers and some Gentile Christians all gathered together in Antioch to share a meal. Peter probably thought that by staying aloof from the Gentiles he was promoting harmony – he did not want to offend the friends of James. But Paul charged that Peter's action violated the Gospel. By joining the Judaizers Peter implicitly supported their claim that Christ was not sufficient for salvation.

Compromise is an important part of getting along with others, but we should never concede the truth of God's Word. If we feel as though we have to change our Christian beliefs to match those of our companions, we are on dangerous ground spiritually.

REFLECT: Know which battles are worth fighting. It's important to maintain your convictions but remember that those who don't know the Lord are watching to see what makes your life different. Let your actions be a blessing and witness to everyone you meet or associate with. They may not agree with you but they will respect your sincerity and be more likely to listen when you present the Gospel to them.

RESPOND: Lord, help me to never waver in my convictions as you give me opportunities to show your love and patience to others.

TO KNOW MORE:
Jeremiah 1 and 2 Corinthians 5 \\

Day 286 | *Shocking*

PRAY: God connect with me here, as I seek you in your Word.

READ: Proverbs 10.10 — Do you remember the first time you saw an old horror movie on late night television as a kid? You didn't notice that the picture was grainy, the sound fuzzy, the plot inconsistent and the sets thrown together. The plastic fangs and overacted shrieks seemed all too real, and you probably spent the night shivering under your covers and catching your breath at the slightest sound.

It seems strange, doesn't it, that if you saw the same movie today it would likely have no effect on you other than to inspire a nostalgic smile? Over the years, you've seen so many dreadful things—both real and fictional—that your sense of what's shocking has been dulled. The same is true with sin. Repeated exposure to a sinful attitude or habit soon leads to acceptance and, frequently, participation—whether it's a moral failure or a willful disregard for the needs of others. Don't fall victim to this destructive spiral. If someone in your life has a sinful habit—like a family member or a close friend—confront that person in love. It's the best thing you can do . . . for both of you!

REFLECT: As Christians, when we openly "wink" at sin it's a sign that we don't take it seriously, that we'd rather be well liked than to risk being considered judgmental. And, when we turn away from doing the right thing with a shrug of our shoulders because it's too much trouble to become involved, we give our unspoken approval to the sin. It's important to stand firm in our convictions and to not let our disregard for sin become part of its support.

RESPOND: Ask God to help you be a positive influence on others and that you will support righteousness and mercy at all times.

Lord, forgive me when I've shown apathy in the face of immorality and injustice and may my life be a light for others to see your compassion and holiness.

TO KNOW MORE:
Psalm 35 and 3 John 1 \\

Day 287 | *Pennies*

PRAY: God connect with me here, as I seek you in your Word.

READ: Luke 21.1-4 — Today's reading tells this story of a woman dropping a Roman lepta or mite (a coin worth about two cents) into a Temple treasury box. Her generosity revealed that Jesus has a unique way of measuring giving. According to this story, affluent people who give their leftovers do not touch the heart of God so much as an old woman on Social Security who drops a dollar bill into the offering plate. Jesus is saying the real issue isn't the amount we give, but the attitude with which we give it.

Think about it. If a millionaire gives $50,000 to the church missions fund, everyone oohs and aahs. Certainly this is a sizeable amount of money, but it's not a very sacrificial gift. (It's not hard to imagine living on $950,000!) But suppose a retiree with only $10 to his name – money that needs to last until the end of the week – gives that money to the missions campaign. Do you see that he has made an incredible offering to God? Not big in terms of monetary value, but huge in terms of devotion and love. And that's the kind of gift God wants from each of us.

REFLECT: Sacrifice means being willing to do without. It also means giving up control. Mary Rhodes gave $1,000 to help build an inner-city gym. This sum was a drop in the bucket in terms of the total amount needed, but it was nearly everything she had. And when she gave her money to the building effort, she gave up her say on how it was to be used from that point on. That kind of "no strings attached" giving pleases God.

RESPOND: What we do with our material wealth is a very good test of our spiritual health. How we treat money speaks volumes about what we truly believe. Take time to evaluate the condition of your heart in terms of what the ultimate priorities in your life truly are.

Lord, help me to be like the widow in Luke 21 – a selfless, sacrificial, generous giver.

TO KNOW MORE: Nehemiah 13 and John 8 \\

Day 288 | *Sorry*

PRAY: God connect with me here, as I seek you in your Word.

READ: Numbers 5.5-10 — "I'm sorry." How many times a week do you hear or say that sentence? People use this phrase to cover a multitude of offenses—anything from "I'm sorry I stepped on your foot" to "I'm sorry I told everyone the secret you asked me not to share."

But what does it mean to be truly sorry? As you might guess, the Bible has a lot to say about the way we should respond when we wrong others. As the Israelites camped in the wilderness after their exodus from Egypt, God gave them specific instructions as to what they should do after committing an offense against another person.

In God's system, "I'm sorry" isn't good enough. When we sin against another person, our first responsibility is to confess the sin and ask for forgiveness. Our second responsibility is to make full compensation or repayment to that person. Suddenly "I'm sorry I ran over your mailbox" becomes "Here's the money to buy a new one and have it put in." It's only when we are willing to make complete restitution that we demonstrate our regrets and our desire to restore relationships.

REFLECT: The principle of making amends is especially important when the wronged are the poor and needy of our society. Think of the many ways in which the less fortunate are taken advantage of or exploited. When we hear of such mistreatment, we may feel twinges of guilt—especially if we've knowingly (or even unknowingly) been involved. But guess what? Guilt is not enough. We need to make good on our apologies in tangible, measurable ways.

RESPOND: Ask God to help you recall people who deserve to be paid back for wrongs you've done them. Then ask Him for the courage and wisdom to make the situation right.

Lord, help me to always have the courage to admit the things I've done that have caused others sorrow or loss.

TO KNOW MORE: Joshua 7 and Luke 19 \\

Day 289 | *Fads*

PRAY: God connect with me here, as I seek you in your Word.

READ: Matthew 13.44 — Have you ever been swept up in the momentum created by a new fad? One day you're a normal, sane person who goes to work, putters in the garden and shops for groceries. The next day you can't stop talking or thinking about the latest hot phone app, a hit song or an amazing new fusion cuisine. The thing about fads is that their meteoric rise in popularity is exceeded only by their speedy fall off the cultural "heat index."

Actually, in the scope of eternity, everything is faddish. Everything that is, except for the Kingdom of Heaven. How we honour God and the way we treat those around us, especially the less fortunate, is what truly matters in life. And reflecting the love of Christ is a never ending "fad" that's been reshaping lives for more than 2,000 years.

REFLECT: Are you placing emphasis on the things that matter? Do you spend more time finding new ways to make your life exciting and amusing than you do reading the Bible and praying? If so, it's time to dramatically adjust where you place God in your life. Only He can give you the unending peace that comes from a meaningful life.

RESPOND: Evaluate your priorities and begin building your life around eternal things that matter the most.

Lord, place in my heart a desire for things that are truly meaningful and keep my thoughts focused on the eternal rather than the momentary.

TO KNOW MORE:
Proverbs 2 and Hebrews 11 \\

Day 290 | *Distractions*

PRAY: God connect with me here, as I seek you in your Word.

READ: 2 Corinthians 11.2 — As Paul was writing his second letter to the church in Corinth, he knew that their pure and simple devotion was being threatened by false teaching. While he didn't want the believers to lose their single-minded love for Jesus, he also understood human nature. Paul knew that keeping Christ first in our lives can sometimes be very difficult – especially when we have so many distractions threatening to sidetrack our faith.

Just as Eve lost her focus by listening to the serpent and David turned from the path of righteousness when he saw Bathsheba, we too can lose direction by letting our lives become overcrowded and confused. In other words, we can soon abandon the two great commandments of Jesus found in Matthew 22.35-40 – to love God with our entire being and to love our neighbours as ourselves.

REFLECT: Is there anything that threatens your willingness to keep Christ first in your life? Ask yourself, "How can I minimize the distractions that threaten my devotion to the One who gave His life to save mine"?

RESPOND: Remember when you accepted Jesus as your Saviour and gave Him supremacy over your life? It may be time to recommit yourself to placing Him first in your heart, mind and home.

Lord, I offer my love and devotion to you and ask that you will help me seek your will in all things.

TO KNOW MORE:
Isaiah 54 and Ephesians 5 \\

Day 291 | *Priorities*

PRAY: God connect with me here, as I seek you in your Word.

READ: John 12.1-8 — One of the most amazing acts of faith in all of Scripture is found in John 12. In this passage, Mary took a jar of expensive perfume, anointed Jesus' feet and wiped them with her hair. This drew the ire of Judas, who was watching with disdain. Of course, not only was Judas the most notorious traitor in history, he was also a fledgling scam artist. As the keeper of the money for the disciples, Judas was the one who collected the offerings given by Jesus' followers. Despite his pious behavior, Judas had apparently made a habit of skimming money from the bag for his personal use.

Mary's unusual and very expensive gesture was not very "religious" according to the customs of the day (or, for that matter, by today's standards either), but it showed clearly that her heart was dedicated fully to the Lord. So, even if Judas' objections concerning the poor had been sincere, he still would have been wrong to question Mary's singular act of love.

REFLECT: Mary's unmistakable devotion should cause us to examine ourselves. Are we willing to give our all to Jesus? If we minister to others for any other reason than our love for God, we will always miss the mark.

RESPOND: Spend some time in prayer showing the same type of adoration for the Lord that Mary revealed when she washed Jesus' feet.

Lord, I pray that I will always place you first in my life and that my actions will consistently demonstrate my love for you.

TO KNOW MORE:
Song of Songs 4 and Matthew 21 \\

Day 292 | *Blessings*

PRAY: God connect with me here, as I seek you in your Word.

READ: Numbers 24.5-7 — From today's reading, we understand that Balak, the king of Moab, was determined to hold onto the land he thought was his. But he was so scared of the Israelites that he hired a sorcerer named Balaam to put a curse on God's chosen people. What Balak didn't count on was God's interference. God refused to allow Balaam to curse Israel. Every time he tried, the curse came out as a blessing. According to Balaam, the Israelites were looking at a prosperous life in the Promised Land. All they had to do was remain faithful to God.

This is not to say that being faithful guarantees material wealth. It doesn't (ask any pastor or worship leader). Yes, God is the source of all blessings and there are faithful men and women who are both godly and wealthy. But the important blessings God bestows on His people are spiritual. The rewards and treasures that await all of us are in heaven where "moths and rust" cannot destroy them.

REFLECT: We must remain faithful to God, not for the material benefits we will reap but for the eternal joys that await us.

RESPOND: Thank God for bestowing daily blessings on your life and for His promise of an eternal home with Him.

Lord, thank you for your many blessings and for your promise of eternal joy in your presence.

TO KNOW MORE:
Joel 3 and John 1 \\

Day 293 | *Humbleness*

PRAY: God connect with me here, as I seek you in your Word.

READ: 1 Peter 5.5 — Have you ever gone to someone older for advice, fully expecting that they will listen patiently and give you a few words of wisdom and encouragement? What if they laughed in your face, instead? You'd probably feel a range of emotions—from embarrassment to irritation to exasperation. And, conversely, what if you kindly offered to share a few quiet words with a younger person but were scornfully rebuffed? You weren't trying to be intrusive; you simply wanted to show that you cared.

The truth is that no one, young or old, has much tolerance for a person who is contemptuous toward the sincere and earnestly expressed needs or concerns of others. Perhaps this is why we read in Proverbs 3.34 that God "mocks proud mockers but shows favour to the humble and oppressed" (NIV). If you find yourself in a position where you are either asking for godly advice or sharing biblical wisdom, remember to do so with the same respect you expect from others—and that you always receive from the Lord.

REFLECT: Pride often keeps elders from trying to understand young people and young people from listening to their elders. Peter told both young and old to be humble and to serve each other.

RESPOND: If you are a young person who needs direction, seek out an experienced elder in your church who has successfully navigated through life's many storms. If you are a mature person, share your wisdom so the next generation can be encouraged by your concern for them and by the work God has done in and through you.

Lord, instill within me a humble heart so that I can both learn and lead as I share in the abundant Christian relationships you have placed in my life.

TO KNOW MORE:
Psalm 132 and Romans 13 \\

Day 294 | *Heaven*

PRAY: God connect with me here, as I seek you in your Word.

READ: Mark 12.18-27 — Jesus said the Sadducees were ignorant of Scripture and, worse, that they didn't understand God's power. Heaven is far beyond our ability to comprehend or imagine (see Isaiah 64.4 and 1 Corinthians 2.9). We must be careful not to create foolish, mocking questions about Heaven that cannot be answered from our human perspective just to sound interesting or start an endless debate.

We need not be afraid of Heaven, though, because of what we don't know. Instead of wondering what God's coming Kingdom will be like, we should concentrate on our relationship with Jesus right now. All that matters is that when we are in the new Kingdom, we will be with Him. How we live now – and how we treat others, especially those less fortunate than ourselves – will make a great difference on the other side of eternity.

REFLECT: Jesus' statement does not mean that a person will not recognize his or her spouse in the coming Kingdom. It simply means that God's new order will not be an extension of this life – the same physical and natural rules won't apply. Our fallen, worldly relationships are limited by time, death and human institutions. But in God's new and restored world, our relationships will be eternal.

RESPOND: The best gift you can give someone today is to share this Good News.

Lord, keep my mind focused on things that are eternal – the things that truly matter – and give me the courage to share your saving gift of salvation through Jesus with others.

TO KNOW MORE:
Isaiah 25 and 2 Timothy 3 \\

Day 295 | *Guidance*

PRAY: God connect with me here, as I seek you in your Word.

READ: Proverbs 20.4-5 — "If you don't study, you'll fail the test." "If you don't save, you won't have money when you need it." "If you don't listen to good advice, you're going to repeat your mistakes." From the time you were a young child, you've heard warnings like these. But what about these words of counsel from Jesus: "Do not store up for yourselves treasures on earth, where moths and vermin destroy, and where thieves break in and steal. But store up for yourselves treasures in heaven, where moths and vermin do not destroy, and where thieves do not break in and steal" (NIV). Just as today's passage advises us to be earnest in our labours and thoughtful in our decisions, the work we do should have meaning and purpose for today, tomorrow and forever. As a result—and this always happens when we "do the right thing"—not only will we bring lasting hope into the lives of others, we also receive the reward of great personal joy and satisfaction.

REFLECT: God provides for us, but He also expects us to be responsible.

RESPOND: Don't take any blessing for granted in your life. Work hard. Work cheerfully and gratefully. And share your abundance with others who are struggling to overcome their circumstances. In the end, the seeds we plant and carefully tend for ourselves and others will grow and bloom.

Lord, thank you for your Word which gives each of us daily guidance for holy living and is an endless source of encouragement and hope.

TO KNOW MORE:
Psalm 64 and 1 Corinthians 2 \\

Day 296 | Denials

PRAY: God connect with me here, as I seek you in your Word.

READ: John 21.15-17 — The apostle Peter was no stranger to blunders. Yet, despite his penchant for putting his foot in his mouth, the Lord never gave up on him, as we see in today's reading. This is one of the most poignant reunions in all of Scripture. The last time Jesus and Peter spoke before Jesus' crucifixion, Peter had vowed to lay down his life for the Lord. Jesus told Peter that not only would he not lay down his life, on three separate occasions that very night he would actually deny even knowing Jesus. Shortly thereafter, Jesus was arrested and tried. During the trial, Peter was confronted three times by people who claimed he was one of Jesus' followers. Three times Peter denied knowing Him, just as Jesus had predicted. When Peter realized what he had done, the Bible says he "wept bitterly" (Luke 22.62). Imagine Peter's emotional state, then, as he was confronted by the resurrected Christ. Three times the Lord asks Peter if he loves Him. Three times Peter answers yes. Three times Jesus instructs Peter to feed or take care of His sheep. With this symbolic gesture, Jesus forgave Peter for his three denials and restored him to ministry.

REFLECT: Christians today are also called to feed Jesus' sheep, that is, take care of His people. Sometimes that care involves actually feeding people or providing food for needy families and the homeless. Sometimes it involves protecting and standing up for the rights of those who are exploited or powerless in our society.

RESPOND: Ask God to give you the wisdom and the opportunity to serve as a "shepherd" to someone, feeding (whether physically or spiritually) and taking care of that person according to Jesus' instructions to Peter in John 21.

Lord, help me to be a loyal and faithful servant who proclaims the truths of your Word and who cares for those in need.

TO KNOW MORE:
Isaiah 40 and 1 Peter 5 \\

Day 297 | *Gifts*

PRAY: God connect with me here, as I seek you in your Word.

READ: Deuteronomy 33.13-16 — God is a gift-giver beyond compare. He knows exactly who you are, what you need and what you can use. For instance, in today's passage you read about the gift of God's blessings for each tribe of Israel, which He makes through Moses. Moses acknowledges the amazing work of God in their midst, then goes through each of the twelve tribes offering a blessing in God's name: long life to one, strength against enemies to another, safety to a third, and so on. God knew each tribe intimately and He knew how best to bless them. He knew exactly what to give them.

God gives different people different gifts and He has given you certain skills, talents and abilities to use for His glory. God desires that all of His children discover and use what He has graciously given them.

REFLECT: When God looks at your life, does He see a grateful heart? Does He delight in seeing the gifts He has lavished on you put to work in loving service to others in His name? That's His desire. So open your "gift" from Him today and put it to good use.

RESPOND: Thank God for His gracious gifts and blessings to you—not only the people and things that make your life richer, but the talents and abilities He has graced you with. Ask Him to give you more opportunities to put these gifts to work, starting today.

Lord, thank you for the unique skills and abilities you have given me. May I have opportunities to use them for your glory.

TO KNOW MORE:
Micah 5 and Acts 14 \\

Day 298 | *Prodigals*

PRAY: God connect with me here, as I seek you in your Word.

READ: Luke 15.11-32 — Some people need to hit the bottom before they come to their senses. The Prodigal Son's outlook was based on a desire to live as he pleased. That isn't so different from the attitudes of most people in our world today. It may take great sorrow and tragedy to cause them to look up to the only One who can help – or it can take the loving words of someone like a parent to direct them to the Lord. Regardless of the way home, God is always there awaiting our return.

REFLECT: Is there someone you can help today who may be searching for true satisfaction but is looking for it in all the wrong places? Be a loving friend or family member and share the one true source of joy and satisfaction with them – the eternal embrace of Jesus.

RESPOND: If you're struggling with self-centered thoughts and selfish desires, you know they bring no joy whatsoever. Begin to think of ways you can help others and you'll be amazed at how quickly your world-view will change for the better.

Lord, guide my steps so I can turn from self-centeredness and begin to bring joy into the lives of others.

TO KNOW MORE:
Jonah 3 and Matthew 7 \\

Day 299 | *Habits*

PRAY: God connect with me here, as I seek you in your Word.

READ: Romans 14.17 — When people become Christians, they often reject many of their old habits and interests and replace them with more wholesome activities. Smoking and alcohol abuse are exchanged for exercise and a healthy diet. Noisy evenings in front of the television while munching on fast food are replaced with enjoyable dinnertime discussions with the family.

Unfortunately, many Christians don't examine their lives beyond the physical changes they've made. They continue to practice many of the same spiritual sins. They gossip or say hurtful things or become jealous when someone else succeeds. While it's important to change your way of life and take care of the body God has given you, don't forget to ask Him to change your heart as well. Then you will become an example of the loving habits Jesus desires to see in all of us.

REFLECT: In Galatians 6.9 we read of an excellent habit all believers should adopt from the Apostle Paul: "Let us not grow weary of doing good, for in due season we will reap, if we do not give up".

RESPOND: Ask God to turn your negative spiritual habits into fruitful routines of loving concern for others.

Lord, I pray you will remove all the bad habits I've accumulated over my lifetime and make me pure and blameless in you sight.

TO KNOW MORE:
Isaiah 61 and Colossians 2 \\

Day 300 | *Weaknesses*

PRAY: God connect with me here, as I seek you in your Word.

READ: 2 Corinthians 12.1-10 — Imagine having the visions that Paul experienced. It would be very easy to become boastful, especially if God had chosen you alone to witness the marvels of Paradise. Apparently it was a temptation even to Paul since God gave him a physical condition that kept his spirit humble. Although God did not remove Paul's physical affliction, even after his repeated petitions for relief, He promised to demonstrate His power through this faithful apostle.

The fact that God's power shows up in weak people should give us courage and confidence. When we are blessed with tremendous talents or resources, we are tempted to do God's work on our own – and that leads to pride. We must rely on God for our effectiveness in reaching out to others rather than on our own energy, efforts or talents. Our weaknesses not only help develop Christian character, they also deepen our relationship with Him.

REFLECT: When we admit our weaknesses, we affirm God's strength. When we are weak, when we allow God to fill us with His power, then we are stronger than we could ever be on our own.

RESPOND: Depend on God and God alone. Only His power will make you an effective minister to others and allow you to do good works that have lasting and eternal value.

Lord, I pray that you will demonstrate your power through my weakness and help me to be humble about the talents and gifts you have given me.

TO KNOW MORE:
Daniel 2 and Galatians 5 \\

Day 301 | *If...*

PRAY: God connect with me here, as I seek you in your Word.

READ: Psalm 74.20-23 — You see a homeless man on the street. He's coming your way. What do you do? Do you say anything? Do you give him anything? You see a mother with three small children, waiting in front of a church's canned goods distribution centre. What do you do?

Let's get real. You may struggle to meet your monthly obligations. And you may not be in a position of power. But someone is. And He is working to help the oppressed around the world. The truth is, we do have an incredible, even infinite source of power available to us: the power of an omnipotent God. There is only one thing He calls us to do. It won't cost us anything but time. It's called prayer. Pray for the poor, the needy, the hungry. Ask God not to let them be constantly disgraced. Ask Him to use you to improve their circumstances and bring encouragement to their souls.

REFLECT: We live in a fallen world. A long time ago, humankind made the choice to go its own way rather than God's. We live with the consequences of that choice. Those consequences include hunger, pain, sickness, crime . . . the list seems endless. But God can and does reach through all that pain and darkness to touch hurting souls with His love and provision. Let us pray that He will do that for the needy today.

RESPOND: Do you know any poor and needy people by name? Do you know some by their faces, having seen them on the street or at a homeless kitchen? If so, bring them before the Lord in prayer. Pray Psalm 74.21 on their behalf.

Lord, "Don't disappoint those in need or make them turn from you, but help the poor and homeless to shout your praises" Psalm 74.21 (CEV).

TO KNOW MORE:
Jeremiah 33 and Hebrews 8 \\

Day 302 | *Maturity*

PRAY: God connect with me here, as I seek you in your Word.

READ: Philippians 2.3-4 — There's an old saying that challenges us not to judge someone until we've walked a mile in his or her shoes. In other words, we need to view life from another's perspective before we become critical or patronizing or egocentric. Having the ability to step out of our own perceptions – and into another's – is the true mark of maturity. But it's not easy. Take a look at how God, through Paul, describes this in today's reading.

How does all this work out, specifically? Well, say we were quick to judge another's aloofness as being snobby. And then later we learn that that person is merely shy or the product of a home that constantly demeaned her. Genuine love is what we're aiming for. Paul tells us that it involves working together with one heart and purpose. It's unselfish, not attempting to merely make a good impression or to cultivate one's self. And it's humble, thinking of others first. When Christ freely demonstrated all of this to us – when we deserved nothing – shouldn't we attempt to do this for each other?

REFLECT: Genuine love does indeed mean walking in another's shoes – before we form an impression, before we make a snap judgment and definitely before we wound another's heart.

RESPOND: Pray for your attitude. Ask to have the ability to see from another's perspective and to be careful to think of others before you think of yourself.

Lord, forgive me for my quick judgments and help me begin to learn what it is to love – genuine love.

TO KNOW MORE:
Hosea 12 and 1 Timothy 6 \\

Day 303 | *Neighbours*

PRAY: God connect with me here, as I seek you in your Word.

READ: Joshua 22.8 — God gave Israel the Promised Land. It belonged to them. But in order for them to fully possess the land, they had to cooperate. Interestingly, two and a half tribes received land on the east side of the Jordan, where no enemies lived. Yet God required these fighting men to share the blessings and the burdens the other tribes faced.

Salvation has a similar dynamic. God gives us salvation without merit, but we must engage in the "battles" of this life in order to fully "possess" it. We can easily focus on ourselves and revel in our own spiritual success, but that isn't the picture God gives us of life in the Kingdom of God. The eastern tribes were entrusted with much, so they were expected to give much. They also had a role within their own tribes by sharing the wealth they gained from their enemies. Mature Christians have something to give out of the abundance of spiritual blessings they have received through their relationship with Christ. God calls us to come alongside others, to encourage and strengthen them in their faith and fight next to them in the spiritual battles they face.

REFLECT: One key way we can participate in others' lives is through the generous giving of our material resources. Joshua reminded the people of Israel before his death that every blessing they possessed, going back many generations, came from the Lord. God told them, "I gave you land you hadn't worked for, cities didn't build and food you didn't plant" (from Joshua 24.13). When we consider His faithfulness to so many generations, we realize that returning His kindness to others is a fully appropriate response.

RESPOND: Ask God to remind you of the ways He has blessed you and then resolve, with the help of the Holy Spirit, to share generously with others.

Lord, help me to be a generous giver out of the abundant blessings you have faithfully provided.

TO KNOW MORE: Deuteronomy 8 and Hebrews 11 \\

Day 304 | *Gossip*

PRAY: God connect with me here, as I seek you in your Word.

READ: 2 Thessalonians 3.11-13 — "Do you wanna' hear a secret about that new family? Listen . . . Can you believe it?!" This is how it generally starts, doesn't it? The names and locations and situations may be interchangeable, but the nature of gossip usually has the same way of unfolding. It has the same furtive glances., the same whispered words, and, usually, the same destructive results.

Of course, 2 Thessalonians 3.11-13 refers to more than "busybodies". Any negative behaviour that hurts others – whether emotionally, spiritually or physically – is condemned throughout Scripture. So, the best way for us to conduct our lives is to "never tire of doing good". Such an attitude of Christ-like graciousness not only edifies and encourages others, it makes our own daily walk so much easier and more enjoyable.

REFLECT: Gossip is tantalizing. It's exciting to hear and it's difficult to not pass on since it gives us a feeling of power. But gossip tears people down and it distracts us from our spiritual responsibilities. If you often find your nose in other people's business, you most likely are not keeping up with your own responsibilities.

RESPOND: Look for a meaningful task to do: sharing the Gospel with a neighbour, offering to help at a soup kitchen, reading God's Word to someone who has difficulty seeing, etc. You will soon discover the joy and satisfaction that comes from serving Christ and furthering His Kingdom.

Lord, forgive me for wasting my time in idle chatter and meaningless activities that don't glorify your Kingdom.

TO KNOW MORE:
Ecclesiastes 4 and 1 Timothy 5 \\

Day 305 | *Forgiveness*

PRAY: God connect with me here, as I seek you in your Word.

READ: Matthew 18.21-35 — "You always hurt the one you love". Think about it: This well-known phrase really doesn't make any sense, does it? Why would a person try to make someone they care for unhappy? The truth is, few people want to hurt a loved one. For that matter, most of us (fortunately for civilization) have no desire to hurt anyone – family member, friend or complete stranger. Usually unkind or hurtful actions or words are the result of job pressures, financial burdens or other problems.

If someone has done something to upset you, remember to follow the example of Christ and offer your compassion, love and forgiveness rather than anger and bitterness. If you do, you will relieve rather than escalate the situation. On the other hand, of course, if you have sinned against another person, ask for forgiveness and ask God to help you never repeat your foolish actions.

REFLECT: The Parable of the Unforgiving Servant illustrates God's total forgiveness when dealing with our sins. Our debts have been paid by Christ and we are set free from our transgressions forever. What a wonderful Lord we serve!

RESPOND: Ask God to help you be as forgiving to others as He has been with you. Remember that harbouring hard feelings and anger causes as much, if not more, sorrow to the unforgiving person as it does to the transgressor.

Lord, just as you have forgiven me countless times for my sins, help me to forgive others who have done hurtful things to me.

TO KNOW MORE:
Genesis 4 and Luke 17 \\

Day 306 | *Advice*

PRAY: God connect with me here, as I seek you in your Word.

READ: 1 Corinthians 12.1-3 — If there was ever an occupation for which there would be an abundance of eager candidates, it would probably be hosting a television show where the host listens to the problems of his or her guests and then offers sober words of sage advice (after a commercial break, of course). Yes, the world seems filled with people who are ready, willing and eager to share their opinions with anyone who crosses their paths.

Now, it should be said, this isn't always a negative thing. Just remember, though, while it's important to seek the counsel of wise and godly people, it's also imperative that we test their advice against the Word of God. If what they say contradicts the laws God has established for His people, turn your back on their advice. And, if you're asked to share your opinions or counsel, turn first to the Scriptures so you don't become a stumbling block to this earnestly seeking person.

REFLECT: How a person speaks and the words they say reveal volumes about their character. Strive to be a person whose comments and observations are an encouragement and point others to the Source of all wisdom.

RESPOND: Ask God to bring people into your life you can pray with.

Lord, I pray that you will bless me with wise and godly friends with whom I can have regular fellowship and who can help me grow in my faith, and that I'll also be an encouragement to them.

TO KNOW MORE:
Deuteronomy 21 and Galatians 3 \\

Day 307 | *Contentment*

PRAY: God connect with me here, as I seek you in your Word.

READ: Proverbs 30.7-9 — If you were given two wishes, what would they be? Agur was a wise teacher who wrote some very smart sayings, one of which can be found in today's reading. He begs God for two favours: first, that he would never tell a lie. Second, that he would get just enough to meet his needs –neither too little nor too much. Now, how similar were your two wishes to Agur's? Agur was wise indeed. First, he wanted a life that was totally open and honest before God and his fellow human beings. That way he'd never be tempted to deceive others or come up with excuses before the Lord. Imagine the freedom of a totally honest life! Second, he wanted neither poverty nor riches. Now, the first part makes sense. Who would ask God for poverty? But the second part may have a lot of people scratching their heads. Why didn't Agur want wealth? Agur knew that if he grew rich, he might put his faith in his money rather than in God. And that, indeed, would be a tale ending in unhappiness and regret.

REFLECT: Being poor can be hazardous to your physical and spiritual health. On the other hand, Jesus pointed out that rich people have trouble getting into God's Kingdom (Matthew 19.23–24). The apostle Paul learned to be content with whatever he had and in whatever situation he found himself (Philippians 4.12). These are essential, lifelong lessons to hold dear.

RESPOND: Make Agur's prayer your own. Ask God to make your life one marked by honesty and contentment. Then trust Him to answer you.

Lord, I pray you will give me peace and contentment in all circumstances and that I will bless others with the abundance you have given me.

TO KNOW MORE:
Psalm 21 and Luke 10 \\

Day 308 | *Angels*

PRAY: God connect with me here, as I seek you in your Word.

READ: Hebrews 13.1-2 — Have you ever considered that you may have met an angel without realizing it? There are a lot of "urban legends" about angelic visitations. Their truth in fact is impossible to verify. But the writer of Hebrews leaves no doubt that as believers, we are to show hospitality to strangers, for some who have done this have entertained angels without realizing it. The Bible has at least three Old Testament stories of people welcoming angels unawares: Abraham (Genesis 18), Gideon (Judges 6) and Manoah (Judges 13). But encountering God's messengers in amazing ways isn't the point here. The point is, we're to love each other with true Christian love. That means showing hospitality to everyone in need, regardless of the circumstances.

REFLECT: Hospitality is simply making other people feel comfortable and at home. And there are a lot of people in this world who would love to experience some warm hospitality. A new family in the community that comes to visit your church; elderly people who live in nursing homes; single mothers with young children; travelling missionaries, etc. Make hospitality a regular part of your life. Whether you encounter an angel or just another human being, you'll be miraculously blessed.

RESPOND: Thank God for the many times you have been shown hospitality and ask Him to increase your capacity to help others.

Lord, I pray you will give me opportunities to show hospitality to others in your name.

TO KNOW MORE:
Isaiah 58 and 2 John 1 \\

Day 309 | *Friends*

PRAY: God connect with me here, as I seek you in your Word.

READ: Judges 1.19-28 — Just a few generations ago, cigarette advertisers promoted the idea that smoking was actually good for you. "Healthful!", "Refreshing!", "Adds vigor!", boasted the ads that appeared in magazines and on the radio. And many accepted that notion without question. Today, we look at the thousands of lives ravaged by heart disease and cancer and shake our heads, wondering how anyone could have believed such nonsense.

It seems the people of Israel in the time of the Judges had accepted some pretty foolish ideas as well. Despite repeated warnings from Moses and Joshua, they no longer saw the urgency of stamping out dangerous influences. Their live-and-let-live attitude allowed some pretty dangerous people to creep into their lives. When God commanded the Israelites to take over the Promised Land, he gave clear instructions regarding the people occupying those lands: "You must destroy them totally and make no treaty with them." Eventually, just as God predicted, the "harmless" Canaanites passed their corrupt ways to the unsuspecting Israelites.

REFLECT: We must avoid the temptation of hanging out with people just because they are popular, fun or simply nice. The Israelites made that mistake, and so can we.

RESPOND: Ask God to bring people into your life who will strengthen your walk with Christ. And pray that you will be a positive and compassionate influence in the lives of those who are seeking Christian friends.

Lord, I pray you will give me opportunities to share your love with others, and I ask that those you've brought into my life will continue to encourage my walk with you.

TO KNOW MORE:
Isaiah 41 and Romans 8 \\

Day 310 | *Needs*

PRAY: God connect with me here, as I seek you in your Word.

READ: Luke 18.35-43 — Beggars in ancient Palestine often waited along the roads near cities because that was where they would be able to beg from more people. Usually disabled in some way, they were unable to earn a living. Medical help was not available for their problems, and the people of that era tended to ignore their obligation to care for the needy. Thus beggars had little hope of escaping their degrading way of life.

But the blind beggar in today's reading took hope in the Messiah. He shamelessly cried out for Jesus' attention, and Jesus said that the beggar's faith had restored his sight. As a Christian, never forget that regardless of how desperate your situation may seem, you can call out to Jesus in faith and He will help you. This includes resolving the major decisions in your life, such as whether to start a family, change careers or buy a home, or overcoming the stresses of daily living which are often too numerous to list.

REFLECT: God loved you so much that He sent His Son to die for your sins. Be assured that He cares enough to answer your prayers in His perfect timing and manner.

RESPOND: Turn to God with problems you are facing, along with the concerns of loved ones in your family, church and community. Also pray that God will help you accept whatever His will is for your life and the lives of others.

Lord, I submit my needs and concerns, along with the needs and concerns of (names), to you for your perfect guidance and resolution.

TO KNOW MORE:
1 Samuel 2 and Mark 10 \\

Day 311 | *Legacy*

PRAY: God connect with me here, as I seek you in your Word.

READ: Acts 9.36-41 — The stories of the bizarre last requests of the dying often find their way into tabloids and news clips. An elderly woman leaves all her worldly possessions to a cat. A rabid hockey fan wants to be buried in the uniform of his favourite team, along with a puck and stick. As Christians, we can easily dismiss these as examples of what the unsaved want as a legacy. The question is, what kind of legacy will we leave behind? How will we be remembered? What relationships will we have invested in?

We learn about a woman named Dorcas in the book of Acts. Now here was someone with a worthy legacy. Note the possible inscription for her headstone: "She was always doing kind things for others and helping the poor." But eulogies weren't needed for long because friends begged Peter to come and pray over her dead body and she came back from death. Once again this much-beloved woman was used by God: many were saved through her miraculous raising from the dead. And somehow, you just know that she continued to serve God through many acts of kindness.

REFLECT: Dorcas was a woman who was given a second chance when she never needed one to begin with. She had friends who cared for her. What was the legacy she left behind? Kindness, relationships, compassion. Dorcas' beloved legacy went from life to death to life again. She didn't waste a moment. And her life continues to be a lesson for all of us to this day.

RESPOND: What legacy will you leave behind? How will you be remembered? Prayerfully evaluate your life. Ask God to help you leave behind a legacy of love and service to Him and to others.

Lord, I pray that my legacy will be one of loving kindness to others and devoted service to you.

TO KNOW MORE:
2 Chronicles 2 and Titus 3 \\

Day 312 | *Thankfulness*

PRAY: God connect with me here, as I seek you in your Word.

READ: Colossians 1.3-8 — In Paul's letters there is a pattern he regularly uses for his openings – one that can be found in verse 3 of our reading today. Before he brings his petitions to the Lord in prayer, he begins with a statement of praise and thanksgiving. This is the way the Lord showed us to pray, as well. In the familiar King James wording, we "hallow" or honour God's name before bringing Him our needs for our "daily bread".

But isn't this how those who love one another communicate? We demonstrate our adoration and respect before everything else. And this theme is another pattern from Paul's letters – the affirmation that we should be filled with a loving spirit. Remember, because of our love for one another, Christians can have an impact that goes far beyond our neighbourhoods and communities. The Bible speaks of Christian love as an action and attitude, not just an emotion. But, above all, it's a by-product of our new life in Christ, the One who demonstrated the greatest love of all.

REFLECT: Christians have no excuse for not loving others. As a Christian, don't base your love on what feels right at the time; instead, respond in prayerful consideration of what is in the best interest of others.

RESPOND: Ask God that He will guide you, through His Holy Spirit, in all that you do and say to others. And remember to share His love with a world that so desperately needs it.

Lord, I am thankful for all the many blessings you have lovingly given me and I ask that you will provide me opportunities to share your love with others.

TO KNOW MORE:
Psalm 143 and Galatians 5 \\

Day 313 | *Medicine*

PRAY: God connect with me here, as I seek you in your Word.

READ: Mark 5.25-34 — Even in the 21st century, the care available to countless millions is little better than what was offered to the woman we read about today who lived 2,000 years ago. This unnamed woman had an incurable condition that caused her to bleed continually. It made her ritually unclean and excluded her from most social contact with other Jews. Her life was miserable and she desperately wanted Jesus to heal her. While she no doubt knew that her bleeding would cause Jesus to be "unclean" under Jewish law if she touched him, her anguish was such that she did so anyway. Rather than respond angrily, Jesus lovingly turned to her and offered the words she longed to hear – that her faith had brought complete healing and she was free to go in peace.

REFLECT: God is always ready to help, just as Jesus demonstrated in this story and in many other instances. We should never allow our fear or sin to keep us from approaching Him. Coming to God for help is the first step in healing a fractured life.

RESPOND: Honestly submit any specific physical problems, spiritual concerns or emotional crises you are having. And ask that He will give you a heart of compassion for the hurts of others.

Lord, I pray that you will bring healing into my life and into the lives of the many people I know who are hurting, including (Names).

TO KNOW MORE:
Psalm 107 and Luke 7 \\

Day 314 | *Love*

PRAY: God connect with me here, as I seek you in your Word.

READ: 1 John 4.7-12 — Name a dozen popular songs from the last few years (or decades) that feature the word "love". Actually your list could probably go on and on given enough time. Yes, the world needs love. It really does. But notice in today's reading that John makes a keen distinction when referring to God's love. He says, "God is love" not "Love is God".

Our world, with its shallow views and attitudes, has turned the Christian expression of love around and contaminated the message these four letters convey. Too often the world says that love is what makes a person feel good, and that it's alright to sacrifice moral principles and others' rights in order to obtain it. But that isn't real love; it's actually love's enemy. In other words, to be honest, it's really little more than selfishness.

REFLECT: God's love isn't like that propagated by a fallen world. Our definition of love must come from the God who is holy, just and perfect. And it must be faithfully expressed toward our Creator and generously toward those around us.

RESPOND: Ask God to teach you to love as He does – faithfully and with compassion toward everyone.

Lord, thank you for loving me enough to send your Son to die for my sins. I praise you and ask that I will be a faithful witness to others of your mercy.

TO KNOW MORE:
Psalm 86 and 2 Corinthians 13 \\

Day 315 | *Betrayal*

PRAY: God connect with me here, as I seek you in your Word.

READ: Luke 22.54-62 — In today's passage we read the poignant story of Peter's betrayal after the arrest of Jesus. When silently confronted with his unfaithfulness, the most vocal and emotionally volatile of the 11 remaining Disciples wept bitterly. He did this not only because he had denied his Lord, but also because he had turned away from a very dear friend – a person who had loved and taught him for three years.

Truthfully, love and promises of commitment are generally not enough to withstand human error and weakness, no matter how much resolve and courage we think we have. We need to be aware of our own breaking points and not become overconfident or self-sufficient in our daily walk with the Lord. Regular prayer and Bible reading are essential for instilling the kind of spiritual tenacity God wants from His people.

REFLECT: Peter learned from his humiliating experience valuable lessons that would help him in the leadership role he would eventually assume. We, too, can learn from our human frailties the things Jesus wants to teach us if we submit our lives to Him.

RESPOND: Pray that God will forgive you of your sinful behaviours and ask that you will gain wisdom from past transgressions so you can mature in your faith and be ready to serve God in whatever capacity He holds for you in the future.

Lord, forgive me for my sinful thoughts, words and deeds and help me to learn from the things I've done so I will become all you want me to be.

TO KNOW MORE:
Ezekiel 7 and Mark 14 \\

Day 316 | *Prayer*

PRAY: God connect with me here, as I seek you in your Word.

READ: 1 Samuel 1.9-18 — Prayer belongs to everyone, regardless of our social status, race or background. Despite the offenses we have committed or the wounds we have caused, we may come to God with our requests. Knowing that He hears them is marvellous in itself, seeing Him respond fills us with joy and wonder.

The first thing to note about Hannah's prayer is that it happened at a specific time. She was at Shiloh at God's Tabernacle after supper (v. 9). Although Jesus taught that it doesn't matter where we pray or worship (John 4.21), it's important to develop a regular habit of prayer throughout the day. Next, we see that "Hannah was in deep anguish, crying bitterly" (1 Samuel 1.10). God wants us to be transparent with Him. Third, Hannah dedicates her all to God (v. 11). Dedicating Samuel to God was not merely a bargain to obtain a child; it was a beautiful act of faith.

REFLECT: Hannah, who had lived for years in shame for her childlessness and had been humiliated by her husband's other wife, had one recourse: prayer. At last her request was granted, and so will any sincere prayers we offer to God.

RESPOND: You can know Hannah's happiness and God's blessings on your prayers. Pray honestly. Pray consistently. And let your whole being enter your prayers, just as Hannah demonstrated.

Lord, I bring my petitions to you in faith that you will answer my prayers for both my needs and the needs of those who are hungry or in despair around the world.

TO KNOW MORE:
Psalm 29 and Hebrews 5 \\

Day 317 | *Clergy*

PRAY: God connect with me here, as I seek you in your Word.

READ: 1 Corinthians 9.1-7 — Most of us have heard stories about divorces of the rich and famous. They are often messy, petty episodes and include one of the partners demanding a living allowance based on the lifestyle he or she has grown accustomed to. Such "necessities" can include a $10,000 a month budget for clothes, a new car every year, several vacations and a palatial estate. In contrast, Paul made the case for his necessities with humility. Paul said that the church must take the responsibility to support God's workers. Christians should provide financial, material and spiritual assistance to people in service to the Lord. Even if you have only a couple of dollars a week to give, the important thing is that you provide regular support.

REFLECT: Prayer is perhaps the most powerful encouragement tool available. What kind of difference could you make in your community simply by praying regularly for Christian leaders? What kind of material help can you provide for your church's clergy? What about the missionaries who are sponsored by your congregation? Depending on their situation, a resource drive could be very helpful. These kinds of initiatives take a bit of time and effort on your part, but they're well worth it.

RESPOND: Carefully and prayerfully consider how you can support God's workers in your community and around the world.

Lord, I pray for the clergy and staff and my church and the missionaries we support. Please provide for their needs and encourage them as they serve you.

TO KNOW MORE:
Song of Solomon 5 and 1 Timothy 2 \\

Day 318 | *Imprisonment*

PRAY: God connect with me here, as I seek you in your Word.

READ: Philippians 1.12-14 — Being imprisoned would cause many people to become bitter or to give up, but Paul saw it as one more opportunity to spread the Good News of Christ. He realized that his current circumstances weren't as important as what he did with them. Turning a bad situation into a good one, he reached out to the Roman soldiers and encouraged those Christians who were afraid of persecution.

You may not be in prison, but you still have plenty of opportunities to be discouraged – times of indecision, financial burdens, family conflict or the loss of a job. How you act in such situations reflects what you believe.

REFLECT: Like Paul, look for opportunities to demonstrate your faith to others, even in bad situations. Whether or not the situation improves, your faith will grow stronger.

RESPOND: Turn your conflicts and concerns over to God and ask that He continue to give you strength and encouragement during times of difficulty. And, if given the opportunity, prayerfully consider serving as a ministry volunteer to those who are truly imprisoned. The kindness you show may be the only opportunity for these men and women to experience the love of Christ.

Lord, I pray that you will encourage me in all circumstances and I ask that you will reveal any opportunities where I can minister to local prisoners.

TO KNOW MORE:
Esther 9 and Romans 16 \\

Day 319 | *Healing*

PRAY: God connect with me here, as I seek you in your Word.

READ: Matthew 15.29-31 — Imagine what it must have been like for the people Jesus healed of their physical impairments. Remember this was a time when physicians couldn't perform surgery on someone with a heart defect. They weren't able to correct a person's eyesight with glasses or contacts. They didn't have vaccines for diseases like polio or chemotherapy for cancer. No wonder the people Jesus touched and made whole rejoiced and praised God. He was their only source of hope. Today, God can still miraculously cures people of their physical problems. But, more important, He offers to everyone deliverance from the pain and anguish caused by our fallen condition. Through the sacrifice of His Son, God makes spiritual healing readily available to all who confess their sins and earnestly come to Him.

REFLECT: Recognize that God is the Great Physician and believe that He is able to cure, if it is His will, any physical problems you are suffering. Also know that His grace is sufficient to heal all of our spiritual wounds and that He can restore us and make us whole.

RESPOND: Turn to God and pray that He will forgive you of your sins and heal the spiritual brokenness in your life. When you do, God will indeed perform a miracle and free you from bondage.

Lord, I pray for forgiveness for the times I have not loved you with my whole heart or loved my neighbour as myself. I humbly repent and ask that you will restore me and guide my steps in the future.

TO KNOW MORE:
Exodus 24 and 2 Thessalonians 2 \\

Day 320 | *Treasures*

PRAY: God connect with me here, as I seek you in your Word.

READ: Proverbs 10.2 — Remember when you were a child and desperately wanted the latest toy or game or piece of sporting equipment—the one all your friends had? You wanted it so badly and nothing else seemed important. You just knew you'd never be happy unless you got what you wanted. Soon childhood turned into adolescence and then adulthood. Along the way, new interests captured your thoughts and previous desires seemed trivial by comparison. Unfortunately, many people will do anything for these fleeting pleasures. The bitter irony is that the more greedy they become and the more aggressively they acquire, the more miserable their lives are. The Bible tells us that we are to save up our treasures in heaven, where their value is never reduced. Remember, don't spend your time plotting ways to get some material possession at any price. Soon these things will seem as meaningless as a long-forgotten and broken toy.

REFLECT: Work to achieve something truly valuable: contentment with what you have, a lifetime of service to God and an eternity in His presence.

RESPOND: Thank God for what you have and ask that He will continue to bless you with the abundance of His grace and mercy.

Lord, thank you for the abundance in my life. I pray that you will continue to meet my needs so I can, in turn, be a blessing to others.

TO KNOW MORE:
Amos 8 and James 5 \\

Day 321 | *God's House*

PRAY: God connect with me here, as I seek you in your Word.

READ: 1 Corinthians 3.16-17 — In today's passage, Paul refers to the church as the "house of God". Just as you would be upset if someone came into your home and physically destroyed it, God becomes angry with those who spiritually defile His house. If a church member uses his or her financial position or status in the community to achieve personal goals that are contrary to God's plan, usually the church splits, new members become discouraged and quit attending and the person who instigated the conflict becomes part of another congregation where he or she resumes a career as a troublemaker.

What happens in the church is a model for what will take place in our lives when we care only about our own desires and forget about placing the Holy Spirit in charge. Ultimately we will be in constant tension that will tear us apart emotionally and spiritually.

REFLECT: If we hold God's Word in reverence and welcome God with our actions and through our prayers, He will honour us and bless our lives and our ministry to others.

RESPOND: Pray for peace and harmony and ask that God will guide your life.

Lord, I pray that I will be a blessing to my church with my attitudes and actions and that I will have peace in my life as I strive to live in accordance with your will and the truths of your Word.

TO KNOW MORE:
Psalm 99 and 1 John 4 \\

Day 322 | *Amazing*

PRAY: God connect with me here, as I seek you in your Word.

READ: 2 Samuel 7.18-24 — Out of all the people in Israel, God selected David to be the leader of His chosen nation. In response, David was equal parts amazed, humbled and thankful that the Lord was so gracious to him. Do you ever feel like David? Are you ever amazed at what the Lord has done for you? Do you ever consider yourself unworthy of God's blessings? If you answered "no" to these questions, you're not alone. The truth is, our society conditions us to expect the best for ourselves. Because we're so focused on what we don't have, it's easy for us to ignore or take for granted the things we do have.

REFLECT: Rather than expecting the best for ourselves, we need to cultivate the spirit of amazement, humility, and thankfulness that David possessed. We need to recognize there are people around us in circumstances much more dire than ours. We need to recognize that our relatively privileged lifestyle is not some sort of birthright but an inexplicable blessing from God.

RESPOND: Praise God for His blessings and ask that He will show you ways to use those blessings to help others. And remember to humbly pray, "Who am I, O Sovereign Lord, that you have chosen to bless me?"

Lord, thank you for your many blessings and I pray that I will maintain a humble spirit in all circumstances.

TO KNOW MORE:
Genesis 32 and Ephesians 3 \\

Day 323 | *Imitation*

PRAY: God connect with me here, as I seek you in your Word.

READ: Ephesians 5.1-2 — Children love to imitate their parents. That's why mothers and fathers have to be careful what they say or do since it will affect the words and actions of their sons and daughters. Just as children imitate their parents, we should imitate Christ. His great love for us led Him to make the ultimate sacrifice so that we might have eternal life.

Remember, the key features of Christ-like love are forgiveness and humility. Love should be the standard for our daily conduct as we deny ourselves, takes up His cross and follows Him in faithful service to those around us.

REFLECT: The love you show for others should be the kind that goes beyond affection to self-sacrificing service – the kind of love that guards against doing things that will hinder your Christian witness.

RESPOND: Ask God to help you be a loving servant to those around you. Pray that others will see His love through your words and actions.

Lord, I pray that I will be a faithful witness to others of your infinite love and that I will have opportunities to share your promise of eternal life through the sacrifice of your Son.

TO KNOW MORE:
Hosea 1 and 1 Peter 1 \\

Day 324 | *Fruitful*

PRAY: God connect with me here, as I seek you in your Word.

READ: Mark 11.15-26 — There are two parts to the unusual incident in today's reading: the cursing of the fig tree and the cleansing of the temple. The cursing of the fig tree was, actually, an acted-out parable associated with Jesus driving away those who bought and sold in His Father's house. The Temple was supposed to be a place of worship, but true worship of God had virtually disappeared. The fig tree offered the promise of fruit, but it produced none. Jesus was showing his anger at religious life without substance. If you go through the motions of faith without putting it to work in your life, you are like the fig tree that withered and died. Genuine faith has great potential; ask God to help you bear fruit for his Kingdom.

REFLECT: Consistently standing up for what is right is seldom a good way to gain friends. The religious leaders hated Jesus for His charges of hypocrisy against them. The way you conduct yourself and the faithfulness of your walk with the Lord, however, are usually enough to silence anyone who tries to criticize your convictions.

RESPOND: God loves to show us how we can be of service to Him and His Kingdom. Ask Him to give you the strength, wisdom and faith to persevere in the tasks He has given you.

Lord, I pray that I can be a faithful servant to you and your Kingdom and that my actions and motives will be consistently honorable.

TO KNOW MORE:
Zechariah 3 and Matthew 18 \\

Day 325 | *Reality*

PRAY: God connect with me here, as I seek you in your Word.

READ: Colossians 1.15-23 — Many false teachers in the early church believed that the physical world was evil, and therefore could not have been created by God. If Christ were God, they reasoned, he would only be in charge of the spiritual world. But Paul explained that both the spiritual and physical worlds were created by Christ and are under His authority.

Many Christians limit their relationship with God to church on Sunday and a quick prayer before dinner. God wants to participate in every activity of your life, including your job, your financial decisions and your friendships. He also wants each of us to involve ourselves fully in bringing the reality of who He is into the lives of those who are in desperate need of His saving love.

REFLECT: By placing God in a spiritual box, we deny ourselves the blessings, guidance and love He wants to share with us. Ask that He will touch every aspect of your life and bless you with His infinite wisdom and perfect guidance.

RESPOND: Jesus Christ has no equal and no rival. Submit everything in your life to the Lord.

Lord, I place everything in my life in your hands and ask that you will guide me as I live to love and serve you.

TO KNOW MORE:
Isaiah 44 and Revelation 5 \\

Day 326 | *Benevolence*

PRAY: God connect with me here, as I seek you in your Word.

READ: Proverbs 14.8-9 — How rarely we find good will around us today. Angry drivers scowl at each other in the streets. People fight to be first in line. Disgruntled employers and employees both demand their rights. There seems to be a permanent cloud of unhappiness everywhere, regardless of the time zone, the climate or the season of the year. But the common bond of God's people should be kindness. Those with good will think the best of others and strive to be gracious in all circumstances. When someone crosses you and you feel your blood pressure rising, ask yourself, "How can I demonstrate to this person the same love God has shown to me?" The truth is, your response will likely stop them in their tracks and quickly improve their outlook on life, and their feelings toward you, as well.

REFLECT: When you see those who are begging on a street corner or are sleeping on a sidewalk grate, your first reaction may be to shake your head and walk away. Take a moment to remember all the reasons you have to feel grateful and why you should show compassion, not disdain, for the less fortunate.

RESPOND: In all circumstances, God expects His followers to lend a helpful hand and offer a compassionate word to everyone we encounter.

Lord, I pray that my attitude will always be one of kindness and consideration toward everyone I meet so they can see your love through me.

TO KNOW MORE:
Job 34 and Jude 1 \\

Day 327 | *Contentment*

PRAY: God connect with me here, as I seek you in your Word.

READ: 1 Timothy 6.6-10 — Everybody would love to get rich quick. Admit it. Wouldn't it be great to have someone knock on your door and hand you a lottery cheque for $10 million? Or maybe some long-lost relative you didn't know existed leaves you his entire estate worth billions. You could deal with that, couldn't you? But then, how much is really enough? If you had the ten million, or even the ten billion, would that really bring contentment? In today's passage, Paul describes peace of mind to his young friend Timothy.

So what are we supposed to do? "Let us be content" with what we have. Contentment is an elusive thing in our culture. After all, our whole society is built on the idea of having more. We must make more money to buy more things. But that philosophy is totally foreign to the way of Christ. When is it so bad to want money and things? When they force our attention away from God and His will for us.

REFLECT: Money itself isn't bad. But the love of money is the root, the source, the cause of all kinds of sin: greed, lust, stealing. All of these types of evil conduct are sourced in wanting more. And many who fall into the money trap have wandered from the faith and experienced many sorrows.

RESPOND: Don't get on the treadmill of greed. Be content with what you have. God will bless you with everything you need. Then you can spend your time and energy pursuing ways to love and serve others. And that's the greatest wealth a person can experience!

Lord, I pray for contentment in all things and ask that I can be a blessing to others in your name.

TO KNOW MORE:
Psalm 37 and 2 Corinthians 4 \\

Day 328 | *Provision*

PRAY: God connect with me here, as I seek you in your Word.

READ: 1 Kings 17.8-16 — Imagine your family has nothing to eat. You've lost your job and there is no way to get more money. Yet, each day you wake up and there is $100 on your nightstand for you to use for food. Today's passage presents an equally amazing scenario. Only this one really happened.

No matter how desperate the situation, there is always hope when God is in the picture. Just look at the stories of Gideon and his three hundred warriors, Joshua and the battle of Jericho, or David and Goliath. God seems to enjoy defying the odds. And He delights in those who step out on faith, like the widow at Zarephath, to think of the needs of others as equal to their own.

REFLECT: In today's story, God miraculously provided food for the widow, her son and Elijah even though it seemed impossible. God wants to provide for you too. Philippians 4.19 states that God will meet our needs with His "glorious riches" made available to us through Jesus. Written almost two thousand years ago, this verse is still true today.

RESPOND: What is it you need? Money to provide for your family? A job? The time to care for the needs of a loved one who lives in another city? Take your request to God and watch what happens.

Lord, I pray that you will not only meet my needs but I ask that, like the widow who shared with Elijah, I will always have compassion for others.

TO KNOW MORE:
Isaiah 41 and Hebrews 13 \\

Day 329 | *Praise*

PRAY: God connect with me here, as I seek you in your Word.

READ: Luke 11.1-13 — When Jesus began to teach his disciples about prayer, he gave them a pattern to follow–a model prayer, in other words. Notice the order in the Lord's Prayer. First Jesus praises God, then He makes His requests.

Praising God first puts us in the right frame of mind to tell Him about our needs. Too often, though, our prayers are more like shopping lists than conversations. Jesus also made forgiving others a central part of our relationship with God. God has forgiven our sins, therefore we must forgive those who have wronged us and be compassionate to those who are in need. To remain unforgiving and uncaring shows that we have not understood how we ourselves, along with all other human beings, need to be forgiven and cared for.

REFLECT: Think of someone who has said or done something that made you angry. Have you truly forgiven that person, or do you still carry a grudge? Think of the poor you pass each day. Do you care about the fears, needs and uncertainties they face each day? Your communion with God in prayer is directly affected by your relationships.

RESPOND: Pray for others, forgive them, care for them and ask God to help you show compassion in all situations. And offer to God the prayer He taught His disciples.

Lord, I praise you in all things and ask that you will meet my various needs and show me ways that I can be a blessing in your name to others.

TO KNOW MORE:
Psalm 105 and Romans 2 \\

Day 330 | *Beauty*

PRAY: God connect with me here, as I seek you in your Word.

READ: Proverbs 15.13-15 — Have you ever known someone who is physically handsome or pretty but their negative attitudes and selfish behaviour make them, shall we say, far less appealing? On the other hand, do you know someone who is barely noticed by strangers yet their kindness makes them beautiful to those who know and love them? Yes, our attitudes colour our whole persona.

We can't always decide what happens to us, but we can choose our outlook toward each situation. The secret to a Christlike attitude is to fill our minds with good thoughts – thoughts that are true, pure and lovely; thoughts that dwell on the good things in life. This was Paul's source of joy as he faced imprisonment, and it can be ours as we meet the struggles of daily living.

REFLECT: Take a moment each day to reflect on your attitudes. Examine what you allow to enter your mind and what you dwell on. Then consciously choose thoughts and attitudes rooted in the Holy Spirit and in His good gifts. This will give your life an infusion of irrepressible joy and free you to turn toward helping those who are less fortunate.

RESPOND: Offer your feelings and outlook to God and ask that He will shape your life according to His will.

Lord, I pray that I will reflect to others the peace and inner attractiveness that can only come from loving and serving you.

TO KNOW MORE:
Ecclesiastes 5 and 1 Peter 4 \\

Day 331 | *Christlike*

PRAY: God connect with me here, as I seek you in your Word.

READ: 2 Corinthians 8.16-24 — Isn't it wonderful to be around someone who allows God to work fully in their life? People are naturally drawn to them, often sharing their concerns and problems, knowing they will be treated with compassion and the advice they receive will be marked by wisdom and insight. Titus was a faithful disciple of Christ. He was eager to serve, took joy in the growth of others, had integrity, was a servant and was concerned for the needs of those around him. As Christians, we should make a commitment to imitate Titus' qualities. True Christian character means acting as our Lord would in all our dealings with people.

REFLECT: Don't worry about whether your neighbours have more money than you'll ever earn. Do not attempt to seek retribution when someone takes advantage of you. Always remember that you are a servant of Jesus Christ and people will look to you, just as they did to Titus, as an example of those who belong to the Lord.

RESPOND: Ask that God will forgive you when you dishonour His name. And ask that you can be a blessing to those around you and can serve the needs of your church faithfully.

Lord, I submit my life to you and pray that I will be kind and tenderhearted and encouraging in all circumstances.

TO KNOW MORE:
1 Samuel 20 and 3 John 1 \\

Day 332 | *Bosses*

PRAY: God connect with me here, as I seek you in your Word.

READ: Romans 14.1-9 — Everyone has someone to whom they must answer in their workplace. Even if you own a company, you are responsible to your employees, a group of shareholders or to the bank that lent you money. Whether or not your supervisor is a pleasant, agreeable person, he or she still expects you to perform your duties to the utmost of your abilities. If you fail too often, chances are you will soon be looking for other employment. In your personal life, it's important that your ultimate authority, or "boss", be the One who created you. Seek God's guidance on a daily basis. If you make a mistake, He won't hold it against you. Likewise, just as Paul commands in today's reading, be patient with others. Restrain your judgments since your words and attitudes can be a burden and a source of discouragement to believers and non-believers alike.

REFLECT: Unlike those who control your paycheck, God is always willing to forgive you for your shortcomings and welcome you back into His arms. Don't be afraid to confess your sins and be eager to acknowledge Him as the Lord of your life. And make every effort to be just as forgiving and open with others as God is with you.

RESPOND: Ask the Lord to guide you in all of your steps and lead you along His paths of righteousness. Pray that He will give you opportunities to serve others regardless of whether you are the employer or employee, the boss or worker in your daily life.

Lord, I pray that I will be patient and kind in all circumstances and that others will be able to see the light of your salvation through my life.

TO KNOW MORE:
Isaiah 53 and Titus 2 \\

Day 333 | *Timing*

PRAY: God connect with me here, as I seek you in your Word.

READ: Luke 3.23 — Imagine the Saviour of the world driving nails in a small-town carpenter's shop until he was 30 years old! It seems incredible that Jesus would have been content to remain in Nazareth all that time, but He patiently trusted the Father's timing for His life and ministry. Thirty was the prescribed age for priests to begin their life's work (Numbers 4.3). Joseph was 30 years old when he began serving the king of Egypt (Genesis 41.46) and David was 30 years old when he began to reign over Judah (2 Samuel 5.4). Age 30, then, was a good time to begin an important task in the Jewish culture. Like Jesus, make a vow to work within God's timing, resisting the temptation to jump ahead before receiving the Spirit's direction. Are you waiting and wondering what your next step should be in life? Don't try to out-think God, but rather trust Him in His perfect timing.

REFLECT: Have you fully submitted your life to God? Do you trust His plan for your life? True contentment and effective ministry to others can only come when we are patient and allow Him to direct our steps. Submit your life to God and ask that He will reveal His will to you.

RESPOND: Ask that God will keep your personal agenda from getting ahead of His timing and that He will forgive you when you become fretful and impatient because others seem to be passing you by or appear more successful.

Lord, I trust you with my life and ask that you will give me the patience to wait until your timing is made clear so I can serve you more effectively.

TO KNOW MORE:
Numbers 4 and Acts 1 \\

Day 334 | *Leadership*

PRAY: God connect with me here, as I seek you in your Word.

READ: Titus 1.6-9 — What are the attributes and characteristics you look for in a friend? Is loyalty important to you? How about compassion? Do you prefer people who have a sense of humour or people who are more serious? Do you care whether the person is popular or not? Is it important that you share the same interests? If you could design your own friend, what would he or she be like? Now, what if we asked you to list the attributes and characteristics that are important for a church leader to have? What things might be on your list? Think about this and then compare your ideas with those of Paul in his letter to Titus.

REFLECT: Why do you suppose God places such strict standards on spiritual leaders? Well, for one thing, they're responsible for teaching others about the Lord and His will. And one of the best ways to lead others is by example. When we look at a Christian leader, we should see attributes and characteristics that we would like to develop in our own lives. By the same token, we should learn to model those attributes so that others will learn from our example.

RESPOND: It's very important to have the right people in church leadership positions today. Do you have what it takes to become such a person, compassionate enough to be a loving servant to others?

Lord, I pray that whenever the opportunity arises to lead others at church or through a ministry outreach, I will serve with a pure heart and intentions that are above reproach.

TO KNOW MORE:
Malachi 2 and 1 Timothy 3 \\

Day 335 | *Fairness*

PRAY: God connect with me here, as I seek you in your Word.

READ: 2 Kings 4.1-7 — Karen thought she was being fair. She always made her two sons evenly divide any candy they were given. But she noticed one day that her nine-year-old, David, was helping himself to the larger piece of the candy bar and giving the smaller piece to his six-year-old brother, Will. So the young mother made a new rule: Whoever did the breaking would get the last choice of halves. After that David made sure the candy bar was equally divided!

God expects us to share fairly with others. Just as He gives us many blessings, He also expects us to be generous with our brothers and sisters in the church. In today's passage we read about a woman with whom God shared His resources. In this story, the woman is both obligated and indebted. She is obligated to her debtors and indebted to God for His provision to satisfy the debt. And, like this woman, we too are obligated to others and indebted to God.

REFLECT: God passes His love and His blessings to us so we can pass them on to others. By doing this we can help quench the fires of famine, drought and starvation, one person at a time.

RESPOND: How generous are you with your resources? What are you doing to pass along God's blessings?

Lord, I pray for a generous heart; one that is willing to freely give to others in the same way that you generously give to me.

TO KNOW MORE:
Nehemiah 5 and 1 Timothy 1 \\

Day 336 | *Welcome*

PRAY: God connect with me here, as I seek you in your Word.

READ: Romans 16.16 — Have you ever been somewhere and felt completely out of place? Unless somebody makes an effort to help you feel comfortable, chances are you'll never want to return. This is what many people experience when they go to a church for the first time. Everyone seems to know each other, have a regular pew where they sit and have plans together after church. There seems to be no room for anyone else.

As a mature believer, you have regular opportunities to help others feel welcome when they are new to your church. Suggest a class they might enjoy. Invite them out to lunch after the service. Call them up during the week and tell them how much you enjoyed getting to know them. You'll not only be helping your church continue to grow, you may be developing a friendship that will last a lifetime.

REFLECT: A kind word and a warm smile are the easiest and most inexpensive things in the world to give someone. They're also the most effective methods when it comes to reaching out and witnessing Christ's love to those searching for a spiritual haven.

RESPOND: Ask God to give you opportunities to welcome visitors to your church so they will feel comfortable and at home.

Lord, help me to notice others when they visit our church and place within me an empathy for their needs.

TO KNOW MORE:
Psalm 19 and 1 John 3 \\

Day 337 | *Marriage*

PRAY: God connect with me here, as I seek you in your Word.

READ: Proverbs 18.1 — Our society values assertiveness. And the truth is, at times, everyone must be aggressive if he or she is to survive in the workplace, on the highway or even in the check-out line. But assertiveness can become selfishness if it isn't tempered by love. God's people should put others before themselves; they should be humble and seek to serve rather than to be served.

This attitude is especially important for those who are married. Chances are one of you is naturally more aggressive than the other. There isn't anything wrong with this; it simply means you'll need to work hard for your temperaments to complement each other. And, in every decision you make together, seek common ground until you are both satisfied.

REFLECT: Marriage is one of God's greatest gifts. It can also be a daily grind if it's marked by self-centredness, bitterness and ill-will. Strive to develop loving attitudes that embody the relationship Christ has with His bride, the church.

RESPOND: There's a fine line between aggressiveness and selfishness. If neither of you cross that line, your marriage will be loving and harmonious, even when you disagree.

Lord, help us to always place you first in our lives so that your love can serve as a model for our marriage.

TO KNOW MORE:
Isaiah 26 and Hebrews 3 \\

Day 338 | *Trouble*

PRAY: God connect with me here, as I seek you in your Word.

READ: 1 Thessalonians 3.1-3 — Are you looking for trouble? Of course not. No one looks for difficulties. Some people think troubles are the result of sin or a lack of faith. And sometimes this is the case. But trouble may also be a part of God's plan. Going through trials can develop character (James 1.2-4), patience (Romans 5.3-5) and sensitivity toward others (2 Corinthians 1.3-7).

Actually, problems are unavoidable in an ungodly world and your troubles may be a sign of effective Christian living. Some people turn to God hoping to escape suffering. But, thankfully, rather than promising escape in every situation, God gives us power to grow through our daily challenges.

REFLECT: Christian life is marked by obedience to Christ despite temptation and hardship. By allowing God to hone and refine you, you will mature to the point where you can be a help and blessing to others who need a word of encouragement and kindness.

RESPOND: Ask God to give you faith and courage during times of hardship. He will help you overcome any adversity and make you stronger in the process.

Lord, I pray you will give me strength and spiritual resolve when I face difficult times and help me to never forget that you are in control of all things.

TO KNOW MORE:
Jeremiah 44 and 1 Thessalonians 2 \\

Day 339 | *Courage*

PRAY: God connect with me here, as I seek you in your Word.

READ: Mark 15.47 — Because of the lowly status women occupied in ancient Palestine, Mary Magdalene and Mary the mother of Jesus, could do very little to help our Lord during His ministry. They couldn't speak before the Sanhedrin in His defense, they couldn't appeal to Pilate for His release, they couldn't stand against the crowds and they certainly couldn't overpower the Roman guards.

But they did what they could. They stayed at the cross when the disciples had fled in fear and panic. They followed Jesus' body when he was laid in the tomb. And they prepared spices for his burial. Because they used the opportunities they had, they were the first to witness the Resurrection. God blessed their devotion and diligence.

REFLECT: Let these brave and faithful women be an example to you in your ministry and outreach to others. Take advantage of the opportunities you have and do what you can for Christ rather than worrying about what you cannot do.

RESPOND: Cast aside doubts and fears so God can honour your efforts and reward you with His presence throughout eternity.

Lord, open my eyes so I can see the needs around me and help me to never turn down an opportunity to serve you simply because it seems too daunting.

TO KNOW MORE:
2 Chronicles 16 and Luke 23 \\

Day 340 | *Attention*

PRAY: God connect with me here, as I seek you in your Word.

READ: Acts 10.4-33 — Many people who feel inferior resort to outlandish behavior so they will get noticed. They may wear T-shirts with offensive slogans so they can silently confront people. They may drink heavily so they can be the "life of the party". They may shop for exclusive designer clothes that will set them apart from the crowd.

By contrast, check out Cornelius in today's reading. Cornelius was a humble man whose kindness brought him unexpected heavenly attention. All too often, we're impressed by skills of a professional athlete or the beauty of a model or the power of a wealthy person. These are things that attract our attention. But God has different priorities and ideals: He notices the one who gives to the lowly and the poor. This was the type of person – a Gentile man with a tender heart – that God pointed out to Peter. Isn't it comforting that we don't have to depend on attention-getting antics for God to notice us?

REFLECT: Cornelius became an incredible tool for good in God's hands, all because he cared about the poor around him. God does indeed notice when we give to the needy – through money, time or effort.

RESPOND: Want to get noticed? Don't rely on athletic abilities, knowledge, or beauty products. Instead, work on a tender and giving heart. God will notice and He will honor your care for others.

Lord, I pray that you will help me to focus on things that are truly meaningful and not the superficialities that the world admires.

TO KNOW MORE:
Psalm 141 and Philippians 4 \\

Day 341 | *Speculation*

PRAY: God connect with me here, as I seek you in your Word.

READ: 1 Corinthians 2.11 — If you've ever read a biography about a key historical figure, you know the author will speculate at some point, "What was he thinking when he made that momentous decision?" If you've ever watched an interview with an athlete who made a crucial error, you know the reporter will probably ask, "What in the world were you thinking when you threw away your team's chance to win?" The truth is, most of us are curious about what makes other people tick. We want to understand why a person decided to do one thing when another action would have been easier or smarter. If the person won't, or can't, tell us, we begin to theorize and come to our own conclusions. The Bible tells us that to guess what others are thinking and then judge them on that basis is not only typically incorrect, it's also morally wrong. Don't hurt others by assuming their motives are misguided. Our task as believers is to be encouragers, not obstacles to spiritual growth.

REFLECT: Don't become impatient or suspicious of others because of feelings and attitudes you are convinced they hold. Instead, give those around you the benefit of the doubt and treat them with the same thoughtful respect you expect to receive.

RESPOND: Ask God to forgive you when you judge too quickly. Remember Paul's admonition to the Ephesians: "Always be humble and gentle. Patiently put up with each other and love each other" Ephesians 4.2 (CEV).

Lord, forgive me when I judge too quickly and may I have a humble and loving spirit toward others.

TO KNOW MORE:
Jeremiah 17 and Romans 11 \\

Day 342 | *Eloquence*

PRAY: God connect with me here, as I seek you in your Word.

READ: Romans 16.17,18 — There are few experiences more enjoyable than listening to a gifted speaker. Whether he or she is lecturing in a classroom, telling a story at a party or delivering a sermon on Sunday morning, their ability to communicate can hold the attention of people and they always leave their listeners wanting to hear more.

Unfortunately, many eloquent people become enraptured with their ability to hold an audience spellbound and start believing that style – or, as Paul defines it in some versions, "fancy talk" – is more important than substance. This attitude is especially dangerous in the church, where a pastor, worship leader or Sunday school teacher has been given the responsibility of explaining and interpreting the Word of God. If his or her interest in exercising an ability to sway others is greater than their commitment to prayerfully studying the Scriptures, division and corruption in a congregation often result.

REFLECT: It's vital to read and study your Bible each day and pray that God will reveal Himself to you through His Word. By doing this faithfully, you will know when others are preaching heresy and will be able to defend the truth against their eloquent but false claims.

RESPOND: Ask that God will give you wisdom and discernment when questions and concerns arise from new Christians and seekers who have become discouraged or misled by false teaching.

Lord, keep my heart and mind focused on the truths of Scripture and give me the words to say when someone seeks my counsel on a spiritual matter that troubles them.

TO KNOW MORE:
Isaiah 56 and 2 John 1 \\

Day 343 | *Justice*

PRAY: God connect with me here, as I seek you in your Word.

READ: Proverbs 31.8-9 — Oskar Schindler – the protagonist of the blockbuster movie Schindler's List – was an unconventional hero. He certainly wasn't a godly do-gooder. In fact, he was a drinker, a gambler, a cheater and a womanizer. He was driven by greed and lust. As World War II began, he saw an opportunity to make a lot of money by employing Jews at slave wages in a Polish munitions factory.

REFLECT: King Lemuel is one of the Bible's mystery men. All we know about him is that he was a king. Some scholars think that he ruled the kingdom of Massa in northern Arabia. Wherever Lemuel ruled, he had come to know the one true God. And he followed some wise sayings his mother had taught him. Today's reading focuses on one of those sayings. Lemuel knew that, as king of his nation, he had a great responsibility to make sure the poor and needy got justice. It was easy to overlook those in poverty and need. It was even easier to abuse them. The poor were often mistreated and mocked for their helplessness. Lemuel knew it was his job not to let that happen. He was an advocate for the helpless. Proverbs 31.8-9 reflects the heart of God and guided King Lemuel. It can also guide you.

RESPOND: When you learn about an injustice speak up! Be an advocate. Talk to your pastor to see if your church can get involved in some way. After all, wouldn't you want someone on your side if you were in their situation?

Lord, help me to be a support, in your name, to those who are alone and have no one else to count on.

TO KNOW MORE:
Psalm 82 and John 7 \\

Day 344 | *Patience*

PRAY: God connect with me here, as I seek you in your Word.

READ: Luke 1.8-17 — In today's reading we find Zechariah offering incense on the altar while praying – perhaps for a son or for the coming of the Messiah. In either case, his prayer was answered. In a remarkable way! Up to this point there hadn't been a recorded revelation from God in more than four hundred years. No wonder he was stunned and frightened.

Yet his fears would soon turn to joy. Despite their age, Zechariah and his wife, Elizabeth, would have a son who would prepare the way for the Messiah. God answers prayer in His own way and in His own time. He worked in an "impossible" situation – Zechariah's wife couldn't conceive – to bring about the fulfillment of all the prophecies concerning the coming Messiah.

REFLECT: If you want to have your prayers answered, be open to what God can do in impossible situations. Wait for Him to work in His way and in His time. And pray that your patience will serve as a positive witness to those who are desperately "praying and waiting" for their own miracle – whether it be for a job, for healing or for another critical situation.

RESPOND: Ask that in all circumstance God's intentions for your life will be accomplished. And always be thankful, no matter how or when He responds.

Lord, teach me patience as you reveal your will for my life in your perfect timing. And I pray for those who have turned to you in their time of need including (names).

TO KNOW MORE:
Daniel 10 and Acts 10 \\

Day 345 | *Encouragement*

PRAY: God connect with me here, as I seek you in your Word.

READ: Philippians 1.3-6 — From the opening of Paul's letter to the church at Philippi, it's apparent that this faithful group of believers was a regular source of joy for the great apostle. In fact, today's passage is just one of several places in this brief letter where Paul described his feelings of elation when considering the Philippians.

So what was it that made this community of believers, who lived in the northeast region of modern-day Greece, so special? Well, most notably, they were eager and willing to be used by God for whatever task He had in store for them. And they did so with a great sense of peace and joy. Their lives were marked by unwavering faith and ever-present grace in all circumstances. Because of their close walk with the Lord, they were able to work together and effectively share the message of salvation with others. Their example is a wonderful testimony that is just as worthy of emulation today as it was two millennia ago.

REFLECT: As a Christian, you can be a wonderful source of joy and encouragement to others. Remember, by having confidence in God's sovereign care for your needs, you will always be effective in your outreach to others.

RESPOND: Strive to become a living witness of Christ's love to those who don't know Him as Saviour. Likewise you can be a source of comfort and assurance to other Christians who need to be regularly encouraged in their faith — even if they are leaders in the church.

Lord, help me to be a source of joy to those who need encouragement and a source of ministry to those who have not given their lives to you.

TO KNOW MORE:
Psalm 60 and Romans 1 \\

Day 346 | *Management*

PRAY: God connect with me here, as I seek you in your Word.

READ: 1 Peter 4.10-11 — What's so hard about being the manager or coach of a sports team? It's simple, right? All you do is put your best players on the court, ice or field and yell at the officials occasionally. Seems pretty easy. Those who know sports, however, will tell you that good leaders can make the difference between a mediocre team and champions. They study the game and know the best players to use in a given situation. They experiment with new strategies to get the most out of their team. In short, they make the best of the resources that are given to them.

In a similar way, Peter encourages Christians to be good managers of the gifts God has entrusted to them. Peter urges us, first of all, to take stock of what we have. Just as a manager may study his or her team to discover their strongest players in a given situation, you need to find out what talents God has entrusted to you. If you're not sure, many churches and Christian organizations have spiritual gift surveys which can help you pinpoint your talents more precisely. Second, act on those gifts! Part of being a good manager is using what you have to the best possible advantage.

REFLECT: One of the Bible's great promises is that if we prayerfully act on behalf of God's Kingdom, He will graciously intervene to help us. His generosity flows through us and He supplies "all the strength and energy" we need (v. 11). With such help available, there's no reason why we can't all be world-class managers.

RESPOND: Take God at His word and act on His promises today.

Lord, help me be a faithful manager of the gifts you have given me so I can effectively serve others in your name.

TO KNOW MORE:
Psalm 145 and Ephesians 3 \\

Day 347 | *Fear*

PRAY: God connect with me here, as I seek you in your Word.

READ: Mark 4.35-41 — Life is unpredictable. Each day we're confronted with decisions and events that cause us anxiety and uncertainty. This is why one of the great comforts of the Christian life is knowing we can rest in the assurance that God is in complete control. Yet, so often we act as if we've never witnessed God's gracious provision and miraculous intervention in our lives.

Of course, in this regard, we're no different than the disciples who had witnessed Jesus cast out demons and cure diseases. Despite this, they quaked in fear when they experienced His sovereignty over creation. His response was to incredulously question their maturity and faith. As you serve Him by serving others, remember that if He can calm the wind and seas, He is more than able and willing to intervene on your behalf in all circumstances.

REFLECT: Just as Jesus said that our Heavenly Father is concerned about the sparrow that falls from its nest, we are guaranteed that He cares about us infinitely more. If you or those around you are going through a time of hardship or indecision, turn your cares over to the Lord. He will never forsake you or turn away from those you pray for.

RESPOND: Ask God to give you peace in all circumstances and confidence in His promises.

Lord, even though my life is unpredictable, I am thankful it is in your hands and that you will guide me faithfully according to your will.

TO KNOW MORE:
Malachi 2 and Revelation 15 \\

Day 348 | Stewards

PRAY: God connect with me here, as I seek you in your Word.

READ: Proverbs 21.20,21 — Easy credit has many people living on the verge of bankruptcy. The desire to meet high expectations and accumulate more and more "things" pushes some people to spend every penny they earn and stretch their credit to the limit. But anyone who squanders all he or she has is spending more than they can afford. As the writer of Proverbs declares, a wise person puts money aside for when they may have less.

As we read in today's passage, God approves of foresight and restraint. But it's also interesting that verse 20, which deals with stewardship, is followed by the promise of blessings in verse 21 that will come to those who care for others. This is because the blessings we receive from God are not only for our benefit and sustenance –they are a resource for us to share, as worthy stewards, with those in need.

REFLECT: Stewardship involves more than budgets and fiscal oversight. It includes acting responsibly on behalf of someone less fortunate and caring enough to help them meet their needs. In this way we are rewarded with the distinct joy that comes from sharing our abundance with those who will appreciate our faithfulness the most.

RESPOND: Take time to examine your lifestyle to see whether your spending is pleasing to God or whether you are just indulging your various "wants".

Lord, please give me the wisdom to use the money and resources you have blessed me with effectively to sustain my needs and to help others.

TO KNOW MORE:
**Psalm 112 and Luke 16 **

Day 349 | *Provision*

PRAY: God connect with me here, as I seek you in your Word.

READ: Psalm 136.1-5 — One of the most effective advertising campaigns in the past couple of decades are the commercials featuring the Energizer Bunny. Nothing can stop or slow down this drum-beating rabbit. It just keeps going and going and going. Guess what? That's a good picture of the love of God. But, unlike a man-made battery, God's love truly is inexhaustible. Throughout history the Lord has hovered over the world, caring for His people and intervening in their lives.

That's the message of the Hebrew poet in today's Psalm: "His faithful love endures forever". How is God's love demonstrated? In creation; in the way He supernaturally delivered His people from Egypt and brought them into the Promised Land. And what is the proper response to such perpetual care and concern? The people of God should be extremely thankful!

REFLECT: The command to "give thanks" is found twelve times in Psalm 136; almost once for every two verses. This isn't just a hymn of praise for Old Testament Israelites. Modern-day Christians can rejoice in the same way. Why? Because God still leads His children. He still delivers. He heals and comforts and provides.

RESPOND: The love of God never ceases. He is forever patient and loving and He's eager to forgive and restore. Ask God to take you to places where you can know Him and His love in deeper ways than ever before.

Lord, I want to experience your enduring love each day. Draw me closer to you and give me opportunities to share your compassion and care with others.

TO KNOW MORE:
Ezra 3 and Jude 1 \\

Day 350 | *Wrecks*

PRAY: God connect with me here, as I seek you in your Word.

READ: Jeremiah 33.10-13 — In Canada when there is a serious car accident, the police usually calls an ambulance and a wrecker truck. In the United Kingdom, however, in a similar situation, the police calls an ambulance and a recovery truck. Both vehicles are basically the same, but their names are quite different. Wrecker seems to emphasize the problem, while recovery emphasizes restoration. Which would you rather have take care of your car?

God is in the restoration business; only He redeems lives. In today's passage He promises to restore His people. Certainly the people of Judah, God's people, and their land, looked devastated and hopeless. But God saw beyond the devastation to future prosperity. Homeless people, alcoholics and drug addicts are called "human wrecks," with the emphasis on "wreck". But God sees the same needy people with eyes of faith, hope and love. He knows that no one is a hopeless wreck. Recovery is always a possibility with Him in the picture.

REFLECT: God wants His people to look at others without condemnation or judgmental attitudes. He wants us to view others with eyes of love.

RESPOND: What can you do to restore the "wrecks" in your world? You can provide hope. You can bring laughter. You can share the love of Christ.

Lord, help me to love others, in your name, without passing judgment or feeling that any life is hopeless.

TO KNOW MORE:
Ezekiel 37 and John 3 \\

Day 351 | *Sacrifice*

PRAY: God connect with me here, as I seek you in your Word.

READ: Romans 12.1-2 — The human body is a marvellous instrument. Despite the incredible scientific advances that have been made in the past few decades, researchers still haven't unlocked all the secrets of a tiny cell, let alone explain the infinite complexities of the brain. It's no wonder God wants us to treat our bodies as holy and blameless before Him.

But notice in today's passage that Paul wants us to be "living" sacrifices. Remember what happened when animals were sacrificed in the Old Testament? They were put to death on the altar. But since Jesus died in our place on the cross, death has no power over those who have given Him their lives. So the sacrifice we're making is to willingly offer our resolve to lead a holy life, to do what is right and pure and to be a loving witness for Him throughout the world.

REFLECT: As our creator, God knows just how special we are. By obeying His laws for righteous living, we acknowledge the incredible gift of life we have been given and we show our thankfulness for the eternal life that awaits us.

RESPOND: Encourage those around you to think on things that are pure and to engage in activities that will be pleasing to Him.

Lord, I offer my body as a living sacrifice to you and I ask that you will help me to be a gentle witness to others for doing what is pleasing and holy in your sight.

TO KNOW MORE:
**Psalm 116 and Romans 15 **

Day 352 | *Simplicity*

PRAY: God connect with me here, as I seek you in your Word.

READ: Matthew 5.13-16 — Being labeled simple or simple-minded is obviously not a compliment. But Jesus seems to put a priority on simple things. He called Himself the Bread of Life, the Living Water, the Rock. Pretty simple, everyday words. And Jesus labeled us sheep, one of the more intellectually challenged animals of His creation. In today's passage, Jesus asks us to ponder deep issues with, once again, simple terms. First He compares us to salt. It's so basic, so essential for the preservation of food, so needed for boosting receptive taste buds. Can you imagine chips or spaghetti or steak without it? Next, He directs our attention to light comparing us to a city on a mountain. Now that's a glow everyone notices! The light and the taste – such easy concepts to grasp and yet so vital in understanding that our mission is to help the world discover the freedom that can only come through Jesus Christ.

REFLECT: Jesus knew we'd get so buried in our efforts to understand why He came and our part in this magnificent plan, that we would lose the unaffected beauty of why He did what He did. So over and over again, Jesus attempted to make the idea of salvation understandable and . . . simple.

RESPOND: We are the salt of the earth. We are the light of the world. Simple? Yes and no. For in Jesus' mind, the simple become tools, the weak become strong, the foolish become wise. So the question is, just how simple can we be?

Lord, show me ways that I can share your love and the truths of your Word with others in basic terms that will resonate deeply and effectively.

TO KNOW MORE:
Leviticus 2 and Colossians 4 \\

Day 353 | Rags

PRAY: God connect with me here, as I seek you in your Word.

READ: Proverbs 8.13 — Have you ever come across and old friend on the street–someone you haven't seen for years and remember as a nice guy? Then you spend a little time catching up. Before long you realize something has changed about your friend. The kind, gracious person you knew as a teenager has become a bitter and angry adult. He says negative things about mutual acquaintances and boasts of his accomplishments. By the time you part, you wish you hadn't seen him so you could remember him as he was.

Scripture tells us that the only truly good and sinless person who ever lived was Jesus Christ. The righteousness of everyone else is like "filthy rags". It doesn't matter how sweet and generous we are: if our hearts are not filled with the presence of the Holy Spirit, disappointments and negative influences will eventually harden and corrupt our attitudes. This is why it's so important to develop "the mind of Christ" as Paul states in 1 Corinthians 2.16b. Only then can we have "the love of Christ" for those around us.

REFLECT: If you submit yourself to God, the first thing old friends will notice when you become reacquainted is the dynamic presence of the Holy Spirit and how He has changed you for the better.

RESPOND: Ask God to be the most important influence in your life. And pray that He will protect you from negative thoughts and attitudes that will stifle His perfect maturing process.

Lord, I pray you will fill me with the loving and compassionate mind and heart of your Son so I can be His comforting hands and feet and voice to others.

TO KNOW MORE:
Psalm 97 and 1 Peter 5 \\

Day 354 | *Satisfied*

PRAY: God connect with me here, as I seek you in your Word.

READ: Isaiah 55.1-2 — The Old Testament contains several promises from the Lord to protect and care for the poor. This passage isn't one of those promises. The focus here is on spiritual not physical needs. It isn't an invitation to dinner but an invitation to salvation. The Lord is inviting people to come to Him, to trust and rely on Him for salvation. He points out there is no need to pursue anything else in life because He is the only one who can bring genuine satisfaction. So, remember that mental list you made earlier? Cross out everything on it except "the Lord"!

REFLECT: Is it reasonable to expect people who are wondering where their next meal is coming from to listen to us when we tell them the only thing that will satisfy them is the Lord and His salvation? Probably not. That's why our ministry should always consider the whole person. When we help take care of people's physical needs, we are sharing God's love and compassion. Then those who are hurting will be more open to considering the salvation He offers.

RESPOND: Praise the Lord for the fact that you have experienced His salvation. Ask Him to help you maintain a perspective on helping the whole person – meeting both physical and spiritual needs – in your ministry to those less fortunate than you.

Lord, I pray that the ministry I'm involved in will be equipped to effectively care for people's physical needs so that we can bring satisfaction to their spiritual lives.

TO KNOW MORE:
Psalm 143 and Romans 3 \\

Day 355 | *Cults*

PRAY: God connect with me here, as I seek you in your Word.

READ: Colossians 2.20-23 — So many people become involved in religious cults today. The tragic consequences are destroyed careers, broken marriages and shattered lives. You can help your friends and family members guard against false religions by asking them these questions if they become involved with a group you don't trust:

- Does it stress man-made rules and taboos rather than God's grace?

- Does it foster a critical spirit about others and exercise discipline harshly?

- Does it "reveal" formulas, secret knowledge or special visions that are more important than the Word of God?

- Does it elevate self-righteousness rather than honouring Jesus?

- Does it reject Christ's universal church by claiming to be an elite group?

- Does it teach humiliation of the body as a means to spiritual growth rather than focusing on the growth of the whole person?

- Does it disregard the family rather than holding it in high regard as the Bible does?

REFLECT: If the answer to any of the above questions is yes then advise your loved one to reject the teachings of the leaders of this group and pray that God will lead him or her to a fellowship of believers who obey the truths of God's Word.

RESPOND: Ask God to give you wisdom when helping others maintain fellowship with a church that upholds God's Word. And pray for those who become ensnared by the false teachings of cults.

Lord, I pray that I will have the words to say when someone I know is having difficulty seeing the difference between the light of truth and the darkness of falsehoods.

TO KNOW MORE: Genesis 3 and Ephesians 5 \\

Day 356 | *Control*

PRAY: God connect with me here, as I seek you in your Word.

READ: Ephesians 3.1-13 — What are the worst circumstances you can imagine? Would it be a place where people are physically and mentally abused? What about conditions where everything is filthy, including the food and water? Not very pleasant. Now try to imagine what it would be like if you were in this awful place and you were badly injured from repeated beatings, it was often cold and there was very little light. What a horrible situation! Yet it was in such environments that Paul wrote many of his letters, even those that were encouraging and tender. How was he able to be thoughtful and productive and consistently positive? It's because this great apostle maintained his firm belief that God was in control of all that happened to him. His faith never wavered even in the worst of circumstances. Do you let the annoyances of daily living convince you that God has lost control of this world? Like Paul, remember that no matter what happens, God is directing both the world's affairs and your circumstances.

REFLECT: God understands your needs and will never forsake you, even in the darkest of situations. And, as you trust more and more in Him, you'll be empowered by His Holy Spirit to share the same confidence and assurance with others who are hurting or in need.

RESPOND: Praise God for His consistent provision, even during the most difficult and uncertain periods of your life. Ask that He will give you opportunities to share His wonderful faithfulness with those who need to hear this encouraging message.

Lord, thank you for never turning your back on me, even when my own actions have caused problems and heartaches, and allow me to be a blessing to those who are hurting.

TO KNOW MORE:
Isaiah 8 and Galatians 5 \\

Day 357 | *Fasting*

PRAY: God connect with me here, as I seek you in your Word.

READ: Ezra 10.5-6 — When was the last time you saw a celebrity or politician show remorse for his or her role in a public scandal? They may even weep and beg for understanding. But how many make a fundamental change in their lives? After they've shaken off the acute embarrassment, many go back to the way they lived before. Rarely do we see sorrow that changes lives.

In contrast to today's quick apologies, Ezra's grief for the sin of his people could not be mistaken. Weeping, he threw himself on the ground in front of the Temple of God, drawing a large crowd. The people responded, crying bitterly and confessing that they had disobeyed God by marrying pagan women. They vowed to do whatever God commanded. Ezra's genuine display of remorse jolted the Israelites. It snapped them back into reality, exposing the true condition of their hearts. By joining Ezra, they were beginning their own restoration.

REFLECT: Ezra put aside his physical needs for a time and focused on his spiritual condition. Often during a fast, people find that their spiritual sensitivity is greatly enhanced. They find it easier to hear God's voice and to express to him what is truly on their hearts. Fasting, in itself, does not make us more spiritual. The Lord wants our fasting to lead to a new awareness of ourselves and others.

RESPOND: Fasting should make us attentive to the pressing hardships that millions face every day. Fasting can help us in many ways. It teaches self-discipline. It helps us understand the plight of the poor. But sometimes it can be a way of telling God that we are putting everything else aside to get right with Him. As Ezra demonstrated, that reason alone can have effects that we cannot imagine.

Lord, I offer my time, my talents and my desires and I ask that any personal sacrifices I make will draw me closer to you.

TO KNOW MORE: Proverbs 27 and John 4 \\

Day 358 | *Sorrows*

PRAY: God connect with me here, as I seek you in your Word.

READ: Matthew 25.34-40 — In today's reading we learn that, for Christians, the "face" of poverty ultimately is the face of Christ. In this discourse about the end times, Jesus begins speaking figuratively about His intimate identification with humankind. Christ willingly made himself subject to the pains and sorrows of this world. Leaving the glory and riches of heaven, He lived most of His life dependent on the kindness of strangers. He may not have literally experienced each of the trials listed in this passage, but He did experience rejection and a life devoid of most of the comforts enjoyed by others.

REFLECT: Jesus is the ultimate representative of the poor and downtrodden. We need to remember that He "was acquainted with the bitterest grief" and "a man of sorrows" (Isaiah 53.3). Why was He willing to endure such suffering? To save us. Recalling this aspect of Jesus' life should increase our appreciation for what He has done for us. It should also increase our compassion for the hurting people we encounter.

RESPOND: We serve Jesus by serving others (2 Corinthians 4.5; Colossians, 3.24). By ministering to our brothers and sisters we are, in fact, bringing comfort to "the body of Christ" (Ephesians 5.30). Since we never know who we're coming in contact with and how God plans to enrich our life through them, we need to keep our eyes open for the neglected, the suffering and the helpless around us. It's something of a mystery, but in helping those who are so closely identified with Christ, Jesus says we end up ministering to Him.

Lord, I pray that you will give me opportunities to serve you by serving those who mourn, who suffer, who are afraid and who live in constant uncertainty.

TO KNOW MORE:
Daniel 9 and Hebrews 1 \\

Day 359 | *Faithfulness*

PRAY: God connect with me here, as I seek you in your Word.

READ: Luke 1.1-38 — In ancient Palestine a young, unmarried woman who became pregnant could get in serious trouble. Unless the father of the child agreed to marry her, she could remain single for life. If her own father rejected her, she could be forced to beg or, worse, to become a prostitute in order to earn a living.

Mary, with her story about being made pregnant by the Holy Spirit, risked being considered crazy as well. Still she said, despite the possible costs, "I am willing". When Mary said this, she didn't know about the tremendous blessing she would receive. She only knew that God was asking her to serve Him, and she faithfully obeyed. Don't wait to see the bottom line before responding to God. Offer your life willingly, even when the results of doing so look distressing.

REFLECT: God will honour your faithfulness just as He honoured Mary. He will grant you the "peace that passes all understanding" in times of uncertainty. He will "lead you beside still waters" when you fear what may become of you when obedience means possible condemnation or derision. He knows what you're experiencing because He suffered everything you can possibly go through, and worse. So rejoice . . . your Heavenly Father is watching over you.

RESPOND: Ask God to help you see beyond immediate circumstances toward the future, and to do so with a glad heart and an open mind.

Lord, whatever your will may be for my life, grant me peace and courage for the journey you have planned.

TO KNOW MORE:
Psalm 116 and Matthew 1 \\

Day 360 | *Good vs. Evil*

PRAY: God connect with me here, as I seek you in your Word.

READ: Psalm 1.3-4 — Surfing late-night television, you've probably come across old movies and TV shows. If you're watching a frontier adventure, you know the good guy wears pressed clothes and is clean-shaven while the bad guy is sloppy and unkempt. If you're watching a crime drama, you know the hero is the square-jawed detective or honest cop and the villain is the snarling punk or oily business executive. And of course, you always know that the good guy will win in the end. The author of Psalm 1 seems to have had this same mindset. Looking around today, it's tough to be as confident as the Psalmist was. In today's society, the wicked seem to prosper. Inevitably the people who succeed in the corporate and professional world are those who ignore basic Christian concepts such as loving one's enemies and ministering to the poor and needy. Why is that? Why does God allow those who flout his will and exploit the less fortunate to prosper? The answer is simple: He doesn't – at least not according to his definition of prospering. Their happiness is fleeting, not eternal, and the day will come when the tears of those who suffer unjustly will be wiped away and they will agonize no more.

REFLECT: God promises that His people will claim the ultimate victory over evil. Let that thought encourage you when you see the proud and arrogant prosper.

RESPOND: Ask God to give you the wisdom, courage and endurance to confront the evils of the world.

Lord, I pray for those who are unjustly exploited and ask for opportunities to provide them comfort and solace during their times of difficulty.

TO KNOW MORE:
Joshua 1 and 1 Thessalonians 5 \\

Day 361 | *Priorities*

PRAY: God connect with me here, as I seek you in your Word.

READ: Mark 10.17-22 — Suppose you're watching the news on a "hidden camera" investigation of a local carnival you were going to visit. A reporter, posing as a new employee, asks the owner about a risky ride. "But what if someone gets hurt?", the reporter asks. "If someone gets hurt, we can probably settle a lawsuit for a lot less than the cost of a new roller coaster," the man replies. After the news report airs, attendance at the carnival falls dramatically, even after the owner claims he was "misquoted". His greed and lack of concern for others likely cost him everything he put into his business.

But do you think this is only about the wealthy of this world? Our reading's rich man's sin was not that he had money but that he loved his money more than he loved God. This kept him from following God. You don't have to be rich to love money. Whenever the desire for obtaining and keeping money becomes an obsession, we're putting that before God. The remedy is not that we need to sell all we have, but instead that we put money in its proper place, after trusting God.

REFLECT: Even if the rich man had sold all his goods at that very moment, the core problem would still remain if he had continued to be preoccupied with money. If Jesus were standing before you and pointed out the deepest desires of your life in relation to money, just what would He see? What would He say? So where is your heart?

RESPOND: Do you need to confess that money has become a barrier in your relationship with God? In total honesty, pray for help in trusting God alone.

Lord, I place my life in your hands and entrust all that I have with you so that my priorities are focused on living a holy life in accordance with your will.

TO KNOW MORE:
Daniel 6 and 1 John 2 \\

Day 362 | Contentment

PRAY: God connect with me here, as I seek you in your Word.

READ: Luke 1.53 — Nicaragua is a beautiful country, but living conditions there can be brutally hard. Julio, living with his family on a mountain by the sea, daily reckoned with the relentlessness of the wind. They had no running water. Six lived in an area the size of a small room. And the only clothes they owned were those they wore. Certainly Julio could be bitter and miserable. Instead, he was eager to share the little he had. Intense joy radiated from him and his family. It's a miracle, really, this type of contentment.

Finding the words "satisfaction" and "hungry" and "good" in the same sentence certainly seems incongruous. Only good things tend to satisfy us. So putting these three words together just can't be possible, can it? Somehow you get the feeling that God is performing another small miracle here. For indeed, Mary was satisfied and content before her God. Poor and single, she still responded to her Lord's call with amazing faith and trust. And among the poorest of the poor, in the heart of places around the world, people like Julio are profound evidence that this same kind of contentment can still happen.

REFLECT: When someone knows the joy of the Lord, satisfaction comes through this relationship, along with love and eternal life. These are the things that really matter.

RESPOND: Pray for the poor of the world – for their physical hunger and for their need for God. Ask Him to give you an attitude of contentment and a greater willingness to share with others.

Lord, I pray for those in need around the world and ask that I can be a source of encouragement and provision out of the abundance you have given me.

TO KNOW MORE:
Psalm 34 and James 2 \\

Day 363 | Words

PRAY: God connect with me here, as I seek you in your Word.

READ: Isaiah 1.17 — On a chilly November day in 1863, a crowd gathered to hear two prominent speakers dedicate a battlefield memorial. The main speaker was Edward Everett, who spoke for nearly two hours. The man who followed him spoke but a few minutes. No one today remembers Everett's speech, but Abraham Lincoln, the other speaker, recited some of the most famous words in history – the Gettysburg Address.

Well-versed in Scripture, Lincoln may have borrowed a page from the prophets of the Old Testament, also famous for their direct, in-your-face style. In the book of Isaiah, God gave His people a few short sentences that pack a punch. In today's verse, God tells us we are part of His wider earthly family. And just as food and safety are the top priorities for our natural brothers and sisters, they're also the number one priority for our spiritual siblings. The oppressed, the fatherless and widows don't have a lot of people looking out for them. That's why it's so important for us to assume our God-given responsibilities as spiritual fathers, mothers, sisters and brothers, doing everything we can to defend them and make sure that they are taken care of.

REFLECT: We may not see any earthly payback for fulfilling our responsibilities to the poor and oppressed, but we can rest assured that our heavenly reward will be something special. If we only do what Isaiah tells us, we will be taking a giant step toward loving people the way God has commanded.

RESPOND: Ask God to bring to mind someone in your community – whether it's a widow, a homeless person or someone else in need – for whom you can assume the role of a spiritual family member.

Lord, I pray you will give me opportunities to be a source of spiritual encouragement to (name).

TO KNOW MORE:
Zechariah 8 and Acts 24 \\

Day 364 | *Value*

PRAY: God connect with me here, as I seek you in your Word.

READ: Psalm 8.6-9 — How much are you worth? If you had to put a price on yourself, what would it be? If you were able to break down the chemicals and compounds that make up your body and sell them on the open market, you might get a couple of hundred dollars. That's not bad money, but it certainly doesn't qualify you as a priceless artifact–except in God's eyes.

You see, God appraises human beings on a much grander scale. For reasons that are beyond our comprehension, we are incredibly valuable in His eyes. Every person with whom we come in contact on a given day is precious to God. This places a great deal of responsibility on us to treat others properly. When we mistreat God's "valuables"–for instance, the poor and needy–in a sense, we are disrespecting Him.

REFLECT: How would you feel if someone were to come into your home and start treating your most expensive possessions as though they were junk? Think about how God feels when we treat his most valuable possessions–people–like garbage. If God says that human beings are valuable, who are we to disagree with Him? And if God cares for His precious possessions, who are we to mistreat them?

RESPOND: Ask God to help you place the same value on human beings that He does. Ask Him to help you learn to treat others with respect and dignity.

Lord, I pray that I will have compassion for those I encounter, especially the poor and needy who are often disregarded by others.

TO KNOW MORE:
Genesis 9 and Hebrews 2 \\

Day 365 | Dilemmas

PRAY: God connect with me here, as I seek you in your Word.

READ: Matthew 16.8-9 — It's Monday evening. You won't get paid until Friday. You have two ice cream sandwiches, a jar of mustard, six grapes and half a roll of breath mints to eat. Your car needs gas and your rent is due the following morning. If you're like most people, at some point in your life you've struggled through a week like this. If you haven't, then don't be too critical of the disciples for their lack of faith.

It's hard not to be discouraged when you don't have enough to meet your needs. Yet, as Jesus said, don't let your anxiety cause you to lose faith. While we can't expect God to help us when we foolishly spend more than we earn on expensive clothes or frivolous entertainment, He will forgive us and help us not make the same mistakes again. If your situation is not caused by careless living, then ask God to help you during times of crisis.

REFLECT: God is always willing to provide you with solutions for meeting your needs. In the same way, He is ever present for those who have no other means of successfully resolving their dire circumstances. Just as He has met your needs during hard times, show the same compassion to others.

RESPOND: Ask God to help you maintain your faith during difficult times. Ask, too, that as He meets your needs you can, in turn, help others who are facing a critical situation.

Lord, I place my trust in you in all circumstances and I pray that, just as you have shown me compassion, I will find ways to serve you by helping others.

TO KNOW MORE:
Psalm 6 and Mark 7 \\